THE CENTURY OF

U. S. CAPITALISM

IN LATIN AMERICA

Diálogos

A series of course adoption books on Latin America

The Faces of Honor: Sex, Shame, and Violence in Colonial Latin America—Edited by Lyman L. Johnson, The University of North Carolina, Charlotte and Sonya Lipsett-Rivera, Carleton University

¡Que Vivan Los Tamales! Food and the Making of Mexican Identity—Jeffrey M. Pilcher, The Citadel

Independence in Spanish America: Civil Wars, Revolutions, and Underdevelopment—Jay Kinsbruner, Queens College

Heroes on Horseback: A Life and Times of the Last Gaucho Caudillos—John Chasteen, University of North Carolina at Chapel Hill

The Life and Death of Carolina María de Jesús—Robert M. Levine, University of Miami, and José Carlos Sebe Bom Meihy, University of São Paulo

The Countryside in Colonial Latin America—Edited by Louisa Schell Hoberman, University of Texas at Austin, and Susan Migden Socolow, Emory University

Senior advisory editor: Professor Lyman L. Johnson, University of North Carolina at Charlotte

THE

CENTURY OF

U.S. CAPITALISM

IN LATIN

AMERICA

Thomas O'Brien

University of
New Mexico Press
Albuquerque

To the memory of
Margaret McLean O'Brien

Library of Congress
Cataloging-in-Publication Data
O'Brien, Thomas F., 1947–
   The century of U.S. capitalism in Latin America
   / Thomas O'Brien.
      p. cm.
   Includes bibliographical references (p.) and
      index.
   ISBN 0-8263-1995-5 (cloth). —
   ISBN 0-8263-1996-3 (pbk.)
      1. Investments, American—Latin America—
History. 2. Business enterprises, Foreign—Latin
America—History. 3. United States—Com-
merce—Latin America—History. 4. Latin
America—Commerce—United States—History.
5. United States—Foreign economic relations—
Latin America. 6. Latin America—Foreign
economic relations—United States. I. Title.
HG5160.5.A3027   1999
332.67´37308—dc21   98-33361
                                                        CIP

CONTENTS

INTRODUCTION

Over the past two centuries entrepreneurs and corporations have played the largest role in defining the terms of engagement under which the people of the Americas created their community of nations. From colonial merchant sea captains such as James Brown to Walter Wriston, the head of Citibank in the 1970s and 1980s, U.S. entrepreneurs conveyed not only commerce and investment to Latin America, but also cultural and ideological precepts. As economic contacts between the United States and Latin America evolved over the past two centuries, the Americans' self-appointed mission to transform their neighbors to the south intensified and became far broader in scope. U.S. merchants and government agents in the late eighteenth and early nineteenth centuries limited their efforts at social change to leaving a few strategically placed translations of religious tracts and promoting the creation of republican institutions in Latin America. As U.S. business interests turned inward in later decades, they contributed to a land hunger which prompted attempts to seize the territories of Latin American nations, most notably Mexico.

But the most intense and pervasive transformational efforts have occurred over the past one hundred years as U.S. businesses invested directly in Latin America. Mining and agricultural enterprises sought to transform peasants into industrial wage workers and instill in them the values of competitiveness, individualism, and promptness essential in the modern work place. Subsequently, mining, petroleum, and utility companies expanded that transformational process to the middle class, hoping to create an effective cadre of white-collar employees.

After World War II, the manufacturing enterprises that typified the U.S. presence in the region undertook herculean efforts to create broadbased consumer societies which would provide an expanding market for everything from Coca-Cola to Chevrolets. These manufacturing multinationals were far more involved in local societies than the mining and agricultural enterprises of the past which depended on their hosts primarily for a labor force and legal protection for their operations. The multinationals of the late twentieth century became intimately involved in local societies whose financial and social policies as well as political climates played central roles in the success or failure of corporate operations.

The transnationals allied themselves with the International Monetary Fund and local regimes to promote economic policies which expanded the consumer market among the middle and upper classes while typically exerting negative effects on the incomes and general well-being of most of the population. The multinationals intensified the application of scientific management practices which sought to gain absolute control over the activities of workers. U.S. manufacturers also promoted the transfer of American labor systems and production standards to local companies that supplied them with inputs for their final products. It is this intensifying effort by U.S. corporations to transform Latin America that has distinguished the twentieth century as the corporate century in U.S. relations with Latin America. It is this story of an ever-intensifying attempt by Americans, and particularly American businesspeople, to transform Latin America into a series of societies compatible with the successful operation of capitalist enterprises that lies at the heart of this book.

Initially, economic relations between the United States and Latin America were grounded almost entirely in international commerce. As indicated in Tables 1 and 2, Latin American exports and imports have played a major role in U.S. international trade throughout the nineteenth and twentieth centuries. By the same token, by the early twentieth century the U.S. would become Latin America's major trading partner, regularly accounting for one-third to one-half of the region's imports and exports. The interactions prompted by international trade certainly increased Americans' and Latin Americans' knowledge of each other and provided for exchange of material cultures, but for most of the past two centuries, such contacts in Latin America were limited to select groups residing in the largest urban areas. By comparison, the effects of U.S. direct investment on Latin America have been far more dramatic.

Table 1. U.S. Exports to Latin America: Selected Years, 1850–1990

Year	Exports in US$mil	Exports to L.A. as % of Total U.S. Exports
1850	20	14
1870	46	10
1890	93	11
1910	263	18
1930	698	18
1950	2,863	28
1970	6,533	15
1980	36,000	16
1990	49,000	12

Sources: U.S. Department of Commerce, Bureau of the Census, *The Statistical History of the United States: Colonial Times to 1957* (Stamford, Conn., 1965), pp. 903–04; James Wilkie, ed., *Statistical Abstract of Latin America, Vol. II* (Los Angeles, 1995) p. 821; U.S. Bureau of the Census, *Statistical Abstract of the United States: 1986,* 106th ed. (Washington, D.C., 1985), p. 810; and U.S. Bureau of the Census, *Statistical Abstract of the United States: 1992,* 112th ed. (Washington, D.C., 1996), p. 800.

Table 2. U.S. Imports from Latin America: Selected Years, 1850–1990

Year	Total in US$mil	% of Total U.S. Imports
1850	174	19
1870	436	29
1890	789	25
1910	1557	26
1930	3061	26
1950	8852	35
1970	39952	15
1980	36000	16
1990	64000	13

Sources: U.S. Department of Commerce, Bureau of the Census, *The Statistical History of the United States: Colonial Times to 1957* (Stamford, Conn., pp. 903–04; James Wilkie, ed., *Statistical Abstract of Latin America, Vol. II* (Los Angeles, 1995), p. 821; U.S. Bureau of the Census, *Statistical Abstract of the United States: 1992,* 112th ed. (Washington, D.C., 1996), p. 800; and U.S. Bureau of the Census, *Statistical Abstract of the United States: 1986,* 106th ed. (Washington, D.C., 1985), p. 810.

Table 3. Total U.S. Direct Investment in Latin America in US$bn:
Selected Years, 1897–1990

Year	US$bn
1897	$.3
1908	.7
1914	1.2
1960	8.3
1970	14.7
1980	38.8
1990	70.7

Sources: Mira Wilkins, *The Emergence of Multinational Enterprise: American Business Abroad from the Colonial Era to 1914* (Cambridge, 1970), p. 110; Wilkins, *The Maturing of Multinational Enterprise: American Business Abroad from 1914 to 1970* (Cambridge, 1970), p. 182; and James Wilkie, ed., *Statistical Abstract of Latin America*, Vol. II (Los Angeles, 1995), p. 956.

As indicated in Table 3, U.S. investments in the region remained modest until the turn of the century, but from that point forward they exploded. Even the devastation of the Great Depression of the 1930s proved to be only a temporary lull in the tidal wave of U.S. capital into Latin America. Beyond the sheer size of that investment is the fact that unlike trade, investment carried with it an aggressive agenda for change in the societies of the region. American businesspeople sought to dramatically alter the work habits and social values of the Latin American working and middle classes. U.S. companies often launched peasants, small planters, and retailers on an economic rollercoaster, as their activities initially created jobs and business opportunities, only to later erode these benefits as the corporations sought to monopolize activity in their respective industries. Much of the exposure to U.S. consumerism since World War II is the work of multinationals in the consumer goods industries, which have found that direct investment in Latin American countries is one of the most efficient means of selling their products abroad. By every measure, it is direct American investments which have had the most pervasive and profound role in transmitting U.S. influences to Latin America. Yet that impact has not been uniform throughout the region.

The first three chapters of this book make only brief references to two of the largest and most important countries in Latin America—Brazil and Argentina. That omission reflects the fact that until the end of World War II, U.S. investment in these two countries remained modest compared to Mexico, Cuba, and others. That imbalance was the result of several factors. Most importantly, Brazil and Argentina did not possess the mineral wealth or offer opportunities for direct investment in agriculture that provided the principal attractions for U.S. investors until the Great Depression. But that relative neglect would rapidly end as U.S. investors shifted their attention from mineral and agricultural products toward manufacturing.

After World War II, U.S. manufacturers of automobiles and other consumer goods would aggressively enter Brazil and Argentina, attracted by the sheer size of their potential markets. But whether investing in mining or manufacturing, in Mexico or Argentina, U.S. businesspeople *did not* operate in a vacuum. Their efforts to reshape cultures and people elicited a wide range of responses from Latin Americans.

During the nineteenth century the region's elites, inspired by Liberal developmental ideas which promoted modernization through free market policies and infusions of external investment, made foreign concessions a central part of national policy. By the early twentieth century, U.S. investors were achieving a dominant position in countries such as Mexico and Cuba. Their development of raw materials, industry, and utilities earned considerable admiration from Latin Americans. Yet these positive responses to U.S. business ventures proved to be only part of the picture.

If corporate America could offer the promise of perpetual material improvement, that process came at a considerable cost of change for many Latin Americans. The loss of peasant lands to large commercial enterprises, subjugation to the rigors of the modern work place, and the deterioration of small business interests in the face of foreign competition created a mounting wave of discontent in Latin America. When the Great Depression spread economic ruin across Latin America, many of its citizens placed the blame for catastrophe squarely on the shoulders of U.S. business leaders and the elites who had welcomed their ventures.

Populist political movements rooted in the middle and working classes challenged the regional elite's political power from the 1930s through the 1950s, and made U.S. enterprises a target of their wrath. Populist regimes instituted policies designed to give the government control of strategic national resources and to replace foreign imports with products from a growing domestic industrial base. U.S. corporations, with the increased assistance of the federal government, responded to both the economic and political threats to their Latin American interests. They modified practices to accommodate nationalist sentiments, and focused increasing attention on direct industrial investment in the region to counter protectionist policies, such as high import duties imposed on their products.

Although U.S. investment would make substantial progress in Latin America in the post-war years, it again became the target of intense popular discontent in the 1960s and 1970s. Revolutionary movements in Latin America called for the complete nationalization of U.S. interests and in a few instances, most notably Cuba and Chile, such movements achieved power and made good on their promise to completely expropriate foreign investments. Yet at the same time nationalist and leftist upheavals also prompted domestic military intervention in even more countries, such as Brazil, Uruguay, Argentina, Peru, and Chile.

The new regimes, while counteracting leftist policies of income redistribution and outright expropriation of foreign property, did not necessarily act as ready allies for U.S. corporations. They frequently pursued their own nationalist agendas designed to shape multinational investment to what they deemed to be the national interests of their own countries. Meanwhile, many of these governments instituted economic policies which shifted income toward the middle and upper classes, creating a larger domestic consumer market. In turn, U.S. manufacturing multinationals redoubled their efforts to promote consumerism and impose stricter controls over workers in their factories. During the 1980s the momentum of revolutionary movements faltered; and military regimes, unable to cope with a mounting debt crisis and increasing popular discontent, surrendered control to civilian regimes.

In the wake of the debt crisis, the United States launched a concerted effort to open Latin America more fully to its trade and investment. These efforts centered on lowering protectionist barriers to foreign trade and investment. Through the International Monetary Fund (IMF), the United States and other developed countries also pressured Latin American governments to reduce social spending in areas such as health and education. Latin America's new civilian regimes have pursued neoliberal economic policies which not only welcomed increased foreign trade and investment, but also set about privatizing many of the state enterprises created in the wake of the Great Depression. In a few cases, such as Chile, those policies have successfully restored economic growth, although the long-term regional success of these efforts remains uncertain. In many countries such as Argentina and Mexico, there are signs of growing social unrest as the working and middle classes experience more sacrifice than prosperity in the economic rebound.

Thus, at the end of the "corporate century," U.S. enterprise and Latin Americans have entered into a new era of intensified interaction. As in the past, that interaction will involve far more than debates about the size and developmental impact of U.S. business in the region. American entrepreneurs have always conveyed more than capital to Latin America. They have carried with them not only technology and new work methods, but an array of values and beliefs which they have attempted to instill in the region. Those values are a complex mix representing some of the best and worst of U.S. culture.

On the one hand, Americans have carried with them beliefs in boundless opportunities for material improvement, and the importance and perfectibility of individual human beings. Armed with that progressive and individualistic spirit, U.S. businesspeople viewed Latin America as an ideal environment in which to fulfill their own potential. Yet U.S. entrepreneurs saw such opportunities in large measure because they perceived Latin America as the antithesis of their own enlightened civilization. The early optimism of leaders like President John Quincy Adams, that Latin Americans might replicate the American republican experiment, gave way during the nineteenth and twentieth centuries to a belief among many Americans that their southern neighbors were a racially inferior people shackled by backward social and political institutions. Americans frequently sought to replace elements of this "inferior" culture with what they believed to be the dynamic and progressive features of their own society.

Although Latin Americans often admired and emulated important aspects of U.S. society, the attempts by foreign corporations to institute radical change and their dismissive attitude toward Latin Americans became an ongoing source of distrust, tension, and overt conflict during the past century. U.S. corporations, which have played such an influential role in the emergence of modern Latin America and its relations with the United States, have developed a complicated and often conflictual relationship with these societies. The story of that relationship has its beginnings at a time when the future world power was no more than a modest collection of British colonies clinging to the shores of the North American continent.

THE CENTURY OF

U. S. CAPITALISM

IN LATIN AMERICA

CHAPTER ONE

MERCHANTS AND THEIR
MISSIONS, 1776–1872

In January 1876 General Porfirio Díaz arrived in Brownsville, Texas, to initiate an uprising to oust Mexican President Sebastián Lerdo from office. Díaz probably chose Brownsville as the launching pad for his rebellion because it was the power base of James Stillman, a noted New York merchant, and one of several American railroad builders, merchants, and financiers who would help fund the uprising. The intersection of interests that made the Mexican general and the American merchant political allies dated back nearly half a century to the arrival of James Stillmnan's father in Mexico.

Charles Stillman landed in Matamoros, Mexico, in 1828 with a consignment of goods from his father's New York mercantile house. The young American merchant would spend much of the rest of his adult life in the northeast corner of Mexico. Over the succeeding decades Stillman and his son James created a business empire that made them two of the wealthiest men in the world. Charles Stillman built a highly successful mercantile operation in northern Mexico, exchanging raw material exports for American machinery and manufactured goods. He also invested heavily in copper, iron, lead, and silver mines in the region.

After the U.S. war with Mexico (1846–1848), Stillman purchased Mexican owned land across the river from Matamoros on the U.S. side of the border. He then created the Brownsville Town Company to sell the property as city lots that would become the city of Brownsville, Texas. When James took command of his father's business empire he became concerned about the policies of President Lerdo. Although a Liberal, who generally welcomed foreign trade and investment, Lerdo had become increasingly wary of U.S. offers of trade agreements and railroad investments, fearing they would lead to U.S. domination of Mexico. Lerdo's resistance led Stillman and his associates to throw their support to Díaz. In return, over the next quarter century Díaz kept his promise to open Mexico to vastly increased U.S. investments. Meanwhile, as Díaz expanded opportunities for American investment, James Stillman became chair of National City Bank's board of directors and from that position, he would make the bank an essential partner of such corporate giants as Phelps Dodge, W. R. Grace, Standard Oil, and General Electric, in helping to finance their rapidly expanding investments in Latin America.[1]

The careers of the Stillmans and Porfirio Díaz personify the intensifying relationship between the United States and Latin America during the nineteenth century, as simple mercantile exchanges evolved into growing direct investment in the region, and eventually gave way to massive undertakings by huge American corporations. As James Stillman's support of Porfirio Díaz illustrated, growing U.S. investment was accompanied by intensifying efforts on the part of American entrepreneurs to shape events in Latin America. Starting with simple attempts of American merchants to spread American ideas of republicanism, such efforts would give way to direct intervention in local politics. Intensifying efforts to reshape Latin America reflected the fact that during the nineteenth century the United States had evolved into a dramatically different society than the republic of small farmers envisioned by Thomas Jefferson and the other founding fathers.

TRADE AND TERRITORIAL EXPANSION

The small farmer working his land with his family is not merely a historical stereotype in colonial America, for farm families comprised the overwhelming majority of Americans in the eighteenth century. Yet smallholder agriculture and the egalitarian social order it underpinned in the countryside did not pervade the length and breadth of the colonies. Even before the end of the colonial era, the economies of the southern colonies had focused on staples such as rice, tobacco, and indigo, geared to production for market and utilizing indentured and slave labor. The southern planter class built its wealth on these crops and translated wealth into social and political power. Joining the planters as part of the colonial elite were urban merchants, especially those in the northern colonies.

Urban merchants like James Brown of Providence, Rhode Island, who carried on an extensive trade with the West Indies, comprised the second important group in the colonial elite. In fact, foreign trade constituted the single most dynamic source of wealth creation in the colonial economy. Central to overseas commerce was the Caribbean, where northern merchants carried on a lively trade. By 1807, Spain's colonies, especially Cuba, accounted for forty percent of U.S. exports to the region.[2]

The growing commercial exchanges between the newly created United States of America and Spanish American colonies enriched a number of merchant families and soon spread beyond the confines of the Caribbean. G. C. and S. S. Howland became the leading New York merchants in the Cuban trade while protégé Moses Taylor parlayed a fortune made in commerce with the island into a distinguished business career in banking and industry. At the same time, U.S. merchant houses such as Alsop and Company and S. B. Hale and Company opened trading ventures in several South American cities including Lima, Peru, Valparaiso, Chile, and Buenos Aires, Argentina.[3] These early representatives of U.S. interests in Latin America had goals beyond the conduct of business.

American leaders, particularly John Quincy Adams who served as Secretary of State and President in the early decades of the nineteenth century, saw the potential for recreating America's republican political institutions in the Latin American environment. American diplomatic representatives, many of them U.S. merchants who resided in Latin American port cities, took on the task of spreading republicanism with a missionary fervor. Representatives such as Joel R. Poinsett, who served in both Chile and Mexico, meddled in local political struggles and even went so far as to draft unsolicited constitutions for their hosts. But even this attempt to promote republican institutions in Latin America had a business related motivation. As Adams noted in explaining his objection to monarchies in Latin America: "The special right we have to object to them [foreign princes] is that they are always connected with systems of subservience to European interests; to projects of political and *commercial preference*."[4]

Despite Adams' intense efforts to promote republicanism and recognition of the new nations for favorable trade pacts, U.S. commerce with Latin America would languish for much of the nineteenth century. Part of the problem stemmed from the fact that both the Latin American and U.S. economies exported primary products such as agricultural goods, leaving them few opportunities to fill each other's needs for manufactures. Damage to local economies during the wars for independence slowed the overall growth of the Latin American economies. Furthermore, the concentration of wealth in a relatively few hands and the fact that most of the population lived outside the money economy, meant that Latin America represented a small market for imports. Once the region's economies began to rebound and expand in the latter half of the century, the British, who had already established commercial dominance in the colonial era, maintained that position until the end of the nineteenth century. As the world's leading industrial power, Britain was particularly well situated to trade manufactured goods for Latin American primary products such as sugar, cotton, beef, and wheat. With its trade anchored initially in Brazil and later Argentina, the value of British exports rose from 6.6 million pounds sterling in 1850 to 55 million pounds by 1913. British imports from Latin America also soared, reaching 76 million pounds by 1913.[5] Only in nearby markets such as Mexico and Cuba did U.S. merchants establish a dominant position prior to the twentieth century. By the early twentieth century, U.S. investments had become an important part of Washington's relationship with its southern neighbors.

The efforts of John Quincy Adams and Joel R. Poinsett to shape the political institutions and economic policies of Latin America derived from more than a pragmatic desire to ensure opportunities for U.S. mercantile interests. Their willingness, even insistence, on spreading American ideas and institutions to neighboring countries reflected both a strong belief among U.S. citizens in their republican political institutions and the conviction that they represented God's chosen people who shared a mission to spread God's word and kingdom on earth. Most Americans detected elements of that kingdom in their own society. Whether couched in these religious terms or in more secular language referring to the benefits of American "civilization," representatives of the new United States envisioned themselves as missionaries devoted to the spread of the benefits of their society to other parts of the world. From the outset then, American business ties with Latin America involved more than a simple exchange of goods. U.S. entrepreneurs also brought with them a missionary zeal to influence societies which they believed did not enjoy the attributes of their own progressive, Christian, republican nation. But that mission soon assumed a much darker motive. As North Americans witnessed the increasing political chaos enveloping Latin America after independence, they frequently sought to dominate or displace Latin Americans whom they came to view as hopelessly uncivilized. That perception derived in part from the legacy of the Spanish empire and the events surrounding its collapse.

Spain's New World experiences proved vastly different from those of Great Britain, due in part to differences in the two societies and to dramatically different environments in which their colonial empires developed. Spain brought to its New World possessions a tightly knit relationship between the Catholic Church and the Crown, a highly bureaucratized government structure, and a pattern of social and economic control by landed elites. In the Western Hemisphere the Spanish attempted to impose these features on some 25 million people who had created elaborate and extensive systems of political rule of their own in the centuries preceding the Spanish conquest. The conquerors successfully destroyed much of the indigenous political and religious elite along with most of the inhabitants of these societies, christianized the surviving population, and eventually installed a European system of large landed estates as an important part of the rural landscape. Yet the process of Hispanization was neither as deep nor as extensive as these accomplishments imply. Indigenous religious beliefs and practices represented a complex mix of pre-conquest and Christian systems. At least through the nineteenth century, the village—the fundamental building block of Indian life—remained the most important and predominant feature of rural Latin America. Ultimately, colonial society developed as an amalgam of Spanish and indigenous cultures.

Not all of Latin America, however, fit this pattern of rural societies dominated by Indian villages with intrusions of large, European controlled estates. For example, in the areas that would become the nations of Argentina and Chile, Spaniards encountered few sedentary Indians. Consequently, they were able to dominate the landscape with large landholdings, most notably the Argentine *estancia* or cattle estate. Their populations evolved into a rich composite of Europeans, Indians, *mestizos* (offspring of Spanish and Indian parentage), and some Blacks. In Cuba, and Portugal's colony of Brazil, the scarcity of sedentary Indian groups led the Spanish and the Portuguese to create vast sugar estates worked by African slaves.

If colonial society promoted an amalgam of cultures, it was not an egalitarian mix. The Crown structured both society and economy around a series of privileges and monopolies. Spaniards born in Spain enjoyed power and authority denied Creoles (Spaniards born in the New World). Within white society, soldiers, merchants, and clergy enjoyed special rights stemming from their institutional affiliations. In turn, all Spaniards enjoyed superior positions to those of Indians and mestizos, as well as Blacks and mulattoes. The economy reflected this social hierarchy in the form of distinct groups with specific rights. Haciendas, Indian villages' control of land, trade privileges for merchants in Spain to conduct business with the colonies, licenses to build and operate *obrajes* (factories), and regulations governing the functioning of artisan guilds offer just a few examples of an economy that Spanish monarchs carved into a series of regulated monopolies. Regardless of the ways in which the Crown shaped and tinkered with the system, however, the Spanish never altered the underlying reality that the success and survival of the colonial economy depended on the Indian population.

Spain built the wealth of its empire literally on the backs of its indigenous inhabitants. Even before the hacienda or great estate emerged as an institution to generate wealth and power, the Crown had assigned Indian labor to individual Spaniards under the *encomienda* system, and distributed labor gangs for public and private use under arrangements variously known as *repartimiento* and *mita*. While payment of wages or payment in kind probably emerged early in the colonial era, especially in the vitally important mining sector, forms of forced labor such as the mita ensured low labor costs for Spaniards' public and private endeavors in the New World.[6]

By the eighteenth century domestic agriculture, the export of silver and gold, and public works in most of the Spanish colonial world depended on Indian labor. Moreover, the funding of the colonial bureaucracy relied in part on Indian tribute. Social control of the all-important indigenous population and the growing number of mestizos or mixed bloods became embedded within a complex hierarchy that reflected both ethnic and class distinctions.

While the vast majority of the indigenous population found themselves at or near the bottom of the hierarchy, the Crown was not entirely indifferent to their plight. Given the heavy dependence of much of the colonial system on Indian labor and tribute, and chastened by the demographic disaster of the sixteenth and seventeenth centuries when the indigenous population shrank to a fraction of pre-conquest numbers, the Crown offered at least minimal protection to the indigenous population and the village institutions that provided the bedrock of Indian culture. Yet by the end of the eighteenth century Spain began to chip away at the paternalistic elements of its colonial institutions.

In an effort to extract greater wealth from the empire, Spain's Bourbon dynasty launched a series of reforms during the second half of the eighteenth century. As a part of that process, the Crown reduced its defense of collective village land ownership and other rights in an attempt to encourage Spaniards to more effectively develop the rural sector. In addition, the increasing sale of public offices and the pressures of economic slowdown turned state officials, charged with defense of the Indians, "into ruthlessly one-dimensional exploiters of Indian lands and labor. . . ."[7] The deterioration of the colonial social contract helped spark popular rebellions in the two principal centers of the colonial empire—Peru and Mexico—between the mid-eighteenth and early nineteenth centuries.

Popular protests decried economic exploitation and posited visions of New World societies free of Spanish rule and Spaniards—pointing to world views considerably at odds with the one which Spain had sought to impose over the previous three centuries. These multiclass, anti-foreign rebellions which offered alternative views of what the future might hold bore strong similarities to events in the nineteenth and twentieth centuries. But the immediate future lay with the Creoles who took advantage of the toppling of the Bourbons by Napoleon in 1808 to address their own grievances against the imperial system through the wars for independence which swept through Spanish America between 1810 and 1825. At the same time that they ended Spanish rule, the Creoles anxiously and successfully avoided mass popular rebellions by Indians and mestizos which would have jeopardized the new Creole dominated social order.

The wars for independence wreaked havoc on the newly emerging nations of Latin America. The protracted struggles exhausted public treasuries, dispersed labor forces, and led to the shutdown of mines and neglect of public works. At the end of these struggles, the Creoles found themselves masters of states with severely circumscribed powers. Such weakened institutions and miserable economic prospects left the rural populations of the region with considerably greater control over resources and their own fates in the immediate post-independence period. Viewed from the perspective of the Europeanized urban Creoles, the forces of darkness and barbarism now held sway over most of their national territories. Furthermore, the Creoles found themselves deeply divided by regional, family, and to a lesser extent ideological loyalties, into warring camps loosely distinguished as Liberals and Conservatives. Conservatives defended the powers of the Catholic Church such as its control over education, and generally considered social experiments to be threats to the existing system of privilege. Influenced by the European Enlightenment, the Liberals espoused the secularization of education and advocated the dismantlement of colonial holdovers such as social privileges and economic monopolies.

Even though Conservatives and Liberals shared common beliefs about the need to reduce the high degree of state economic regulation inherited from the past, and to promote greater internal and international commerce, they would find it extraordinarily difficult to implement that strategy. Not only would peasant communities vigorously resist attempts to privatize village lands, but urban merchants and artisans fought deregulation as a threat to mercantile monopolies and guild privileges. Crippled economies, diminished state control over the all-important rural labor force, and divided elites created conditions of intense political instability. Mexico, the one Latin American nation lying in the shadow of the new North American republic, epitomized the difficulties of this period. Internal disruptions and its proximity to the United States would cost Mexico dearly as expansionary forces captured the official imagination of its northern neighbor. There were strong economic motivations for Americans to question the ability or right of Mexicans to exist as a separate nation.

During the early decades of the nineteenth century, merchant James Brown's descendants in Providence found the waters of international commerce to be exceedingly treacherous. The mercantile fortunes of the Brown family entered a prolonged period of decline and eventual disintegration. In 1838 the family sold the last of its sailing vessels.

The Browns' problems typified a general malaise afflicting U.S. international trade in the early decades of the nineteenth century. Much of the international trade with the Southern Hemisphere resulted from opportunities created by European wars which interrupted the flow of goods from the colonial powers to their American possessions. With the end of the Napoleonic Wars in 1815 those opportunities came to an abrupt end as the Europeans resorted to colonial policies that largely excluded American traders. The outbreak of wars for independence in Latin America further disrupted American trade in the region. But these reversals did not spell the end for the Browns and other U.S. merchants. As the seas of international commerce grew more dangerous, the Browns expanded their activities in land speculation, with their investments reaching as far west as Illinois. Other U.S. merchants financed canals and railroads to make the land more attractive to small farmers, while still others helped finance the rapid expansion of cotton plantations in the South. In the first half of the nineteenth century these activities encouraged the U.S. to promote territorial expansion on behalf of economic interests.

Small farmers and slave owners seeking cheap, fertile land, and Northern merchants interested in sites on the West Coast from which to trade with Asia formed a fragile alliance in favor of expansion. These forces had already triggered a series of land speculation booms within the United States that led to the forced displacement of Indian tribes who stood in the way of this process.[8] Land speculation also cost Mexico a part of its national territory.

In 1836 Stephen F. Austin, a land speculator and the largest landowner in Texas, found his influence in Mexico City being undermined by the Galveston Bay and Texas Land Company. Fearing defeat for his own schemes by a powerful corporate rival with backing from New York financial interests, Austin threw his support behind the Texas war for independence.[9] As

U.S. contact with Mexico intensified during and after the separatist war, American views of Mexican society came to reflect the racialist perspective winning acceptance in the United States.

The early optimism of Adams and others that the Americas could share a progressive republican future gave way to a far more negative ideology in succeeding decades. Influenced by European thinkers, and anxious to justify their displacement of Native Americans and enslavement of Africans, a growing number of Americans accepted racialist interpretations of humanity. Racialism envisioned humanity as comprised of superior and inferior races. As the abolitionist movement clearly demonstrated, not all Americans harbored racist views. But a growing number of Americans assured themselves that they comprised an important part of the superior Anglo Saxon race as opposed to the degenerate Indian and African races with whom they shared North America. These fortunate Anglo Saxons soon drew a similar distinction between themselves and Latin Americans, particularly their closest Latin neighbors, the Mexicans. These theorists of racial superiority depicted Mexicans as a mongrelized race inclined to laziness, hard drink, and violence. Surely no clearer evidence of this existed than the unrest which had disrupted Mexico ever since independence.[10]

Many Americans at all different levels of society believed that Latin Americans were inherently inferior. In 1849 the noted historian Francis Parkman variously described Mexicans as "ignoble," "brutish," and "squalid." About the same time, an American trapper denounced Mexicans as "depraved, indolent, untrustworthy, dishonest, cowardly, servile, ignorant, superstitious, and dirty ..."[11] Although such views did not necessarily represent the perspective of all or even most Americans at this time, racism did provide the ideological justification for the American assault on Mexico.

Now equipped with an ideology that would justify the conquest of Mexico, a coalition of mercantile and slaveholding interests combined with land hungry freeholders called for war, and in 1846 U.S. military forces crossed the Rio Grande. Yet, at the height of its power, the expansionist coalition faltered. Many who accepted racialist dogma now faced the contradictory conclusion of their own logic—Anglo Saxon race superiority would lead to the absorption of millions of people from an inferior race. Furthermore, the war renewed conflict in the U.S. congress over slavery, raising the question of whether territories acquired from Mexico would be slave or free. These factors deterred and ultimately fractured the coalition, resulting in the partial rather than the total dismemberment of Mexico.[12] But if the Mexican War marked the disintegration of the expansionist coalition, it did not mean the end of territorial aspirations of businesspeople involved in Latin America.

William Aspinwall's Panama rail concession from the government of New Granada (Colombia) in 1848 promised to dramatically improve transportation between the east and west coasts of the United States. Aspinwall's Panama Railroad Company completed the line in 1855 at a cost of $8 million. Until the transcontinental railroad joined the eastern and western halves of the United States, the Panama railway remained the most effective means of transit and transport between two coasts. But the concession carried with it an implicit surrender of sovereignty by New Granada, and its operation did nothing to improve relations between Americans and Latin Americans. On two occasions before the Civil War, the United States intervened militarily to protect the railway from local threats. Meanwhile, Americans who utilized the railroad took comfort in the fact that U.S. marines protected them much like the U.S. cavalry guarded white settlers in the American west from Indian attack. "Thus were Panamanians equated with the 'savage' Indian tribes of North America whose animality could be kept in check only through Uncle Sam's organized military might."[13] Panamanians held equally negative views about Americans and on more than one occasion struck out at what they perceived to be threats from foreigners.

In April 1856, a riot erupted in Panama City, the western terminus of the Panama railway. Crowds destroyed a number of U.S. businesses in the city, and then in a second wave they attacked the railway company, destroying the station and tearing up portions of track. The riot sprang from the tensions which had grown between Americans and Panamanians since the railway venture had been launched. The railroad triggered economic growth but that new prosperity also brought inflated land prices. An influx of Jamaicans took many of the new jobs with the railroad. And finally, the railroad displaced the muleteers and boatmen who had once carried most of the region's overland commerce. The railroad also brought a flood of over 500,000 people passing through the isthmus—many of them Americans with less than complimentary assessments of Panamanians. Both the transients and those Americans who stayed to create businesses in the area echoed the sentiments of their countrymen, that Latin Americans in general and Panamanians in particular were obstinate, proud, and lazy. John L. Stephens explained to his business partner William Aspinwall that in Panama they were "dealing with a population as backward as any on the face of the earth."[14] Such views, when combined with the economic impact of the railroad, provided ample motivation for the popular uprising in Panama City in 1856.

In an effort to short-circuit Aspinwall's Panama transit monopoly, the New York shipping magnate Cornelius Vanderbilt secured a concession from the Nicaraguan government, which led to the establishment of the American Atlantic and Pacific Ship Canal Company in 1849. Although the proposed canal would never be built, the concession included transit rights across Nicaragua. Vanderbilt used those rights to create the Accessory Transit Company. The Transit Company provided a system of stagecoaches and steamboats to carry passengers and cargo between the Nicaraguan coasts. This transit system, when linked to Vanderbilt's shipping interests, provided a relatively quick and inexpensive route between the east and west coasts of the United States at the height of the California gold rush. But by 1853 Vanderbilt had become locked in a struggle with two former partners, Charles Morgan and Cornelius Garrison, over control of the company. The civil war that erupted between Nicaraguan Liberals and Conservatives in 1853 further endangered Vanderbilt's interests.

Seeking to oust the Conservatives from power, the Liberals secured the services of William Walker, an American soldier of fortune with proslavery leanings. Walker departed San Francisco for Nicaragua with the blessings and eventually the financial assistance of the city's mayor, Cornelius Garrison. Walker succeeded in ousting the Conservatives, but then installed himself in power, with the intention of converting Nicaragua into a slave territory. Garrison, who had gained control of the Transit Company, was pleased to be rid of the meddlesome Nicaraguan government, but in 1856 Vanderbilt managed to regain control of the company. At this turn of events, Morgan and Garrison induced Walker to cancel the company concession and grant them a new one. Incensed by Morgan and Garrison's duplicity, Vanderbilt joined Walker's enemies in Central America in a successful war to oust him from power. Although President Franklin Pierce's administration had granted the Walker regime diplomatic recognition, the American mercenary's proslavery policies made him a prime target of antislavery interests and ensured that the U.S. government would do nothing to intervene on his behalf. When Walker again invaded Central America in 1860, he was captured, and executed by a firing squad.[15]

Walker was driven and eventually destroyed by more than the obvious economic motivations involving commerce and slavery. Walker "clearly saw Nicaragua as an extension of the less and less boundless West, an extension that promised rewards of mythic as well as economic dimensions."[16] Latin America beckoned both the mercenary and the entrepreneur not only as a place for profit but as a frontier where the United States could renew itself once more through the conquest and civilizing of primitive nature. But the fulfillment of that mission was less and less likely to come by means of outright territorial conquest.

By the late 1850s the regional and slavery controversies in the United States had fractured the old expansionist alliance, preventing concerted government action on behalf of expansionist schemes. Meanwhile, changing conditions in Latin America would also discourage further attempts at territorial expansion while at the same time encouraging increased U.S. business activity.

LATIN AMERICAN LIBERALS AND
AMERICAN INVESTORS

In the second half of the nineteenth century, some of the more contentious political struggles in Latin America had begun to subside, reducing the possibility that such conflicts would create opportunities for U.S. expansion as they had in the case of Nicaragua. That gradual trend toward political stability marked the emergence of Liberals as the dominant political faction within respective elites. By the 1870s, most Latin American nations had entered a long period of Liberal rule. It is now apparent that the differences between Conservatives and Liberals emerged more from personal, family, and regional rivalries than serious ideological differences. Neither group seriously advocated granting political rights to the masses. Moreover, Conservatives had already initiated programs to commercialize agriculture, promote exports, and encourage foreign trade and investment before the onset of the Liberal age. Nevertheless, the Liberal regimes of the last quarter of the nineteenth century rapidly accelerated these economic initiatives. More importantly, Liberalism as implemented in Latin America proved distinctly different from the versions then operative in North America and Europe.[17]

The agenda of Liberalism in Latin America certainly sounded some familiar notes for nineteenth-century Americans and Europeans. Advocates of constitutionalism, individualism, and the free market would find these concepts receiving strong and consistent verbal support from Latin American Liberals. Indeed, Conservatives but especially Liberals acted forcefully to transform the rural institutions withholding land from the marketplace. In the 1850s in Mexico, the Liberals under President Benito Juárez instituted laws designed to place land controlled by peasant villages and the Catholic Church on the open market. Over the next several decades, governments in Central and South America would enact similar legislation.

Although Latin American constitutions and laws asserted individual rights and relieved their Indian populations of tribute payments, these laws hardly proved to be liberating experiences for most of the people living in these countries. Despite their disdain for what they viewed as the backward practices of Spanish colonial rule, the region's elites frequently replicated some of the very same policies and institutions. Divestment of land from the Church and Indian villages usually led to further growth in the number and size of haciendas. The state frequently initiated or spurred economic activities by granting monopolistic concessions. Thus, the monopolistic and privileged characteristics of the colonial economy and society survived and grew in the nineteenth century. If tribute could be dispensed with, such as in the case of Peru, which abolished the Indian head tax in 1854, equally onerous burdens survived or were created. In nations such as Chile and Argentina where peasant villages did not dominate the rural landscape, control of labor became the central issue. In Chile the state sanctioned *inquilinaje*, a form of service tenantry in which campesinos secured the use of land from estate owners in return for services provided to the estate, and *enganche*, a form of contract labor through which workers paid off debts to mine owners and others. In Argentina, the state created a legal system which punished gauchos or seminomadic cowboys by sentencing them to labor on the emerging estancias or cattle estates.

The ideological underpinning for laws expanding monopolistic economic opportunities for the elite while stripping away village lands and imposing harsh labor obligations on the rural population, derived from a mixture of Liberal philosophy and elite social values. As one study of nineteenth-century Peru notes: "The newly emerging elites selectively grafted notions of a constitutional political culture, liberal legal norms, and bourgeois cultural values and patterns of consumption onto old hierarchical norms of social conduct."[18] In effect, Latin American elites envisioned themselves as pioneers of progress and civilization in populations comprised largely of "barbaric" Indians and mestizos. Such a self-conception would, of course, be quite familiar to Americans who harbored similar views about North American Indians and African Americans. But in Latin America those views applied to nearly the entire population of every nation. In turn, those beliefs justified policies that exacerbated acute inequalities of wealth and subjected much of the population to thinly disguised versions of forced labor. Because those who ruled Latin America firmly believed that their own people constituted an inferior backward culture, they never envisioned their nations as comprised of equal citizens. That perspective would make it extremely difficult to create nation-states backed by broad popular support. Yet the elites could point to their successes in the economic field to justify this harsh regimen. As a result of the Liberals' drive to generate exportable products, Latin America's foreign commerce grew by forty-three percent between 1870 and 1884. Increasing political stability, market reforms, growth in international trade, and encouragement to foreign investors created new opportunities for adventurous U.S. entrepreneurs like Henry Meiggs.

Henry Meiggs stands out as a U.S. business pioneer in Latin America. In addition to his adventurous spirit, Meiggs was forced by business failures and bad debts in California to seek new opportunities abroad. After arriving in Chile in 1855, Meiggs built rail bridges, and directly entered the business of rail construction. Between 1869 and 1870 he signed contracts with the Peruvian government to build more than 1,000 miles of rail line. These railroads proved to be one of several grandiose projects which drove up Peru's national debt. When Peru defaulted on its national debt in 1876, Meiggs issued his own currency to keep the projects going until he signed a new contract with the state in 1877. But by then Meiggs's health had begun to fail, and he died a few weeks later, his railroads uncomplete and the government that financed them effectively bankrupt.[19] But for all of the high drama associated with Henry Meiggs and his exploits, most of the interaction between U.S. business and Latin Americans would now derive from the activities of large corporate entities rather than entrepreneurial adventurers. That development grew directly out of changes in the U.S. economy and society.

While Latin American liberals set about reshaping the political and legal structures of their societies, even more dramatic changes swept across the United States. By the beginning of the nineteenth century, the pastoral landscape comprised of self-sufficient farmers that had earlier typified American society had begun to change. Market forces encouraged more farmers than ever before to experiment with commercial agriculture. Yet even more momentous changes were in store as the first factories appeared on the American landscape. With a rich endowment of natural resources but a relative scarcity of labor, the United States possessed a favorable environment for innovations to reduce labor requirements. Furthermore, federal and state policies encouraging private economic initiatives provided a political and legal structure that supported experiments in industrialization. As a result factories integrating the various stages of a production process under one roof began to play an increasing role in the economy.[20] The Civil War briefly interrupted the pace of U.S. industrialization, but it resumed with a vengeance by the end of the 1860s. Textiles, iron, steel, machinery, and of course, the railway industry, propelled the United States forward into the industrial age in the decades after the war. These dramatic changes did not enjoy universal support in the United States.

The regimen of factory life and the uncertainty of wage labor grated on skilled workers accustomed to higher wages and a more casual work environment in which they had virtually complete control. Many Americans would abandon factory life in search of a better job or in hopes of finding a homestead on the ever-moving frontier. Others for whom wage labor had become a permanent reality organized unions in attempts to defend their incomes and work conditions. These developments marked the breakdown of the old social order and the emergence of a new one more compatible with the changing realities of U.S. society.

At the beginning of the century the urban work place, whether a merchant's store or a craftsman's workshop, constituted an environment characterized by informal work practices and paternalistic relations. However, in succeeding decades those personalistic relationships gave way to more impersonal ones based on the payment of wages. Loyalty now counted for less than efficiency. Indeed, the emergent middle class began to define a set of values such as individualism, sobriety, and initiative which they believed distinguished them from their workers. But if such arrangements brought greater efficiency in the work place they also undermined a social stability once grounded in a patrimonial order. The entrepreneurial middle class found solace and at least a partial solution to social unrest in Protestant revivalism which stressed the perfectibility of mankind. In this manner "a nascent industrial capitalism became attached to visions of a perfect moral order based on individual freedom and self-government. . . ."[21] The middle class posited, in sharp contrast to its ideal of the energetic individualist, a much darker picture of the working class—now viewed as beset by indolence, intemperance, and an attachment to backward concepts of mutualism. To alleviate the sad and sometimes threatening state of working people, U.S. business leaders now marched bravely forward with a social gospel that, when accepted by their workers, offered the hope of social stability and work place discipline.

Middle class values of sobriety, individualism, and hard work now formed a central part of the Protestant social gospel. In turn, prominent businessmen like William Earl Dodge, whose mining company would make major investments in Mexico, found personal inspiration and positive business effects in American Protestantism. After all, sobriety and hard work exemplified the values which Dodge and other capitalists wished to instill in their workers to make them more efficient. Dodge's strong religious beliefs and his commitment to social reform found their clearest expression in his support for temperance. He served for many years as a leader of the American Temperance Union, and became a powerful advocate of temperance among the working class.[22] Dodge and innumerable other U.S. businessmen shared strong religious beliefs in the perfectibility of their fellow man and the need for social reform as a part of a process that would fulfill a religious mission and be good for business at the same time. Armed with the new values and products of the American industrial revolution, their firms ventured forth into Latin America.

The Singer Company became a corporate pioneer in Latin America. The company grew out of I. M. Singer's invention of a practical sewing machine in 1851. By 1855 the firm committed itself to marketing its product nationally by opening regional sales offices, each staffed by demonstrators, salespeople, and mechanics. That strategy combined with its use of the installment plan allowed the company to overcome the public's lack of familiarity with the new machines, and build a network of 530 stores in the United States by 1879. Singer began selling its machines in Latin America during the U.S. Civil War. By the 1880s the company expanded its business in Mexico, the Caribbean, and South America by opening regional stores just as it had done in the United States. Nor was Singer alone in the effort to bring the products of the U.S. industrial revolution to Latin America.

By the early 1880s, Thomas Edison also attempted to market U.S. technology to Latin American consumers. The Edison Electric Light enterprises had begun exporting lighting and electrical equipment to Brazil, Chile, and Argentina, and setting up lighting systems throughout much of Latin America. Edison interests, incorporated as the Tropical American Company in 1881, began selling phone equipment to eight different phone companies in Latin America. Yet the Edison companies did not enjoy great success. The support services required for electrical equipment proved considerably more complex than those needed for sewing machines. The electric enterprises were failing by the mid-1880s and Tropical American sold out to British interests in the 1890s.[23] Singer proved to be one of the few successful cases of a U.S. manufacturer exporting its products to Latin America at this time. U.S. merchants also had a mixed experience in Latin America.

The rapid growth of Latin America's foreign trade in the 1870s did not translate into substantial increases in U.S. commerce for several reasons. First, British business interests had decades of experience in Latin America, they enjoyed the necessary financial support system to carry out international exporting, and in most cases, British products remained superior to

American ones. Through most of the nineteenth century Great Britain remained the leading trading partner for all Latin American countries, with Americans challenging that position in only a few nearby markets such as Mexico. Second, U.S. businesspeople found numerous opportunities in their domestic economy that did not entail the risks of business abroad, such as fluctuating currency exchange rates. Much as they had done with land speculation in the antebellum period, many of America's leading merchants turned to investments in the domestic economy. Moses Taylor, who had made his fortune in the Cuban sugar trade, invested in domestic banking, mining, steel, and railway ventures. Before his death in 1883, William Dodge's firm began to invest in mines in Arizona. The Philadelphia merchant house of M. Guggenheim's Sons undertook similar ventures in Colorado. The banking house of J. P. Morgan grew out of a Connecticut merchant house, while the Brown family of Providence moved from land speculation to textile manufacturing. With so many lucrative domestic opportunities, it is little wonder that U.S. businesses devoted only limited attention to Latin America even as political stability and free market policies made it a more attractive environment for foreign capital. However, the domestic pattern of mercantile investments in industry and banking established a pattern which U.S. commercial houses mimicked in Latin America as they followed up trade opportunities with direct investments.

In Honduras, the Valentines, a family of New York merchants, secured a mining concession from the Honduran government in 1880, and established the New York and Rosario Mining Company. The firm would soon become the largest mining company in the country. The Valentines also secured control of the wharf and railway at Puerto Cortés on the Honduran Atlantic coast. Similarly, Augustus Hemmenway in Chile moved into mining investments from his activities as a merchant, and the U.S. firm of Alsop & Company followed the same course in Bolivia. On the other side of the Andes, Samuel B. Hale moved from trade to finance and helped float loans for the Argentine government. In Cuba, Drake Brothers and Company parlayed their position in the sugar trade into direct investments in sugar plantations.[24] The Drake ventures, however, paled in comparison to activities of the Boston merchant house of E. Atkins and Company.

By the mid-nineteenth century, Edwin Atkins had built an important business on the sugar trade with Cuba. However, like so many other U.S. merchants in the years after the Civil War, Atkins devoted increasing attention to his domestic investments, especially the Union Pacific Railroad, where he served as vice president. As a result, the senior Atkins sent his son Edwin to Cuba in 1869 to assume responsibility for the company's activities in the sugar trade. By then Cubans had launched a rebellion against Spanish colonial rule which would drag on for a decade.

The war and the abolition of slavery in 1886 dealt devastating blows to the Cuban and Spanish planters who dominated the island's sugar production. After regularly extending credit to the planters, firms like Atkins and Company now found themselves with unpaid advances. By 1882 the Sarrías, a prominent family of sugar growers, could no longer meet their obligations to Atkins, and he foreclosed on their plantation, Soledad. Within a decade, Atkins developed the property into a 12,000-acre estate, with a work force of 1,200 and the latest in sugar processing equipment.

The Boston merchant took considerable pride in the fact that over the years he reorganized and reinvested in the estate so that, "The place was thoroughly organized and everything went like clockwork." The reason for Atkins' diligence, as he explained, was that he "wanted every acre to pay something." Although Atkins came to love Cuba and its people, he obviously saw his own work ethic and dedication to reinvestment and productivity improvement as a far cry from the habits of what he termed "the luxurious, indolent Cubans." Surely, if the diligent Bostonian became the master of Cuban sugar estates in Cuba it was a lesson in the triumph of the Yankee work ethic over Latin indolence.[25]

Certain of the superiority of their values and their methods, U.S. merchants would not hesitate to involve themselves in the internal affairs of their hosts. Such inclinations became apparent in the activities of a pair of Irish brothers who Americanized themselves and their firm in the process of building one of the leading foreign enterprises in Latin America.

William Grace arrived in Peru from his native Ireland in 1851 and by 1854 he had become a partner in Bryce and Company, a firm selling naval stores to ships in Peru's main port of Callao. Business was brisk as the harbor bustled with New England whalers, merchant vessels bound for California and ships carrying guano, the fertilizer product which underpinned Peru's economy. By 1860, when his brother Michael joined him in Peru, William had become one of Peru's leading merchants. Because of health and business concerns, William shifted his residence to New York City in 1866, leaving Michael to manage the Peruvian interests of what became W. R. Grace and Company. Meanwhile, William established New York City as the company's headquarters for shipping goods to South America. He also became a business partner of prominent financiers including James Stillman. Among the ventures which William help support were the efforts of James Scrymser to connect the United States and Latin America with a network of telegraphic cables (see Chapter Two).

Under the leadership of the two brothers, W. R. Grace and Company became the most important U.S. merchant house in Peru. Under Michael's direction, the firm became a source of supplies and credit for the Meiggs railway ventures in the 1870s. During that decade the company's interest expanded into products such as guano and sugar. The company's interest in sugar involved not only trade, but also production of cane in Peru. Much like Edwin Atkins, the Grace firm financed the operations of sugar planta- tions. But when the guano beds and state guano revenues began to fail at the end of the 1870s, much of the economy fell into depression. With planter debts mounting, the Graces foreclosed on the Alzamora family's sugar plantation, Cartavio. The brothers had now entered the sugar grow- ing industry.[26] Although Grace and Company would eventually pour capi- tal into the plantation to expand its holdings and upgrade its mill, those investments would have to wait, for Peru had plunged into a disastrous war with its Chilean neighbors.

Although the War of the Pacific pitted Chile against both Peru and Bo- livia, it quickly resulted in sweeping Chilean victories including the cap- ture of the Peruvian capital, Lima. When hostilities broke out in 1879, Peruvian national finances had already dissolved into chaos. With the rich- est of the guano deposits exhausted, Peru had defaulted on its foreign loans in 1876. Any hope for recovery lay in the province of Tarapacá where Peruvians and Europeans had built refineries to extract nitrate of soda from the desert. That apparent substitute for guano in the Peruvian economy now lay in the iron grip of the Chilean government. Additional foreign loans were out of the question until Peru's European creditors or bond- holders were satisfied.

In 1886, Michael Grace launched himself with consummate confidence into this seemingly impossible situation upon becoming the agent of the British bondholders in negotiations with Peru. Finally, in 1890 the Peruvi- ans and the bondholders signed an agreement, known as the Grace Con- tract. The agreement granted the bondholders long-term control over Peru's national railroads and earned the Graces a hefty commission. But more significantly, the contract played a pivotal role in opening up much of Peru to direct foreign investment and established "the Graces' increasing influ- ence in the making of inter-American relations. . . ."[27]

Much like his counterpart James Stillman in Mexico, Michael Grace had enmeshed himself deeply in a Latin American nation's internal affairs. Grace, Stillman, and other U.S. investors unhesitatingly took on that task, confident that their business interests would serve the long-term reform and development of Latin America.

Grace and Stillman's activities indicated that the U.S. mission in Latin America now superseded William Walker's vision of conquering a new physical frontier. Now U.S. businesspeople had set themselves on a mission of reform. They would displace what they viewed as incompetent or inefficient leaders like Sebastián Lerdo, and open economies like Peru's, to the forces of U.S. capitalism. Their capital and technology, combined with their business acumen and a set of values championing individualism, hard work, and sobriety would reform Latin American societies much as in the United States. Such a bold and presumptive mission to other cultures might be expected to prompt vigorous opposition from the targets of reform. But U.S. entrepreneurs like Stillman already had important allies in Latin America among the Liberal elites who now ruled the region. These groups had already committed themselves to vigorously promoting foreign investment as an essential means of stimulating national development. With the acquiescence and often energetic encouragement of these elites, a new age of U.S. business involvement was dawning with enormous consequences for Latin America and its relations with the United States.

In this new era Latin American elites and U.S. businesspeople would launch their respective societies on the most intense period of encounter that they had ever experienced. Rapidly expanding industries in the United States would come seeking raw materials and new markets. But the vision and ambition of these modern industrialists would reach far beyond the desire for profit or their predecessors' desire to affect the course of political events in host countries. They would seek a thoroughgoing transformation of Latin Americans. They would attempt to create a working class and a middle class adaptable to the intense and ever-changing demands of the modern work place and to instill the values and desires of their own consumer society.

SUMMARY

In the first century after the United States achieved independence Americans steadily developed their society's involvement with the nations of Latin America. Early American efforts to promote trade along with republicanism and Protestantism gave way to territorial expansion in the war against Mexico and mercenary expeditions like those of William Walker in Nicaragua. A coalition of small landowners, merchants, and slave owners prompted these aggressive acts to achieve their own economic goals. Those acts also expressed a popular American belief that Latin Americans were inherently inferior to their own Anglo Saxon race.

Divisions in the expansionist coalition and domestic industrialization shifted the U.S. focus away from territorial aggrandizement and back toward commercial relations with Latin America. However, Americans continued to believe that Latin Americans lacked the ambition and the drive to manage their own affairs and develop their own economies. The Europeanized elites of Latin America shared some of those perspectives. The Liberals who came to power in the second half of the nineteenth century viewed their Indian and Mestizo populations as inherently inferior to themselves. As a result they promoted a development strategy that included European immigration, the breakup of communal rural landholdings, and foreign trade and investment.

The Latin American Liberals' policies represented an open invitation to U.S. businesspeople to involve themselves more intensely in the region's economies. Charles and James Stillman, Michael and William Grace, Edwin Atkins, and William Aspinwall were among the Americans who exploited these opportunities. Their interests came to include railroads and plantations as well as more traditional merchant activities. In this process, U.S. entrepreneurs took on more than business endeavors. The activities of businessmen like James Stillman in Mexico and Edwin Atkins in Cuba demonstrated the American belief that they were on a mission to transform the course of Latin America's politics as well as the work habits of its people. However, as the riots against the Panama Railroad Company demonstrated, the Latin American popular classes did not always welcome U.S. involvement with the same enthusiasm displayed by the ruling elites. In the decades ahead Americans would expand the scope and intensity of their transformational mission. In response, Latin Americans would welcome some of U.S. influences, while vehemently, even violently, resisting others.

CHAPTER TWO

THE GOLDEN AGE,
1876–1921

Shortly after the end of World War I, Ralph Ingersoll, a young mining engineer, tossed his bags into the bed of a Ford truck and crossed the border between Arizona and the Mexican state of Sonora. Along with his luggage, Ingersoll carried his engineering skills and the common assumption among the U.S. professional classes that his skills would ensure both business efficiency and significant benefits for the Latin Americans with whom he would work. Ingersoll had been transferred by his employer, the Phelps Dodge Corporation, from the company's operations in Arizona to its mines in Mexico. More specifically, Ingersoll would be one of dozens of engineers assigned the task of carefully measuring the mine shafts and calculating the amount of ore extracted from them. Ingersoll's efforts were intended to oversee the Mexican contractors who managed the mine workers and who were paid according to output. In addition to efficiency in the mines, Ingersoll was certain that Americans could improve what he perceived to be the sorry state of the Mexican "race."

Soon after his arrival in Mexico, the American engineer became convinced, "that all Mexicans are children and have to be treated accordingly. The engineer has to be a sort of amateur god."[1] Ingersoll described Mexicans as carefree, innocent, prone to drink and violence, and lacking basic hygienic habits and a proper work ethic. Yet Ingersoll was equally convinced that U.S. managers could cure Mexicans of their thirst for alcohol, and their poor hygiene habits. In fact, he reported that, "I was told it takes just four years to complete the Americanization of the Mexican. . . ."[2] Yet Ingersoll was not blind to the harsh realities of working for the American corporation. Visiting the home of one of his labor contractors named Angel, he reported the lamentable state of that home. Ingersoll then hurried to explore the living conditions of his personal assistant Soloman:

> If the wealthy Angel lived like this, in what kind of shack did my poor Soloman exist, who lived solely on the dollar and a half with which he was daily rewarded for his faithfulness to me? I found him in one of the company-built houses half-way up the hill. Its interior was almost identical with that of Angel's home! The only difference was that Soloman shared his castle with another family, and everything—children, wives, and dirt—was doubled. And the company houses were one-room shacks about fifteen feet square![3]

Ingersoll's epiphany came at the height of U.S. business success in Latin America during the early 1920s, and illustrated the extremes of the U.S.'s impact in the region. American corporate efforts to affect change in Latin America went far beyond the comparatively feeble efforts of John Adams to promote republicanism or even James Stillman's initiative to alter the political leadership of Mexico. American business made enormous strides in improving the efficiency of Latin America's export sectors, including the efficiency of Latin American labor. Those reforms included attempts to change the work patterns and even the personal values of many Latin Americans. However, those attempts themselves were prompted by the belief that Latin Americans were inherently inferior. This belief is evidenced by the fact that few corporate reformers attempted to treat the Latin American working and middle classes as equals with their U.S. counterparts. Beneath the prosperity of this era, Latin Americans developed a deep-seated resentment over their treatment by Americans, which would boil and eventually erupt to the surface. Popular anti-Americanism provided an ironic end to the golden age of U.S. business in Latin America.

THE NEW INDUSTRIAL GIANT

After touring the states of Ohio and Michigan in 1873, Moses Taylor, the president of National City Bank, returned to New York brimming with confidence about the area's future and urging his associates to invest there. Having made his initial fortune in Cuban sugar, the New York merchant had fashioned his wealth into a vast business empire which included railroads, banking, and finance. The states of the old west like Ohio and Michigan formed parts of that empire. Given that interest and the surge in the U.S. economy after the Civil War, Taylor's enthusiasm is not difficult to understand. Yet within months of his investment advice, the U.S. economy plunged into a prolonged period of depression, threatening even the mighty economic edifice that Taylor had built.

The 1873 crisis was not just one of the periodic panics which staggered capitalist economies in the nineteenth century. The events of 1873 marked the beginning of price declines that would harry both manufacturers and producers of primary products around the globe for the next quarter century. Increased output of industrial and agricultural goods along with improved transportation helped flood world markets with cheaper goods. This new environment contributed to further improvements in productivity as producers scrambled to reduce costs in order to maintain profits in the face of falling prices. As a result, the challenge of falling prices provided one of several stimuli to a massive renovation of the industrial process, particularly in the United States.

Between the Civil War and the First World War the United States emerged as the world's leading industrial power. Iron production increased 900 percent between 1860 and 1895, and steel output shot up 800 percent in the last two decades of the century alone. At the same time that these more traditional heavy industries powered the American economy, U.S. entrepreneurs created newer, science based industries such as electric power, chemicals, petroleum, and telecommunications. By the 1920s U.S. businesses had become world leaders in these innovative industries. While the challenge of the Great Price Depression served as a stimulus to this second industrial revolution in the United States, many other factors made this dynamic response possible.

In the same period companies moved beyond the informal arrangements of family enterprises, creating organizational structures composed of specialized departments from accounting to marketing. Furthermore, leading investment houses, particularly J. P. Morgan, became directly involved in financing mergers to create corporate giants like General Electric and U.S. Steel that controlled both markets and critical technologies. By floating corporate stock issues, J. P. Morgan and his associates gained control of 721 directorships in 112 of the country's leading companies. While all of these developments facilitated U.S. industrial expansion after the Civil War, the most radical changes occurred in the technology and methods of the work place.

Despite the emergence of the factory system, skilled workers had retained considerable control over the work process thanks to their craft knowledge and unions enforcing rules that governed work practices. Breaking the grip of skilled labor on the production process became a primary task of industrialists in the late nineteenth and early twentieth centuries. Owners set engineers the dual tasks of studying in detail the productive process and breaking it down into simple motions to be replicated by machines. Through increased mechanization, new technologies, and scientific management, corporate leaders secured increasing control of the work place, allowing manufacturers to create production systems characterized by the continuous flow of standardized products through assembly lines, as later epitomized by Henry Ford's automobile plants.[4] Nor did this dramatic reshaping stop at the factory door.

Companies driving each other to the brink of ruin by intense price competition among largely indistinguishable versions of the same product helped propel the merger movement. But because consolidation could offer only a temporary solution to this crisis, business leaders developed a far more dynamic strategy to address this problem—the creation of a consumer society.

Gradually abandoning religious proscriptions against ostentatious displays of material wealth, businessmen, eventually seconded by Protestant religious leaders, promoted the idea of consumption of products and services as a panacea for life's problems. Human fulfillment could be achieved through material consumption without jeopardizing one's eternal salvation. Indeed, where Americans had failed to sense the need for such products and services, they would be taught to need and consume by a vast network of advertising and marketing firms. With time payment systems, a cornucopia of new consumer goods would be laid before the public to ease the trials of their daily lives and ensure that U.S. industry did not drown in a sea of overproduction. John Wanamaker, the Philadelphia department store magnate, captured these trends when he explained his use of time payments to sell pianos: "[We] tell customers how easy it is to possess these things. . . . We tell how easy it is to possess a piano despite its seeming large cost. At length desire ripens. And where desire is earnest, the means can always be found."[5] Yet the creation of this new world of material wonders did not go unchallenged.

For much of U.S. society the second industrial revolution and the creation of a consumer society meant dramatic and often unwelcomed changes in their lives. Skilled workers resisted the loss of control in the work place through union activities and more subtle methods such as featherbedding and petty forms of industrial sabotage. By the turn of the century many workers had also turned to radical philosophies such as anarchosyndicalism which postulated worker control of industry as the solution to the exploitation of capitalism. Labor radicalism struck fear in the hearts of American corporate leaders. In 1919 Frank Vanderlip, the president of National City Bank, noted:

> Here with full employment, high wages, constantly bettered conditions, and I believe, a really marked tendency toward greater fairness and sympathy by employers, there has developed the most general unrest and dissatisfaction. The dissatisfaction is deeper than any mere claim to higher wages. It is a challenge of some of the fundamentals of some of our present social and capitalist order.[6]

In the face of this radical threat, corporate leaders adopted a strategy of taming labor militancy by offering education in basic skills and American values along with improved medical services, retirement, and profit sharing plans designed to make workers feel part of a large and beneficent corporate family. And corporate reformers would soon try out their reformist experiments in Latin America.

At the turn of the century, business leaders saw the international market as an important supplemental outlet for the surging output of goods that often strained even the prodigious appetite of domestic consumers. U.S. exports to Latin America increased by nearly 600 percent between 1880 and 1913. By the latter date, the United States had also become the leading export market for eleven of the twenty-one Latin American countries. The United States had now emerged as an industrial power which could meet the growing need for finished products in the southern hemisphere, and could find there some of the primary products it needed to fuel its growing industrial plant. The First World War would further strengthen these trade ties, as the war interrupted Latin America's commerce with many of its traditional partners in Europe. By 1917 the United States accounted for half of all Latin American exports and imports. By the late 1920s, with the British clinging to their last bastion of trade domination in the region in Argentina, it was clear that the United States had become the region's principal trade partner. As impressive as the growth of U.S. trade was, the expansion of direct U.S. investments proved even more spectacular.

Direct U.S. investment in Latin America totaled only $308 million in 1897, but it grew to $1.2 billion by 1914 and then soared to $3.5 billion by 1929. Initially, those investments were concentrated in the regions where geographical proximity, longstanding commercial ties, and the exercise of power by Washington ensured a strong competitive advantage for U.S. business. In 1897, the Caribbean Basin and Mexico accounted for two-thirds of U.S. investment in Latin America. By 1929, Cuba and Mexico still accounted for more than 40 percent of direct U.S. investment, but by then South American countries possessed an equally large share of the total. Those investments also tended to concentrate in nations like Peru and Chile that possessed the greatest opportunities for mining, agriculture, and utility development. Numerous domestic and foreign factors spurred the age of massive U.S. corporate investment in the decades between the Spanish American War and the early 1920s.[7]

Up until the First World War the U.S. petroleum industry generated petroleum far more rapidly than it could be absorbed by the domestic economy. In turn John D. Rockefeller's Standard Oil Company, a dominant force in the refining and marketing end of the industry, began seeking foreign outlets for its surplus by establishing refineries and marketing networks in countries like Spain and Mexico. By 1914, Standard faced a new competitive challenge as Royal Dutch Shell began reducing the transportation costs of supplying far flung markets by developing international sources of crude oil to supply regional demand. Furthermore, the breakup of the Standard Oil monopoly in 1911 left one of its constituent parts, Standard of New Jersey, short of crude supplies to feed its refineries. With these dual stimuli, Standard of New Jersey launched an intense investment campaign in Mexico, Peru, and Venezuela to secure markets and develop new sources of crude oil.[8] A combination of market and supply considerations also led to substantial U.S. investment in agriculture.

In 1899 Boston Fruit Company, a firm specializing in the banana trade, merged with the interests of Minor C. Keith, a nephew of Henry Meiggs, the builder of Peru's railways. Keith had become involved in banana growing while building a railroad in Costa Rica. The new firm, the United Fruit Company, would become the dominant force in the banana trade in Central and South America.[9] For companies that relied heavily on advanced technologies, the motivations could be considerably more complex.

The General Electric Company operated in a new science based industry where technology played a critically important role. G.E. relied on protection of its patent rights to control markets and bar other entrants into the industry. These characteristics of the industry pushed G.E. into Latin America. When G.E. began to invest directly in overseas power generation, particularly in Latin America, it formed the American and Foreign Power Company (AFP) to manage those assets. During the 1920s, AFP expanded its operations to eleven Latin American countries, investing a total of $500 million. As a result of these steps, G.E. could control markets and technologies in Latin America through its direct ownership of power generating companies in countries like Mexico, Cuba, Brazil, and Chile.[10] Meanwhile, banks and investment firms became an inevitable part of this corporate thrust into Latin America.

Holding seats on many of the boards of these corporations and serving as critical sources of financing, firms such as J. P. Morgan and James Stillman's National City Bank soon became deeply involved in Latin America. Morgan and National City Bank provided financing for such corporations as American Smelting and Refining and General Electric. National City Bank also moved directly into South America by opening its first branch in Buenos Aires, Argentina, in 1913, followed by the establishment of branches in Brazil, Uruguay, Chile, and Cuba. U.S. financial institutions soon added to these activities by purchasing interest-bearing bonds sold by Latin American governments as a means of generating loans. In fact, Morgan, National City, and other U.S. banking houses formed a South American Group, sharing these loan offerings among themselves and British bankers.[11] Of course, U.S. enterprise brought more than technology and capital to Latin America; their version of U.S. culture and the objective of spreading it far and wide in the Western Hemisphere were also an essential part of the package.

While an earlier generation of U.S. businesspeople had brought to Latin America a faith in their version of Protestantism and their republican form of government, this new generation of the entrepreneurial elite shared a grander vision and ambitions. Central to this vision "was the notion that the United States must assume the burdens of uplifting the Latin populace so that they could join in helping to fulfill the New World's unique destinies."[12] The business elite grounded that idea in pseudoscientific racist philosophies. Those philosophies asserted that there were measurable physiological differences between humans, which created a hierarchy of superior and inferior races. Yet many U.S. business leaders who ascribed to these theories also believed that the citizens of civilized societies could reform and uplift the denizens of barbarian nations. In this manner, American racist beliefs defined Latin America as a series of backward, largely uncivilized societies, but capable of advancing to higher levels with U.S. assistance.[13] U.S. business leaders would play perhaps the most important role in this new mission to reform and uplift the supposedly backward peoples of Latin America.

The U.S. corporate mission of reform included a commitment to the reorganization of the work place—an essential aspect of the second industrial revolution. Such commitment meant training Latin American workers and middle class employees, not merely in specific skills, but in basic values of competitiveness, individualism, respect for professional qualifications, punctuality, and so forth. Yet this ambitious corporate program of Americanization in Latin American societies could not have advanced without the support of Latin American elites.

ALLIES IN LATIN AMERICA

The late nineteenth century witnessed the complete triumph of Liberalism in Latin America. President Porfirio Díaz (1876–1911) proved to be just one of a series of strongman rulers pursuing liberal polices who achieved power at this time. For example, Justo Rufino Barrios (1873–1885) in Guatemala, and Bartolomé Mitre (1862–1868) and Domingo Sarmiento (1868–1874) in Argentina established regimes that pressed ahead with agendas of social secularization, agricultural commercialization, export promotion and encouragement of foreign investment.

Much like their counterparts in the United States, Latin American elites found support for their strategies in a pseudoscientific philosophy. Positivism, grounded on the philosophical musings of the Frenchman August Comte, called for a scientific elite to rationally and objectively plan national development. The Latin American elite mixed Comte's ideas with social Darwinism which argued that societies progressed as a result of internal struggles, with superior human beings emerging as dominant over inferior humans. The Latin American positivists' motto, "Order and Progress," summed up a strategy of national development through authoritarian political institutions and a survival-of-the-fittest social philosophy. The authoritarian regimes of this period struggled mightily to achieve the goals of economic growth within an environment of social stability, if not social rigidity.

In Mexico President Díaz gave new life to the Ley Lerdo which had launched a frontal assault on the landholdings of peasant villages. Díaz further accelerated the process with new edicts that placed more and more village and public land in the hands of domestic and private investors. The new viability of the real estate market sprang in part from dramatic improvements in transportation, particularly railroads. U.S. companies drawn by Mexican government subsidies, and the country's new reputation for political stability extended the national rail lines from 700 to 5,700 kilometers between 1876 and 1884.[14]

Land and railroad policies in Mexico reflected the larger aims of the new regime to expand exports and encourage foreign investment. Both efforts succeeded as U.S. investors poured hundreds of millions of dollars into agricultural land and railroads. But mining proved to be the center-piece of the Díaz regime's economic development vision. A new mining code combined with dramatically lower transport costs provided by the railroads, and the regime's reputation for protecting foreign investors, spurred a massive infusion of capital. Given Mexico's close proximity to the United States, U.S. capital poured in at rates matched only perhaps in Cuba where the United States controlled the island's international finances and intervened periodically to protect U.S. interests. But if the influx of U.S. investment proved exceptional in the Mexican case, efforts to attract such investment and in general pursue a Liberal agenda proved no less intense elsewhere in Latin America.

In Argentina, a succession of nineteenth-century Liberal rulers such as Mitre and Sarmiento, effectively opened the nation to foreign trade and investment. On Argentina's broad plains, the pampas, the British helped build a rail network that exceeded 31,000 kilometers by 1913.[15] The com-bination of favorable government policies and a rapidly expanding rail network, allowed Argentine landowners to generate a series of export booms in wool, cattle, and grain. In Guatemala, Barrios restored liberal rule and used state powers to promote coffee production and exports and begin a prolonged effort to link the nation's capital to the Caribbean coast by rail-road. In the Argentine and Guatemalan cases, the Liberal strongmen pro-duced spectacular economic growth.

The most successful Latin American experiments in free market devel-opment led to impressive export growth. Between 1883 and 1913, Mexi-can exports grew at an average 4.5 percent per annum, compared to 7.6 percent in Argentina, and 3.7 percent in Central America. A significant proportion of such export expansion can be attributed to a massive inflow of foreign investment from the United States and Europe into Latin America which reached $7.5 billion dollars on the eve of World War I.[16]

As the world teetered on the brink of war, Latin America's Liberal elites could survey their own societies and economies with considerable satisfaction. But Latin American rulers, much like their political counter-parts in the United States, believed that their Indian and mestizo popula-tions lacked the assertive, competitive instincts essential to national development. As a result of that perception, Liberal regimes from Mexico to Argentina promoted European immigration schemes designed to incor-porate what they believed to be more vigorous races into their national

Macro Economics

populations. Liberal governments also continued their assault on peasant village lands. Privatization of peasant lands created increasing strains and conflicts within villages and with the society at large. Those stresses increased as a result of the labor systems that governed the lives of most rural residents.

But in many Latin American countries, the struggle between modernizing elites and more traditional rural populations centered on control of labor rather than land. In Argentina the semi-nomadic *gauchos* or cowboys had long since been reduced to the status of laborers on the great cattle estates by a judicial system that required rural residents to be employed, and frequently sentenced lawbreakers to forced labor. In Guatemala, coffee estate owners used advances of money, seed, and other items to tie Indians to debt agreements they could pay off only through long-term labor commitments on the estates. In Peru and Chile, mines, plantations, and other enterprises relied on *enganche*, a form of labor contract also based on debt. Latin American governments provided legal sanctions and armed force to bolster the functioning of these systems, and utilized forced gang labor to carry out public works projects.[17] Repressive labor systems kept national wage levels low, thereby creating a deterrent to labor-saving innovations designed to lower costs. And while labor repression might reduce national wage levels, the systems themselves absorbed substantial private and public resources in the cost of enforcing these labor practices. The situation in the urban labor market did not prove to be significantly better.

The paternalistic conditions familiar to U.S. artisans a century earlier still prevailed in small Latin American businesses, but labor relations in large undertakings such as the ports and railroads proved less favorable to workers. In these larger enterprises, domestic and foreign capitalists sought to remove control of the work process from workers and place it in the hands of managers. Those conditions, combined with a national wage market depressed by repressive systems like enganche, and the generally disparaging attitude of the elite towards their own work force created explosive conditions soon after the turn of the century. Workers were not the only disenchanted urban group.

The Latin American middle class grew rapidly due to the increasing number of shopkeepers, small merchants, and tradespeople such as blacksmiths and cobblers. Also clinging, however feebly, to middle class income and status were a wide array of clerks and white-collar professionals employed by state and private enterprises. Most of the people in this group owed their positions to the success of the Liberal growth model, and remained fairly conservative in their social and political views. But even as they became enfranchised, middle class voters found their political voices muted by elite political institutions and ballot fraud. Many middle class families discovered that their incomes failed to keep pace with inflation. With limited political power and often under severe economic stress, their loyalty to the ruling order rested largely on continued economic growth. In the absence of an inclusive sense of nationhood, the elite would have to rely on the performance of the national economy to ensure its continued hold on power. The task of maintaining national prosperity proved to be a daunting one.

Several factors limited the beneficial effects of the impressive export growth generated by Latin American economies at the end of the nineteenth century. The reliance of many Latin American nations on a single export product exaggerated the effect of periodic price collapses in raw materials such as Argentine wheat, Chilean copper, Guatemalan bananas, or Cuban sugar. Such price swings made it difficult, if not impossible, for such economies to maintain high export revenue growth rates for more than a decade or two. Even in optimum growth periods, export sectors often lacked sufficient linkages to the local economy to stimulate significant domestic economic growth. In addition, population growth that averaged 1.5 percent in Latin America between 1850 and 1912 meant that much of the increase in export revenue simply sustained existing income levels. As a result, successful development would require Latin exports to grow at an average annual rate of 4.5 percent. Between 1850 and 1912, only Argentina and Chile consistently achieved that level of export growth.[18] Other problems involving price declines and productivity stagnation also troubled the export miracle in Latin America.

Although the Great Price Depression (1873–1896) had largely ended for industrial products by 1897, products of special importance to the Latin American economies such as coffee, sugar, and copper experienced long-term price declines that lasted into the 1920s. Declining exchange rates which increased the amount of local currency Latin Americans received for their exports and increased export volumes helped sustain total export revenue despite falling prices. But such factors could not alter the reality that Latin American economies now participated in a world system where improved transportation intensified competition among the producers of minerals and unprocessed food products. Furthermore, Latin American production methods and structures had changed only marginally since the mid-nineteenth century.[19] The survival of labor repression stands out as one of the most important and pervasive factors inhibiting productivity improvement. Debt peonage, enganche, and other forms of labor repression provided low-paid labor for hacendados, planters, and mine owners, while simultaneously diminishing any impulse to invest heavily in labor-saving devices. In Peru's vitally important Cerro de Pasco mining region, peasant resistance to the expansion of the enganche systems stymied efforts by the local elite to continue developing the region. In Chile the struggle between hacendados and the rural population led landowners to settle for a low-paid and ill-disciplined work force, contributing to an agricultural sector that could no longer feed the nation, much less export food products, despite rich natural endowments. The export boom clearly had proven less than miraculous in promoting national development and benefiting national populations in Latin America.

By the early twentieth century, serious questions had arisen about the ability of the export model to promote national development and of the existing order to generate productivity improvements. Latin American elites had already begun to address these problems by turning to U.S. investors. The elite would seek not merely investment, but renovation of technology and labor systems. As Peruvian president Augusto Leguía (1919–1930) put it, " . . . [I]f I could have my way, Peru would be practically American within ten or fifteen years."[20] In turn, a U.S. consular official in Chile precisely identified the problem U.S. business intended to solve:

> . . . [I]n Chili, as in practically every Spanish speaking country, man in the eyes of the governing classes, possesses no commercial value, not even at all in comparison with the economic value of a jackass. In these countries the ruling classes cannot and will not appreciate that man, in the economy of the nation, is an automated machine representing a capital value . . .[21]

U.S. businesspeople clearly saw the advantage to themselves and the elite in bringing the latest in technology and labor management techniques to the solution of this problem. That process had its roots in the early Liberal efforts to stimulate economic growth in Central America.

CORPORATE PIONEERS

In Central America popular resistance frustrated the attempts of elites to pursue the Liberal agenda with the same success as their peers in countries like Mexico, Argentina, or Chile. Furthermore, monoproduct export economies with few significant linkages to the domestic economy, labor repressive systems, and capital-poor financial systems raised important obstacles to national development. Perhaps most daunting of all were the tropical climates and often rugged terrain of the Caribbean coastal regions that made access to the important markets of Europe and the east coast of the United States difficult if not impossible. Furthermore, peasants strongly resisted abandoning the security of their highland villages for the opportunity to labor in the hot tropical sun of the Caribbean coast. Under these conditions, local elites turned to foreigners to develop these regions, initially for the purposes of building transportation networks, and later to raise an important new export product—bananas. Such considerations encouraged the Costa Rican government to contract with Henry Meiggs in 1871 to build a railroad from the capital San José to the Caribbean.

Meiggs agreed to build a railroad that would allow Costa Rica to export its coffee to Europe and the U.S. east coast. However, Meiggs, fully engaged by his business activities in Peru left the actual work to his nephew, Minor Keith. Keith relied on banana growing to support the railway enterprise during the construction phase. Growing bananas on land ceded to the railroad not only funded construction, but became Keith's principal undertaking. By the 1890s, Keith had become the world's leading banana producer, and his interests had spread from Costa Rica to Panama, Colombia, and Nicaragua. The merger of his interests and those of the Boston Fruit Company in 1899 created the dominant force in the industry—the United Fruit Company (UFCO). But United Fruit did have competitors—the Vacarro brothers who operated as the Standard Fruit and Steamship Company, and Samuel Zemurray who headed the Cuyamel Fruit Company. The Vacarros entered the trade in Honduras the same year that UFCO was created, while Zemurray, a Russian émigré to the United States, undertook independent operations in the same country by 1911. Given the dismal prospects of the Atlantic coastal region, Central American governments offered the companies low taxation rates on bananas, and concessions for the construction of wharves and railroads to support the *fruteras*' main activities—the shipping and marketing of bananas.

The U.S. fruit companies focused on the purchase of bananas from small independent growers on the coast. For example, United Fruit's most important thrust into Nicaragua came as a result of its purchase of the Bluefields Steamship Company. Through its new subsidiary, UFCO secured exclusive navigation rights on the Escondido River in 1904. UFCO effectively gained control over hundreds of small growers who depended on the river as the only viable transportation route to the port of Bluefields. When the small planters attempted to break the UFCO monopoly in 1909 by refusing to sell their bananas to the giant frutera, United Fruit with the aid of the Nicaraguan government, crushed their strike. The strike brought to the surface economic and racial justice issues affecting U.S. enterprise in Latin America. With the strikers languishing in jail, a local newspaper noted that "Had the planters been white men, they probably would have been given better treatment, but what right has a Nicaraguan, and especially a nigger— as some of the Bluefields S.S. Co's people said—to rebel and find fault with the treatment meted out to them?"[22] According to fruit company spokespersons, it was simply a matter of removing an impediment to a profitable business.

At the time of the strike, UFCO's profits depended on its control of transportation and marketing sectors of the industry, rather than the actual production of fruit. As of 1911, United Fruit's own properties would account for only 35% of the bananas it exported.[23] But events such as the 1909 planters' strike brought to the fore the company's contentious relations with small Central American growers, and its inability to impose quality control on the planters. That problem, combined with concerns over the danger from crop disease, prompted UFCO and other fruit companies to integrate their operations backward from marketing and transport into production. By 1929, United Fruit produced almost half of the bananas it shipped. The fruit companies' control of rail and steamship lines, when combined with a substantial portion of the plantations, allowed the fruteras to dictate quality control standards and prices to the small producers.[24] Over three decades, the companies had directly penetrated the production process and established a long-term and highly influential presence on the Atlantic coasts of Central American countries.

In the production of minerals the direct penetration of the production process proved a necessity from the outset because of prevailing conditions in this industry. The successful mining economies of Mexico, Chile, and Peru suffered from serious drawbacks that threatened long-term prosperity. In Mexico, attracting labor into the mines remained a major problem. Most peons preferred to remain on the land and avoid the dangers of mining. Mine owners offered not only wages, but a share in the output of the mines to attract workers. Even when wage workers accepted employment in a mine, they usually worked as a team under the supervision of its most skilled member, thereby creating conditions reminiscent of a U.S. work place dominated by skilled workers. The relatively low cost of labor allowed mine owners to rely on hand tools and workers' knowledge to carve narrow, twisting tunnels into the rock as they followed the course of the richest veins of ore. Similar conditions and technologies characterized

Chilean copper mining, while in the Chilean nitrate region and in Peru, owners turned to the process of enganche to secure labor. In Peru's Cerro de Pasco region, merchants extended credit to peasants who were required to work off the debt with their labor. The merchants then contracted to provide that labor to the mining company or to labor contractors who supervised the workers in the mines. The nitrate refiners of northern Chile operated the system somewhat more directly, hiring labor contractors to scour the countryside in the Central Valley, offering cash advances to peons who signed contracts to work in the refineries. Like debt peonage, enganche provided an inefficient, low-paid work force that led mine owners and nitrate refiners to cling to outdated technologies.[25] Given the gloomy prospects of a mining sector marked by poor technology and productivity, the Latin American elites readily welcomed U.S. companies to revamp this sector of their economies.

The Guggenheim brothers helped pioneer large-scale mining enterprise in Latin America. After building two smelters in Mexico, they turned their attention to acquiring a variety of Mexican mining properties which they operated after 1900 as part of the American Smelting and Refining Company (ASARCO). By 1911 ASARCO's Mexican investments had reached $100 million. The brothers extended their reach into Chile, acquiring the Braden Copper Company and its El Teniente mine in 1909. A few years later they purchased a mining property known as Chuquicamata, and they converted it into the world's largest open-pit copper mine. The Anaconda Company represented the second largest U.S. mining enterprise in Mexico, largely as result of its acquisition of William E. Greene's Cananea copper mines in 1907. The company also invested in Chilean mining, and in 1923 it acquired the Guggenheim interests in Chuquicamata for $70 million when the Guggenheims launched a bid to take over the nitrate industry. Meanwhile, interests connected to Anaconda had established a dominant position in Peruvian mining.

In 1899 James Ben Ali Haggin sold his Anaconda Mining Company to the Rockefeller interests in a deal financed by James Stillman's National City Bank and J.P. Morgan. The deal marked one of the high points in the career of a major U.S. mining entrepreneur. Despite his distinctive middle name, Haggin had grown up in Louisville, Kentucky, the son of a prominent lawyer. His exotic middle name was bestowed upon him by his mother, the daughter of a Turkish Christian who had earlier emigrated from Turkey to England. Haggin initially followed in his father's footsteps, becoming a lawyer, and eventually setting up a practice in San Francisco. With several partners, Haggin begin investing in various mining properties, most notably the Anaconda mining properties in Montana.[26] Three years after the sale of Anaconda, Haggin again turned to Morgan to finance the creation of the Cerro de Pasco Corporation. The company acquired over 700 claims in the Cerro de Pasco region, and began a total revamping of the area into a modern mining operation.

A host of other U.S. companies joined in the rush to develop Latin American mines, including the Phelps Dodge Corporation which extended its copper mining interests from southern Arizona into the neighboring Mexican state of Sonora. Latin American governments went to great lengths to ensure a convenient working environment for the companies, allowing them considerable legal latitude in securing their claims, and using force when necessary to assist them in maintaining order among their labor forces. As for the companies, their investments signaled the beginning of a massive renovation of Latin American mining.

Since the end of the U.S. Civil War, engineers had reshaped the mining industry, developing rationalized systems of developing ore veins, and new equipment to replace the picks and shovels of the past. By the end of the century, mass extraction and refining methods associated with open pit mining allowed the successful exploitation of low grade ores. These steam and electricity driven technologies, combined with low labor costs, made Latin America an extremely attractive field for development, promising to deliver mineral products to the United States at costs lower than domestic operations. Meanwhile, a combination of technology and market considerations drove U.S. petroleum companies to invest in Latin America.

Standard Oil of New Jersey's early stake in Mexico came through its majority holdings in Henry Clay Pierce's Waters-Pierce oil company, which by 1887 operated two Mexican refineries. But at the turn of the century, Standard's operations remained confined to marketing and refining even as the California prospector Edward L. Doheny's oil discoveries on Mexico's Gulf Coast laid the initial foundation for his Mexican Petroleum and Huasteca Petroleum Companies.

Before Edward Doheny ever arrived in Tampico to search for oil in 1900, he had already traveled far from his boyhood roots in Wisconsin. Doheny had devoted twenty years of his life to mine prospecting in New Mexico and Arizona. Then in 1892, he traveled to Los Angeles where his $1000 investment in a tar pit helped set off the Los Angeles oil boom. Unlike other independent oil men he was unwilling to limit his endeavors to the production side of the business, and set up his own marketing operations. That same aggressive entrepreneurial spirit led him to Mexico to open the country's first commercial oil fields.[27]

By 1910, Doheny had competition in the area of exploration from the British engineer and businessman, Sir Weetman Pearson, and his oil company, El Aguila. Meanwhile, Royal Dutch Shell's strategy of developing fields around the globe had set the standard for competition in the international oil business. U.S. oil companies like the Texas Company and Gulf now joined Doheny and Pearson in the exploration and production part of the industry. By 1917, even Standard entered the game, purchasing a small production company in Mexico. Standard's investments in Mexican exploration and production exceeded $32 million by 1922. Shell joined the competition, acquiring Pearson's El Aguila company in 1922.[28] The contest for oil resources also spread to South America.

In 1913, Standard purchased the most important oil fields in Peru from the British owned London and Pacific interests. Through its Canadian subsidiary, the International Petroleum Corporation (IPC), Standard invested $30 million in the fields over the next decade, and secured control of Peru's domestic oil market.[29] However, given the riches of the Mexican fields, which as late as 1922 accounted for 95 percent of the oil produced in Latin America, Standard largely ignored another opportunity in Venezuela.

Shell entered Venezuela in 1913, and Standard effectively abdicated any interest there until it purchased a British oil company in 1922. Even then Standard would not make its own commercial discoveries of oil in Venezuela until 1928. Despite its halting entry into Latin America, by the 1920s Standard derived as much as 40 percent of its international profits from the region. Those impressive earnings resulted from high prices for oil and lenient tax treatment, at least until a revolutionary government in Mexico began raising rates in 1921. Latin American governments were generally inclined to be lenient because Standard and other U.S. petroleum companies enjoyed distinct advantages over local entrepreneurs in terms of access to capital and technology.

Oil exploration often produced years of dry holes and losses that only a large company's deep pockets could sustain. Technology offered another key advantage to large corporations. Standard's first successful discovery in Venezuela came when the company switched from cable to the newer rotary form of drilling.[30] Given the barriers to oil development, Latin American governments proved quite amenable to favorable treatment for foreign petroleum companies. Venezuela represented a particularly notable case. The industry journal *World Petroleum* observed in May 1930 that "probably nowhere else do oil companies enjoy advantages equal to or greater than those which the government of Venezuela grants them for the purpose of stimulating operations."[31] The same advantages prevailed in Standard

Oil's Peruvian operations where the government's taxes amounted to only 5 or 10 percent of company revenues.[32] Concerned about the long-term sustainability of domestic oil reserves, the U.S. government added to these benefits by encouraging overseas exploration and development via tax breaks and diplomatic support for U.S. oil companies seeking to undertake international explorations.

Prior to World War I, government policy toward U.S. foreign investment in Latin America had largely been reactive in form, relying on dollar diplomacy, that is, controlling the finances of nations in the Caribbean Basin as a means of protecting U.S. business interests. However, Washington occasionally pursued a proactive policy to promote U.S. values, and business interests in the region—most notably, after U.S. forces occupied Cuba in 1898. Major George M. Barbour, who headed the military occupation government's sanitary commission in Cuba, epitomized American perceptions of and goals for Latin Americans at this time. Barbour concluded that "Under our supervision, and with firm and honest care for the future, the people of Cuba may become a useful race and a credit to the world; but to attempt to set them afloat as a nation, during this generation would be a mistake."[33] Under the leadership of General Leonard Wood, the military government developed a school system modeled directly on U.S. primary and secondary institutions, a civil code that offered standard U.S.-style legal protection on such matters as patents and copyrights, and more significantly, a revamped landholding system on the eastern end of the island. That system allowed U.S. companies to invest $95 million in sugar plantations and mills by 1914. Over the next two decades, U.S. companies began modernizing mill processes, using electrical power, new machines, and increased operational control by engineers and technicians. By 1924, U.S. sugar investments had reached $750 million and U.S. companies controlled well over half of Cuba's output.[34] In this case government assistance had not been directed specifically at the sugar industry, but at making the island's environment conducive to U.S. investment in general. Washington adopted a somewhat similar approach in Guatemala that benefited the General Electric Company.

During World War I, the U.S. State Department placed considerable pressure on the Guatemalan government to sequester all German property. Guatemala's president, Manuel Estrada Cabrera, resisted pressure by Washington due to the significant role of German citizens in the local economy. He finally relented when the U.S. War Trade Board refused to sell replacement parts to the German-owned Empresa Eléctrica de Guatemala, threatening to plunge the country into darkness. In February 1919, the Guatemalan government ordered the seizure of all German assets, and installed U.S. citizen Donald B. Hodgkin as the custodian of enemy property.

As Guatemala succumbed to U.S. pressure, the State Department encouraged General Electric officials to purchase the Empresa Eléctrica. G.E. had recently extended its interests to Panama and now sent a representative, Henry W. Catlin, to explore the opportunity in Guatemala. Catlin soon arranged to purchase a controlling interest in the Empresa Eléctrica. When Guatemala's national assembly refused to approve the Empresa's new operating concession, G.E. threatened to cut off the Guatemalan government's access to the New York financial market. Given G.E.'s financial backing from J.P. Morgan and National City Bank, the Guatemalans could not treat the warning as an idle threat. Secretary of State Charles Evans Hughes also pressured the Guatemalan government on behalf of G.E. Finally, in 1923 the national assembly relented and approved a fifty-year concession.[35] Meanwhile, technology, market considerations, and a degree of government assistance drove the expansion of other high-tech businesses in Latin America.

The childhoods of Hodgsdon and Hernand Behn may well have influenced the two entrepreneurs to pursue richly diverse international business careers. Sosthenes and his brother were born on the island of St. Thomas in what was then the Danish West Indies. Their father was of German extraction but he had been born in Venezuela, while their mother was the daughter of a local merchant. When their father died, their mother married the local French consul. Their stepfather saw to it that the boys received part of their education in Europe, and then brought them to New York City where he had become involved in trade with Cuba. Their family ties gave the brothers connections with the New York financial community, relationships which secured Hodgsdon a position with the Morton Trust Company. Their financial activities led to the brothers' appointment to the board of directors of the Puerto Rico Telephone Company in 1914. The Behns took an active interest in the company's management. Their success caught the eye of the National City Bank which was financing the operations of the Cuban Telephone Company. When the Cuban company encountered problems, the bank brought the Behn brothers in to manage the firm. By 1916, the brothers had taken charge of the Cuban firm, and in 1920, with the financial backing of National City Bank, they formed the International Telephone and Telegraph Company (ITT) to manage their Cuban and Puerto Rican interests. By 1930, ITT had purchased phone companies in ten Latin American countries with major holdings in Mexico, Peru, Argentina, Chile, and Brazil.

The Behn brothers did not attempt to build a single integrated system but rather a confederation of national telephone companies and manufacturing firms linked by financial controls and U.S. technology. Yet while the individual companies might not be integrated, they did need to access an integrated international cable system if they were ever to be more than small local operations. It was here that the U.S. government had indirectly assisted ITT.

James A. Scrymser, a business partner of J.P. Morgan and William R. Grace, had established the All-America Cables Company to build cable lines that connected Galveston to Mexico City, Central America, and the west coast of South America during the 1880s and 1890s. However, Scrymser could not extend that network to the Atlantic coast because of monopolistic concessions controlled by the British-owned Western Telegraph. During World War I, the State Department threw its support behind All-America Cables' efforts to break the Western Telegraph monopoly. By 1919, the British monopoly crumbled under the diplomatic and legal assault, and All-America Cables completed a cable network that now ran up the Atlantic Coast through the Caribbean and into the United States. In 1927, with All-America controlling over 31,000 miles of cable, ITT acquired the company, thereby ensuring its Latin American operations of access to their own Western Hemisphere network.[36] Washington facilitated similar developments in radio communications.

In 1919, President Woodrow Wilson urged Owen D. Young, president of G.E. to create a dominant U.S. presence in the radio industry. With that encouragement, G.E. purchased the British controlled American Marconi company, and with American Telephone and Telegraph, Western Electric and United Fruit created the Radio Corporation of America (RCA). The purchase of American Marconi gave RCA ownership of Pan American Telegraph, which controlled British Marconi's interests in Latin America. RCA's early dominance in Latin America became a virtual monopoly in 1921, when with the backing of the U.S. government, it negotiated an agreement with German, French, and British radio interests to surrender their rights in South America to a board dominated by Americans.

In the cases of G.E., ITT, Standard Oil of New Jersey, and RCA, Washington had played a role in establishing an expanded corporate presence in Latin America. But, the drive of modern corporations to exploit natural resources and protect markets and technology proved far more important factors than state intervention. Indeed, the companies that invested directly in Latin America had a far more significant ally in their own corporate ranks—the great investment houses of New York.

U.S. loans to Latin America which had topped $350 million in 1914 exploded to $1.5 billion by 1929. The rise of the New York banking community to world prominence resulted from several different factors. First, the Great War ended London's reign as the world's financial center. Second, when the growth of the U.S. economy slowed during the 1920s and more income accumulated among the middle and upper classes, the economy's most likely investors, sought higher return investments for their customers in new opportunities abroad. Finally, the export growth of Latin American economies gave them the revenue streams capable of sustaining larger debt payments. J.P. Morgan, National City Bank, and a host of smaller investment firms such as Kuhn Loeb and J.W. Seligman joined in the Latin American loan boom, often dividing up large loans among themselves. Latin American elites supported and encouraged such loans that offset lost government revenues when export earnings dipped, compensated for capital depleted due to profit repatriation by U.S. companies, and allowed the elites to build massive new public works projects as symbols of modernization.[37] For Latin American leaders, these loans and the other bargains they had struck with U.S. multinationals paid enormous dividends.

The continuation of Latin America's export boom after the turn of the century owed a great deal to U.S. corporations. The fruteras invested some $70 million in Central America, built 800 of the 1,200 miles of national railroads in the region, improved ports and waterways, and tripled the export of bananas from Guatemala, Honduras, and Nicaragua by 1920. In Mexico, with U.S. companies controlling 81 percent of the mining industry's capital, the value of silver exports doubled in the 1890–1905 period. Mexican copper production in the same period shot from 5,650 to 65,449 metric tons. Thanks largely to the Cerro de Pasco Corporation and its investment of more than $25 million, Peru's production of metals more than doubled between 1910 and 1930. From 1912 to 1926, the U.S. companies, which accounted for 90 percent of Chile's copper output, had invested $170 million and increased production from 41,000 to 200,000 tons. Their growth in turn generated millions of dollars in tax revenues and in payments to labor and local merchants. The Cerro de Pasco Corporation returned 55 percent of its $310 million in revenues to the local economy between 1916 and 1930. In Cuba, the U.S. sugar companies' investments of $750 million pushed sugar production from 4.1 to 5.3 million metric tons between 1919 and 1925. American and Foreign Power created a national power grid, transformed the sugar industry through the increased application of electric power, and brought electric service to a quarter million Cuban consumers.[38] U.S. corporate leaders looked with immense pride upon their accomplishments in these decades. Yet the U.S. companies had wrought changes far more profound than even these striking economic statistics suggest. Perhaps the most dramatic of those changes occurred in the work place.

THE MISSION OF TRANSFORMATION

Prior to the end of the nineteenth century, only a tiny proportion of Latin Americans relied on regular wage labor in a factory setting to earn their daily subsistence. Much like their counterparts in the antebellum United States, these Latin American wage workers operated in conditions approximating the craft shop with substantial controls in the hands of skilled laborers, or where unskilled workers exercised their own form of control through high rates of absenteeism and frequent job changes. Indeed, Latin American elites often expressed their dismay over the apparent indifference of their countrymen to the wonders of wage labor, and their willingness to accept subsistence lifestyles. The rural population gave the elite particular reason for discouragement.

Despite Liberal reforms, most of the rural people of Latin America clung with a fierce determination to the land and the culture it supported. Over the generations they divided and subdivided parcels of land to the point that subsistence was no longer possible, and exploited the most rugged of terrains to find plots on which they could scratch out subsistence. When the land itself proved insufficient to support them, they accepted or had forced upon them service tenant arrangements. Under such arrangements, peasants could cultivate plots on the large estates in return for supplying a third or more of their crops to the hacendado. When all else failed enganche might mean weeks or even months in the mines or on the plantations, but rural workers always maintained the hope that they could use these oppressive jobs to preserve their life on the land. Such commitment drove Latin American entrepreneurs to distraction. The elite sincerely hoped that the Americans would transform not only technology, but the Latin American popular classes themselves. The Americans would certainly try.

In terms of technology and work methods, the fruit companies ranked among the least innovative of the large American corporations that commenced business in Latin America at the turn of the century. Even when the fruteras entered the production process, they often tried to avoid direct involvement in the management of labor. In Costa Rica, for example, UFCO contracted with large planters to produce bananas by renting land to *colonos* or small growers. Yet over time in Honduras, Nicaragua, and Guatemala, the company entered production directly, dividing large landholdings into smaller farms, each with its cadre of managers, supervisors, and timekeepers.

Securing a work force proved to be a major undertaking everywhere the fruteras went. In Honduras the number of peasant migrants proved insufficient to meet the needs of the companies, and by 1927 the fruteras had brought as many as 4,000 West Indians to the Honduran coast. West Indians comprised less than 20 percent of the fruit companies' labor force in Honduras, but they constituted the majority of UFCO's 7,000 workers in Costa Rica, where the vibrant small-grower coffee economy of the highlands proved a powerful anchor for the vast majority of the population.[39] For most Latin American peasants, work on the plantations represented a temporary situation allowing them to supplement incomes from subsistence plots. Even those totally dependent on wages saw wage labor as a means to achieve subsistence. Unlike the Americans they did not view wage labor as vital to achieve a higher level of civilization defined by the accumulation of material goods. In 1903, a U.S. consul reporting on UFCO's operations in Guatemala explained this reality quite succinctly:

> There are no strikes, but the poor are not anxious to work. They can live cheaply on the native products, such as corn, rice and fruit, that they are not compelled to work much, since clothing and rent cost them practically nothing. Notwithstanding an advance in wages it is difficult to get men, and this when there are plenty of idle hands.[40]

Due to the peasants' less than ardent commitment to wage labor, the companies instituted task systems, paying workers according to the task performed. As the fruit companies entered production more directly, their operations took on more of the qualities of industrial enterprises. Reflecting the managerial revolution in the United States, UFCO developed a rationalized administrative structure with a division manager overseeing a series of functional departments that included agriculture, engineering, accounting, and merchandise. The company transformed Puerto Barrios, Guatemala, from a sleepy village into a modern port complete with electrical conveyors to feed fruit into refrigerator ships, electric lamps that allowed the work to continue night and day, and even a radio station to coordinate shipping schedules and broadcast American programs. On company farms, managers, supervisors, and timekeepers carefully planned the development of each farm, utilizing irrigation systems, fertilizer, and other devices, while keeping tight control over the work force.[41]

Not all Americans shared the corporate leaders' admiration for these models of American efficiency springing up on the Central American landscape. Upon visiting Puerto Barrios in 1931, U.S. journalist Carleton Beals described the reaction of highland peasants as they arrived in the port to work for United Fruit:

> [T]he bafflement and resentment of the highlander at the terrors of the hot country, his amazement and resentment of the restless energy of the blond beasts from the north, at the throb of this constant belching forth of bananas, more bananas, the constant buzz of this dirty port on the edge of the tropic seas . . . .[42]

The harsh realities of Puerto Barrios were exceeded only by the even harsher conditions of work on the banana farms.

Most of the work on a banana farm such as the clearing of new lands, required unskilled or semiskilled laborers who would endure arduous, back breaking, and not infrequently dangerous work. The frutera managers sought to extract as much hard physical labor as possible in the shortest time possible, knowing full well that many of their workers would desert them or fall victim to diseases such as malaria. That strategy created extremely harsh working conditions reminiscent of the early factory system of the industrial revolution.

For Central American peasants drawn by promises of a material paradise, the fruteras offered a rude and harsh introduction into the realities of early industrial labor systems requiring promptness, prolonged hours of physical exertion, and permanent adaptation to wage labor. But in Chile's copper and nitrate industries, the Guggenheims introduced truly radical changes required by modern mass extraction and refining techniques.

The new mining technologies eliminated the individual miner with hand tools who could search out the most promising ore face. Now steam shovels would carve out huge chunks of earth, load it on railway cars, and ship it to highly mechanized refining plants. These conditions required that a significant number of the workers comprise a permanent trained force familiar with machine operations—a far cry from the work force employed by the fruteras. In 1919, the general manager of the Guggenheims' El Teniente mine described the type of labor system they were trying to create:

> In Chile, as all over the world, labor problems are our most serious difficulty. But . . . we are hopeful of minimizing the difficulties by paying good wages, by providing good living conditions, by fair and

considerate treatment and by getting the workmen themselves to co-operate with the management in the solution of difficulties as they arise in a liberal modern spirit and so preventing them from assuming serious proportions.[43]

Utilities such as AFP and ITT required an even more refined labor force, with a large number of engineers, technicians, clerks, and skilled workers to install and manage the high-tech equipment that lay at the heart of their enterprises. For skilled workers, the high-tech industries often raised serious issues about loss of control in the work place which their U.S. counterparts had already grappled with. Changes could be equally drastic and disruptive for the middle class and the peasantry.[44]

The Latin American middle class directly interacted with U.S. corporations, both as small businesspeople and white-collar employees. For tens of thousands of shopkeepers and small planters in the region, the arrival of large U.S. enterprises brought beneficial effects. The increased regularization of the banana trade by U.S. companies encouraged the growth of a class of small growers. But those relationships also had a negative side. The small Central American banana planters who flourished with the coming of the fruit companies soon faced extinction at the hands of the same fruteras. As the fruit companies produced more bananas directly, they reduced their reliance on local planters. Furthermore, their direct production and control of transportation allowed them to dictate terms to local growers, many of whom abandoned their businesses. Shopkeepers in the banana and mining regions also discovered that U.S. enterprises represented a mixed blessing when their company stores competed with and threatened to overwhelm local merchants. The expansion of large corporations had an even more serious and pervasive effect on the middle class inhabitants of Peru's Chicama Valley.

At the end of the nineteenth century, the Chicama Valley, located on Peru's north coast, was home to thousands of prosperous small farmers, and a large group of busy merchants operating out of towns like Trujillo. However the expansion of large sugar companies, including W.R. Grace and Company's Cartavio Sugar Company, dramatically altered this picture. Upon gaining control of the local boards that administered the region's water supply, the large growers drove as many as 5,000 independent farmers out of business by 1930. The companies also imported and sold retail products and supplies, undercutting the business of the local merchants and contributing to the general decline of the valley's towns.

Among those who struggled to make ends meet under these deteriorating conditions was Raúl Edmundo Haya. Haya, the son of a school teacher, attempted to make a living in Trujillo by founding several local magazines. When the magazines failed, he helped establish and edit a newspaper, *La Industria*. He also set up a stationary business but when that company failed in 1910, Raúl Edmundo had to seek work as an accountant on one of the large sugar estates to supplement his meager income as a newspaper editor. In the face of the general decline of the valley's middle class and his own precarious economic existence, he made sure all three of his sons received good educations. His oldest son Víctor Raúl set his sights on a career in law, but even white-collar professionals faced a difficult environment in the U.S. corporations.[45]

Latin American white-collar employees encountered strong bias in the American corporate world. U.S. companies consistently favored Americans in hiring professionals, even replacing local managers with Americans when they took over companies in the region. When Latin Americans did secure jobs in management they earned salaries lower than U.S. citizens working in the same positions. Thus, for the Latin American middle class the arrival of U.S. companies proved a mixed blessing, offering new opportunities but also introducing competitive threats and a professional career ladder tilted by bias. For peasants the changes weighed even more heavily on the negative side.

Most peasants in Latin America had few encounters with U.S. corporations in the early decades of the twentieth century, but those they had usually resulted in adverse effects upon them and their communities. Aside from the relatively small group who made the transition to occasional or permanent wage labor in mines and plantations, the only other peasants who normally encountered U.S. companies were those who faced the loss of their land to these corporations. The most notable case occurred in Mexico where U.S. investors acquired 100 million acres of Mexico's national territory by 1910. In eastern Cuba, thousands of small plots disappeared before the onslaught of large U.S. sugar companies. In Peru, the Cerro de Pasco Corporation also acquired agricultural properties, but its greatest impact on peasant holdings came as a result of the lead and arsenic that poured from its smelter and cut a swath of destruction through the crops and livestock of nearby peasant communities. Such conflicts of interest brought social unrest. In response, U.S. companies created institutions to serve as mechanisms of social control and instruments of the Americans' self-appointed mission of reform.

Perhaps no single institution better expressed the Americans' dual purposes of control and reform than the company town. In the United States capitalists such as George Pullman and Milton Hershey had created company towns as a means of controlling their workers, ensuring their dependence on the corporation, and as an institution of social uplift. In Latin America, U.S. companies would repeat those experiments on a grand scale. U.S. mining, petroleum, and banana companies created numerous towns from the tropical coasts of Central America to the cold rarefied altitudes of the Andean highlands. Providing workers with at least rudimentary housing was one means of persuading laborers to suppress their distaste for permanent wage labor. The company store offered foodstuffs which might be in short supply in more isolated areas. By paying workers in company scrip redeemable only at the company store, U.S. corporations had a powerful device to hold their laborers in the work place. In addition, the towns offered a more overt type of control in the form of police forces hired by the company or at times provided on an as needed basis by local governments. By banning the sale of intoxicants within their boundaries, the towns tried to eliminate a major cause of absenteeism while they also fulfilled the reformist purpose of delivering working families from the curse of alcoholism. In 1904, a UFCO employee sought to explain the beneficial effects of the company's settlements:

> The directors of the UFCO . . . have always readily fallen in with any suggestion for the welfare of the men. In Costa Rica there are two preaching school masters doing good work, both are on the pay rolls of the company. The parents are encouraged to bring their children where they locate. The Division Manager ever ready to encourage efforts for the welfare of the men says, "since mission work has been in operation in the Zent district, the difference that has occurred in the life of men speaks for itself." It is the Company's desire to make all the divisions model communities with regard to social order and material well being, and to encourage the saving of money . . .[46]

Other messages of uplift and reform came in more subtle and worldly forms.

Looming over the main square of most company towns stood a large clock, an ever-present reminder of the need for prompt arrival at work, and of the importance of "spending one's time wisely." The very structures of the corporate villages carried messages as well. Residences were inevitably segregated by nationality, and white-collar nationals enjoyed superior housing to that occupied by their working class brethren. The company headquarters and the manager's home dwarfed other buildings, thereby giving physical expression to the corporate hierarchy. The typical grid pattern of streets, and the designation of specific areas for working, resting, eating, and sleeping expressed the corporate emphasis on rationalized functions. With increasing frequency, those functional areas included a school for workers' children during the day, and for workers themselves at night or on weekends. Changes in the company town reflected changes in the work force and in corporate policies toward them. Perhaps the most notable example of such changes came in the Guggenheim operations.

Because increasingly mechanized mines and plants required a more skilled labor force, the Guggenheims pursued a series of measures designed to create a better trained, safer, and more contented work force in their U.S. operations. They soon carried those efforts into their overseas operations. In Chile, the Guggenheims created personnel offices to screen job applicants to ensure a high quality pool of laborers to draw from. In 1916, the Guggenheims set up a welfare department at their Braden operations to see to the health, educational, and recreational needs of their workers. By the early 1920s the Guggenheims had raised the concept of the company town to a new level. Workers would no longer simply be anchored to the corporate village by scrip, a company store, and schools. Now the town would be an institution which would also distract them from drink with movies and teach them competitive values with organized sports while binding them to the company through such shared values. Other American mining and oil companies followed similar policies, setting up sports teams and creating social programs in their towns. Meanwhile, the United Fruit Company made particular strides in health and sanitation.[47]

Soon after the turn of the century, UFCO began setting up hospitals in its largest operations, and in 1912 the company created a separate medical department. The frutera's concern with health stemmed from the effects of malaria, pneumonia, and tuberculosis on UFCO workers. At their peak in 1924, the three diseases killed more than 500 of the company's employees. By 1926 the frutera had launched an all-out campaign to combat malaria. In the four years after the program was initiated, it halved malaria infection rates in the company's Costa Rican division.[48] Even the frutera's company towns had become mechanisms for reform and uplift for their workers. Nor were the company towns the sole means for spreading the American message.

Concerned as they were with exporting agricultural and mineral products, most U.S. companies had little interest in creating a consumer society. However, a few important corporations, particularly General Electric, took an intense interest in the formation of a consumer society. By the 1920s, G.E. had shifted its focus in the United States from simply producing power generating equipment to manufacturing and selling electrical appliances. It soon directed the same intense advertising campaigns at Latin American audiences, extolling the wonders of radios, toasters, and clothes washers. The company opened appliance stores in the region, staffed with local employees trained in the art of modern salesmanship, and wielding the most enticing of consumer offers—time payments. G.E.'s efforts generated from its in-country base complemented programs by a range of U.S. corporations that were exporting their goods to Latin America. As in the United States, newspaper ads sold more than a product, they offered access to an ideal world of self-improvement and material luxury. Buyers of RCA radios now had the world at their fingertips, and those who bathed with Palmolive would enjoy the pleasures of their own physical beauty. Beyond these very obvious attempts to peddle the wonders of consumer society, Latin American also saw an even more eye-catching display of images of this ideal world on movie screens.

American movies became regular entertainment fare in cities throughout Latin America during the 1920s. The wondrous images bore testimony to the technological wonders and achievements of U.S. society. Film images of enormous factories, the skyscrapers of New York, spacious homes, and a plethora of consumer goods sent a graphic message of success through the American way to people across the Western Hemisphere. The films of the period suggested through their plot lines that human ills and unhappiness could be resolved through the ameliorating effects of consumerism. Meanwhile, U.S. corporations enjoyed an important ally in their effort to make that vision of a U.S.-made modern society a reality.

American Protestantism inspired both by evangelical impulses and the new social sciences launched intense overseas missionary efforts in the late nineteenth century. The message the missionaries carried to Latin America did not constitute some pristine expression of Christianity but a solidly American one. American Protestantism had long since come to terms with modern capitalism and had accepted many of its values of individualism and competitiveness as its own. Frederick Gates, a leading Baptist clergyman and an advisor to the Rockefeller family, saw very specific economic benefits emerging from Protestant overseas missionary activity:

Missionaries and mission schools are introducing the application of modern science, steam and electric power, modern agricultural machinery, and modern manufacture into foreign lands. The result will be eventually to multiply the productive power of foreign countries many times. This will enrich them as buyers of American products, and enrich us as importers of their products. We are only in the very dawn of commerce, and we owe that dawn, with all its promise to the channels opened by Christian missionaries . . .[49]

U.S. investors in Latin America received additional benefits from missionary activity because of the compatibility of the Protestant message with their own business interests. Missionaries who taught the importance of cleanliness, promptness, and individual betterment, as well as the evils of drink were welcome additions to sugar and banana plantations in the Caribbean Basin and the mining camps of South America. The interweaving of business, religion, and a missionary sense of reform that had marked U.S. enterprise at the start of the nineteenth century had intensified and expanded by the early decades of the twentieth. Yet, much as with the material achievements of U.S. business in Latin America, corporate welfare, religious evangelism, and social reform had a dark side as well.

At the turn of the century, racism had reached a new level of intensity in the United States. Jim Crow laws, lynchings, attacks on black communities, and the Klu Klux Klan all flourished into the 1920s. Racist thinkers now cast their views in the form of supposedly scientific propositions. They claimed that IQ tests proved that white Americans and Western Europeans were superior in intelligence to Blacks, Latins, and Eastern Europeans. Those views enjoyed wide acceptance among the corporate reformers and religious missionaries who devoted their energies to Latin America. These Americans who extolled the possibilities of training Latin Americans to be diligent, efficient workers and explored the potential for creating a consumer society in the region, did so in part because they still believed that their neighbors to the south were inherently inferior to themselves. For the U.S. missionaries of progress, reform was important and indeed necessary because Latin Americans did not belong to the gifted white race. Even relatively moderate, reform-minded individuals believed that capitalism could not help but benefit their less fortunate neighbors to the south. One such individual was federal judge Charles Anderson of Boston.

Judge Anderson was no political or social reactionary. He had been one of several federal judges who dismissed charges brought against scores of political radicals by Attorney General A. Mitchell Palmer during the Red Scare of 1919–1920. In 1922, Anderson visited his son in Tela, Honduras, where he was working for the United Fruit Company. Upon his return, he wrote the following to Victor Cutter, the president of UFCO:

> I was very much interested in the general aspect of the relations of a company like yours to Central America. It seemed to me that your Company has been doing a great work of civilization, and without faults of exploitation and disregard of local and native rights incident to so much of the advance of big business into new regions, and in dealing with weaker, so-called inferior races. If my impressions are

consonant with the facts, you and the others responsible for the management of the United Fruit have cause for just pride.

Though bitterly opposed to so-called imperialism and extension of American domain in the Philippines, I have always expected that your generation or the next would see America held responsible for ordered conditions as far as the [Panama] Canal. . . . As an American citizen and a New Englander I was immensely gratified at what I saw of the way that work is being done.[50]

Corporate managers often had a far less idealistic view of their mission. At their worst, U.S. professionals viewed Latin American workers as drunken, violent beings or at the other extreme, they considered their employees to be child-like creatures in need of guidance since they were easily misled. Such ideas sharply curtailed corporate reform efforts. As Frank Ingersoll discovered, social welfare programs for Latin Americans such as housing, medical services, and education usually fell short of the standards set in the United States because corporations assumed that Latin American workers did not enjoy the level of civilization needed to fully appreciate or benefit from such services. U.S. perspectives on the Latin American middle classes proved to be almost as demeaning.[51]

U.S. managers hired Latin American white-collar employees, but usually only at the lowest levels of their organizations. They viewed Latin American professionals, even those with technical degrees from U.S. institutions, as a cut below the average American. If the region's middle class represented the most likely base for the new consumer society which the Americans hoped to build, it still did not measure up to American standards of intelligence, rationality, rugged individualism, and competitiveness. Even at its most benign, the U.S. mission of reform grew out of smug sense of American superiority.

SUMMARY

By the beginning of the twentieth century, the emergence of United States as the world's first modern industrial society had dramatic effects on its relationship with Latin America. Not only had the United States achieved the dominant role in the region's international trade, but American corporate giants now played critical roles in such key sectors as agriculture, mining, petroleum, and utilities. U.S. multinationals flocked to the Southern Hemisphere to exploit natural resources, expand markets, and protect their control of important new technologies. Latin American elites welcomed and encouraged the U.S. investment surge, trusting that U.S. technology, work methods, and financing would rescue their economies from the inefficiencies of repressive labor systems like debt peonage.

Latin America's rulers were not disappointed with their open door policy for U.S. investment. U. S. companies dramatically increased production of products ranging from Cuban sugar and Guatemalan bananas to Chilean copper and Venezuelan oil. Furthermore, many of these companies introduced new, more efficient work methods, and transferred elements of welfare capitalism, such as education and improved housing, to their Latin American operations. Even the United Fruit Company, not renowned for enlightened labor policies, created a health care system for its workers. Small businesspeople in Latin America also benefited from the Americans' promotion of exports of agricultural products like bananas, and their creation of large labor forces that served as potential new markets for local shopkeepers and merchants. Other members of the middle class found white-collar jobs in the U.S. corporations. The companies also sought to instill values of competitiveness, hard work, and individualism in blue- and white-collar workers. Yet this picture of economic development and social uplift also had its dark side.

U.S. corporate reformers carried with them a deep seated belief in the fundamental inferiority of Latin Americans. That belief, grounded in the pseudoscientific racism of the age, caused corporate managers to limit their reform efforts in the belief that Latin American workers could only be "civilized" to a limited degree. It also led them to give preferential treatment and pay to U.S. employees, and to treat Latin American employees as second class citizens within corporate society. Furthermore, American corporate policies to speed up the work process, and intensify competition within the work force often ran counter to communal values of cooperation and egalitarianism prevalent in much of Latin American society. Small businesspeople found that the arrival of the Americans produced mixed blessings, providing opportunities to some, but threatening others with withering competition, or domination of the type experienced by small banana growers in Central America. As U.S. corporations accelerated economic growth in the region they also created intense frictions between themselves and significant segments of Latin American societies. Those frictions would turn into outright conflict when the economic boom of the 1920s came to an abrupt and disastrous end. The reformers, planners, and dreamers of the 1920s did not stand at the doorway to a better tomorrow—they stood at the edge of the abyss.

PHOTOGRAPHS

Bananas grown by local
planters are loaded on a
United Fruit Company
steamer along the banks
of the Escondido River
in Nicaragua. The com-
pany's domination of
shipping facilities helped
it to take effective con-
trol of the smaller planters' operations. Source:
Scientific American.

American *fruteras* even-
tually attempted to re-
duce the labor intensity
of handling fruit with
machines like this banana
loading device. Source:
Scientific American.

The homes U.S. fruit companies built for their managers in Central America provided a physical expression of the power and status of the companies' American employees. Source: Adams, *Conquest of the Tropics*.

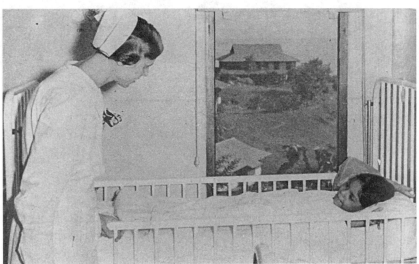

Although the fruit companies' Latin American workers often labored under harsh and unhealthy conditions, the *fruteras* did provide medical services such as this hospital. Source: Wilson, *Empire in Green and Gold*.

The Phelps Dodge company town in Nacozari, Mexico, with its orderly streets and basic social services symbolized the attempts of American corporations to Americanize their Latin American workers. Source: Ingersoll, *In and Under Mexico*.

(Opposite, above) Argentine workers in American-owned slaughter houses launched a massive strike against the companies in 1917. Source: Archivo general de la Nación, Buenos Aires, Argentina.

(Opposite, below) A huge steam shovel extracting ore at the Guggenheim's Santa Elena nitrate plant in Chile typified the mass extraction technology employed by the Guggenheims in both the nitrate and copper industries. Source: Asociación de Productores de Salitre de Chile.

As indicated by this turn of the century power plant in Cuba, early electric enterprises in Latin America were small locally owned operations that survived with the bare minimum technologies. Source: William Jared Clark, *Commercial Cuba.*

(Opposite, above) When General Electric entered Latin America, it bought out and consolidated local firms and introduced the latest and largest energy generating equipment such as found at this G.E. power plant in Brazil. Source: Geiger, Goode, *General Electric Company in Brazil.*

(Opposite, below) James Stillman, who with his father Charles, created an enormous business empire in Mexico and helped establish Citibank as one of the leading foreign financial institutions in Latin America. Source: Citibank.

Two Cuban children enjoy Coca-Colas in turn-of-the-century Havana. Coke became one of the most successful American consumer products ever introduced into Latin America. Source: The Coca-Cola Company.

Early radio transmission stations such as this one in Argentina helped launch radio as an American dominated communications media and a powerful tool for advertising U.S. consumer products.
Source: *Pan American Bulletin*.

By the 1950s Buenos Aires' street cars had been enveloped by a sea of automobiles, many of them American made. Source: Ministerio de Obras Públicas de la Nación, Buenos Aires, Argentina.

Lazaro Cardenas, President of Mexico (1934–40) whose national-ization of the oil industry in 1938 established him as one of Latin America's leading nationalists.

As this scene from a Panamanian television show demonstrates, during the 1950s t.v. became another important American-influenced communications medium and advertising mechanism. Source: *Broadcasting and Cable Magazine.*

Nelson Rockefeller, whose family controlled vast investments in Latin America, meets with one of the region's best known economic nationalists, President Getulio Vargas of Brazil. Source: U.S. National Archives, Washington, D.C.

Fidel Castro (center) with some of his comrades during their struggle to overthrow Cuban President Fulgencio Batista. Once in power, Cuba's revolutionary leader nationalized all American companies on the island including the holdings of corporate giants like General Electric, ITT, and United Fruit. Source: Corbis.

The G.E. manufacturing plant in Rio de Janeiro, Brazil, symbolized the company's growth beyond power generation and into the consumer products field. Source: Geiger, Goode, *General Electric Company in Brazil*.

(Opposite, above) By the 1960s, U.S. consumer products manufacturers were employing tens of thousands of Latin Americans such as these Brazilian workers assembling refrigerators. Source: Geiger, Goode, *General Electric Company in Brazil*.

(Opposite, below) Although U.S. car makers were slow to begin manufacturing passenger cars in Latin America, they eventually joined their European and Japanese competitors in creating large scale operations such as this engine assembly plant in Mexico. Source: Banco Naciónal de Comercio Exterior SA, Mexico City, Mexico.

U.S. based multinationals even transferred the manufacture of the ultimate American consumer good, the television, to Latin America. Shown here are Mexican women assembling sets. Source: Banco Naciónal de Comercio Exterior SA, Mexico City, Mexico.

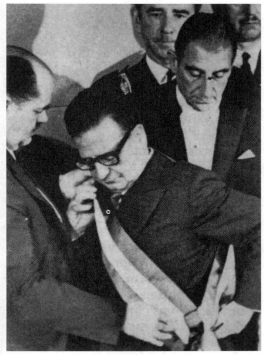

Nelson Rockefeller arriving in Rio de Janeiro during his 1969 tour of Latin America which stirred numerous anti-American protests. Source: Corbis.

President Salvador Allende of Chile accepting the presidential sash at his inauguration in 1970. Soon after his inauguration Allende launched widespread nationalizations of U.S. companies including Anaconda, Kennecott, and ITT. Behind Allende is former President Eduardo Frei, a moderate whom the U.S. government had strongly supported. Source: Associated Press.

Walter Wriston, who as chairman of Citibank, oversaw the bank's massive loan program in Latin America which nearly led to disaster during the debt crisis of the 1980s. Source: Citibank.

CHAPTER THREE

RESISTANCE AND POPULISM, 1922–1939

Christmas Eve 1900 brought a special gift to Elías Lafertte, a fourteen-year-old worker in one of the great nitrate refineries scattered across Chile's northern desert. His grandmother, Juana Urrutia, had decided to make a pilgrimage of thanksgiving to the Virgin of Andacollo. The trip would allow the boy to escape the scorching heat and grinding monotony of the nitrate fields. Together they would journey over six hundred miles south with other workers to the city of La Serena in the province of Coquimbo. There they would join in the festivities surrounding the Virgin's feast day. The celebration would include religious services and processions, public ceremonies and dances, culminating in a day-long bout of public feasting and drinking.

The year's end also brought good news for the U.S. mining magnate Daniel Guggenheim. One of his agents reported the discovery of large deposits of low-grade copper ore in the same Chilean desert region traversed by Elías Lafertte. Such ores represented a potential bonanza for Guggenheim and his six brothers who controlled the largest privately owned mining enterprise in the world.

Their father Simon, the son of an immigrant Swiss tailor, had brought his sons into his wholesale goods business and then led them into investments in Colorado silver mines in 1879. In later years, the brothers helped pioneer open pit mining techniques with their investments in the Bingham Canyon mine in Utah. Those techniques permitted the profitable exploitation of the type of low-grade copper ores discovered in Chile. After some years of hesitation, Daniel Guggenheim finally committed to Chilean mining, and eventually he and his brothers invested nearly $40 million in the initial development of Chuquicamata, a mining property in the northern desert. But Daniel Guggenheim saw what he believed to be an even greater bonanza in the outdated nitrate refineries dotting that same desert. He assured his brothers that "nitrates will make us rich beyond the dreams of avarice!"[1]

In 1930, Daniel Guggenheim and Chilean President Carlos Ibáñez agreed that the Guggenheims and the Chilean government would form a joint venture, the Chilean Nitrate Company (COSACH), to take control of and develop the industry using the Guggenheims' modern mining techniques. But this new company soon closed most of the old refineries causing massive layoffs, and then itself faced collapse with the onset of the Great Depression. The Depression and the COSACH debacle helped topple Ibáñez from power. In the 1932 election to replace him, the Communist Party's candidate Elías Lafertte denounced the Guggenheims as imperialists and called for the immediate nationalization of the company. Although the former nitrate worker fell far short of victory in his quest for the presidency, popular pressure forced the incoming government to dissolve the joint venture with the Guggenheims.

The intersection of the lives of Elías Lafertte and Daniel Guggenheim illustrates the mounting unrest directed against U.S. enterprise in Latin America in the years after the golden age of U.S. investment. Mounting protests in the late 1920s became militant, even revolutionary, movements directed against U.S. interests as the effects of the Great Depression crippled Latin American economies during the 1930s. In response, U.S. corporations would ally themselves with the Roosevelt administration in an effort to defend their investments and continue their penetration and transformation of Latin American societies. Those efforts would profoundly affect the relationships between U.S. corporations and their Latin American hosts for the next half century.

The collapse of the New York stock exchange in October 1929 proved to be more than just the end of another speculative bubble—falling stock prices marked the beginning of a worldwide collapse in commodity prices, trade, production, and lending. The global economy's mighty engine shuddered to a halt with catastrophic consequences for much of humanity.[2] Those developments spurred the growth of dynamic populist movements which seized the political stage during the 1930s and 1940s, bringing with them dramatic changes in the way U.S. companies would be treated. The crisis in the United States brought political realignment with the election of Franklin Roosevelt.

In attempting to deal with global economic catastrophe and a rising tide of anti-Americanism in the hemisphere, Roosevelt forged a new policy toward Latin America and a new partnership with American businesses operating there. By the time the United States entered World War II the Great Depression and the events it triggered had permanently reshaped the relationship between U.S. business and Latin America. The unbounded optimism that unfettered U.S. corporations would fashion the region into a series of prosperous consumer economies had vanished. The elite's open door policies had given way to strident economic nationalism. As for U.S. business leaders, they would have to redesign their methods of operation in the region, and they would work far more closely with their own government to protect their investments in Latin America.

RESISTANCE

Although the elites of Central America had strong reasons to welcome the *fruteras* and encourage their continued presence in their countries, relations between the dominant classes and U.S. companies did not prove nearly as harmonious in other parts of Latin America. The elites did not abandon their commitment to Liberal policies encouraging foreign investment, but many members of the group found their interests at odds with those of the Americans. A typical case involved the Cerro de Pasco Corporation. Its acquisition of hundreds of mining claims in the Peruvian Andes had profited wealthy Peruvian owners and relieved many of them of the ongoing operational problems such as capital scarcity and inferior technology. However, the Cerro de Pasco Corporation's monopoly, once in place, effectively excluded the national elite from profits in the mining sector—a situation that they refused to accept.

In 1900, the Peruvian government had granted a concession to the Empresa Socovanera de Cerro de Pasco for constructing a drainage tunnel in the mining district. The creation of a drainage system appeared to offer a solution to the mines' constant flooding problems. In turn the Empresa's government concession granted it a twenty percent share of the mines' ores. The Cerro de Pasco Corporation, however, objected strenuously to construction of the tunnel and refused to share its ore with the tunnel company.

The Cerro de Pasco managers pointed out that the drainage tunnel offered no real benefit to them because electric pumps could now effectively drain the mines. However, the importance of the drainage company derived less from the service it might provide than from the composition of its board of directors. The Empresa's organizers and directors included some of the most powerful figures in Peru. They expected and insisted on a share of the profits that Cerro de Pasco would extract from Peruvian territory. As the battle escalated, the Peruvian government stepped in and used its troops to halt the shipment of the company's ores. Despite backing from the U.S. State Department, the company finally conceded the inevitable, issuing $60 million in new stock to the Empresa as a means of sharing its profits with the powerful Peruvians who controlled it.

 Such conflicts constituted part of a process by which members of the elite and U.S. businessmen crafted a working relationship to provide powerful national figures with a direct share in the profits generated by U.S. companies. As one American diplomat observed, the resolution of the dispute established the fact "that rich Americans who have secured mining property worth many millions and upon which they have expended many millions, may be made to divide those millions with natives."[3] Elsewhere elite conflicts with U.S. business took on a more violent form.

In April 1920, Henry Catlin of the General Electric Company desperately sought to escape from the rebel forces that were seizing power in Guatemala. Catlin fled to the U.S. legation in Guatemala City. From there the legation's marine guard escorted him to Puerto Barrios where he boarded the U.S.S. Niagara as it weighed anchor on April 27. Catlin's sudden and unceremonious departure resulted from his business dealings, which had antagonized a considerable number of leading Guatemalans. In carrying out his mission to acquire the German-owned electric company for G. E., Catlin (see Chapter Two for detailed discussion) had arranged to purchase the firm for about one-quarter of its estimated market value, thanks to the good offices of Donald Hodgsdon, the American appointed to oversee German property in the country, and the cooperation of President Manuel Estrada Cabrera. The three men then agreed to jointly purchase all German coffee estates in the country. Under the latter agreement, the three would acquire estates worth $8 million for only $3 million. The Unionista Party now challenging Estrada Cabrera's long reign made the president's dealings with Catlin a central issue in its campaign. When that opposition turned to armed rebellion, Catlin reportedly encouraged the President to shell his own capital as a means of deterring advancing rebel forces. Not surprisingly, the triumphant Unionistas made Catlin's expulsion a top priority. But earlier in Mexico a similar inter-elite struggle over U.S. investment had occurred on a far larger scale and served as the prelude for a more consequential revolution.[4]

Porfirio Díaz had risen to power in 1876 with the direct assistance of U.S. business figures like James Stillman. In the decades that followed, Díaz rewarded those supporters with a virtual open door policy for U.S. companies in Mexico. Those policies, along with Mexico's natural riches and its proximity to the United States sent U.S. investment in the country soaring to $1 billion by 1910. The Mexican elite, however, found that the realization of their dream had turned into a nightmare. They now had to compete directly with U.S. investors in agriculture and mining. Their protests fell on deaf ears as the increasingly ossified Díaz regime proved unresponsive to the demands of local power brokers in northern Mexico where most of the U.S. agricultural and mining investments were concentrated. Among those severely impacted by this unequal contest was the Madero family. The Maderos' smelter in the city of Torreón symbolized the dominant position they had established in Mexican mining. But when the Mexican government allowed the Guggenheim brothers to build a competing smelter in nearby Valardina, the Guggenheims quickly gained the upper hand in the mining industry.[5] The Madero family's mounting discontent over threats to their prosperity prompted Francisco Madero to challenge Díaz for the presidency in 1910. Díaz blocked Madero's election bid, but the split within the ruling class gave other sectors of Mexican society an opportunity to vent their grievances over the impact of U.S. corporations on their lives.

Although the growth of the Mexican economy had prompted prodigious growth of the middle class, considerable discontent emerged among small businesspeople, white-collar employees, and professionals. For small businesses the coming of U.S. companies could prove a boon when they accelerated national economic growth, and created a larger wage labor force. But by creating company stores, U.S. corporations often deprived local businesses of access to the market represented by new work forces. They also competed with small businesses by selling low-cost retail products imported duty free. Small farmers or ranchers faced extinction through the loss of land to American investors. White-collar employees in U.S. companies discovered that there were few jobs above the level of clerk that Americans deemed them competent to occupy and always at salaries lower than their U.S. counterparts. All of these groups suffered severe economic setbacks as a result of a serious downturn in the Mexican economy, beginning in 1907, and they all suffered virtual exclusion from the authoritarian political structures of the *Porfiriato*. The mounting discontent of the middle class sectors added to what had already become overt discontent among the popular classes.

Peasants who had a long history of resisting the encroachment of large estates on their property faced a growing threat to their interests during the

Porfiriato. Under Díaz, domestic and foreign interests enjoyed free reign in acquiring vast stretches of Mexican territory, including lands controlled by peasant villages. U.S. businesses played a particularly prominent role in this process by acquiring 100 million acres of the national territory. By the time of Madero's electoral challenge to Díaz, peasants under leaders like Emiliano Zapata had already taken up arms against the regime. Mexican miners soon joined them in their protests.

Despite the creation of company towns and wage scales considerably above national averages, workers developed conflict laden relations with U.S. mining companies. Mining was arduous and often extremely danger- ous work, and Americans treated Mexicans as inferior beings deserving of only low wages and harsh treatment. Mexican workers also protested against fundamental changes in the work place instituted by American corpora- tions in the name of efficiency.

Through an army of timekeepers and engineers, U.S. mining companies sought ever-tighter control over the work gangs who labored in the tunnels far below the earth's surface. They created a complex hierarchy of job types and corresponding pay scales to encourage competitive rather than group work practices. Furthermore, workers viewed corporate welfare policies to discourage drinking and encourage healthier activities as simply additional elements in the expanding array of American control devices.

Many of these issues came to a head in 1906 at William E. Greene's Cananea mine. When Greene's company sought to extract more work from its miners by switching from an hourly to a piece work system, the workers resisted. They struck, demanding higher wages, shorter work days, and guarantees that 75 percent of the work force would be Mexican. The company rejected their demands, and violence soon erupted. When the company proved unable to crush the strike, the governor of the state of Sonora allowed Arizona territorial rangers to enter the state and suppress the labor uprising. The strike was noteworthy not only for the clear nationalist theme that ran through it, but because the strike leaders included a Mexican timekeeper and a supply clerk for the company. Their efforts symbolized the growing alliance between the middle and working classes that would challenge both the Díaz regime and its U.S. corporate allies. Throughout Mexico, workers, peasants, and elements of the middle class rallied around Madero to oust the dictator and reshape the relationship with U.S. business.

After Díaz fled into exile in 1911, Madero succeeded to the presidency but his agenda reflected his own elite background, focusing on political change rather than fundamental social and economic reform. When one of Díaz's generals arranged the assassination of Madero in February 1913, the revolutionary factions battled each other for power.

From the perspective of U.S. business leaders and President Woodrow Wilson, none of these groups represented a satisfactory replacement for Madero or Díaz. However, the Constitutionalists, whose numbers included elements of the middle class and the elite, seemed far less likely to war on American business than the more radical peasant and worker contingents led by the likes of Emiliano Zapata and Pancho Villa.

Fearing the cost of a long-term military intervention, Wilson settled for the short-term occupation of Mexico's principal port, Veracruz, beginning in April 1914. The U.S. government used the occupation as a means of funneling weapons and supplies to the Constitutionalists, helping them to final victory over their more radical rivals. The Constitutionalists and other revolutionary forces then drew up a new constitution. The Constitution of 1917 reasserted national sovereignty over vital natural resources, guaranteed land to peasants, and assured workers of basic rights.

The Mexican constitution's nationalist and social provisions reflected the views of the revolutionary forces and offered a clear warning to U.S. business about the potentially explosive consequences of their mission to Latin America. U.S. business made its perspective on the revolution and the constitution quite clear when Delbert Haff, representing Phelps Dodge and American oil companies, met with the Mexican finance minister Luis Cabrera in El Paso in March 1916. Haff warned Cabrera that his government must honor Mexico's existing foreign debt, respect existing concessions, and put an end to speculation that the government planned to nationalize the oil industry.[6] In summary, U.S. businesspeople intended to defend at every turn the prerevolutionary status of their investments. Yet Americans also treated the case of Mexico as an isolated incident, even as resentment toward U.S. business continued to build throughout Latin America.

The First World War intensified the conflict with American business as U.S. involvement increased and inflationary pressures created new unrest in the region. In 1919 strikes erupted in Peru and their targets included the Standard Oil fields and the Cerro de Pasco Mining Corporation. In the capital of Lima, protesters attacked the headquarters of the W. R. Grace Company and other foreign and domestic institutions which they felt exploited them in the midst of the misery caused by inflation. These uprisings in Peru lacked coordination and they were not exclusively or even primarily anti-American in tone. But they did offer a clear warning that U. S. business and its elite allies would be held responsible for the consequences of their modernization schemes. Argentine workers sent the same message in a major conflict with U.S. meat packing companies.

The U.S. meat packing giants, including Armour and Swift, invested in the Argentine industry after 1905, controlling sixty percent of its output by the beginning of World War I. In the plants surrounding the Argentine capital of Buenos Aires, the U.S. companies introduced the production techniques common to continuous process manufacture. The companies had reduced killing and dismemberment of animals to a series of simple individual tasks to be carried out along an assembly line. The division of labor, when married to continuous processing techniques, enabled the firms to employ fewer skilled butchers and produce more product at a faster rate. It also meant that in the event of strikes, the meat packers could call on the large numbers of unemployed, unskilled immigrant workers in Buenos Aires to serve as scabs.

The companies further encouraged division among workers by assigning specific tasks to different ethnic groups. As a result, the companies could reinforce ethnic divisions with differences in skill levels. The fact that skilled Argentineans might look down on the unskilled Poles and Italians who labored alongside them in the packing plants hampered, but did not preclude, labor organization.

In late 1917, the 15,000 workers in the packing houses around the Argentine capital launched a massive strike against their employers. The workers demanded safe and healthy working conditions. Faced with a drive system in which supervisors and foremen abused workers to extract more work from them, the strikers demanded an end to these practices. Cognizant of the suffering of the unemployed in the workers' community, the organizers also insisted that available tasks be shared among all the workers. For their part, the companies felt most threatened by the strikers' demand for union recognition.

Unions would challenge the labor-intensive meat packing companies' right to hire, fire, and reassign thousands of workers at will. Recognizing the enormous threat represented by unions, the companies' managers rejected the workers' demands out of hand and attempted to break the strike. The meat packers brought scab labor from the swollen ranks of the unemployed and relied on the Argentine military to protect their plants and transportation network. From its onset in late November, the strike became a bitter conflict between workers on one side and corporate and government institutions on the other. Although the packing house workers would enjoy the support of skilled workers such as bakers and railway workers as well as many local merchants, the company-government alliance eventually proved too much for them and the strike collapsed by the end of January 1918.

Yet even in defeat, the workers had sent a clear warning to corporate America and its allies in Latin America. The radical transformation of the work place achieved by U.S. companies and the ill treatment of workers would not go unchallenged. Two decades later when Argentine workers redefined those issues into a nationalist campaign, the outcome of their struggles would be dramatically different. But in the meantime workers elsewhere in the region had already initiated that process.[7]

NATIONALISM

Ethnic divisions promoted by corporations were nothing new to the banana workers at United Fruit's operations in Guatemala. Because most of the country's peasants resisted wage labor on the banana plantations, the company brought thousands of West Indians to Puerto Barrios to supplement its labor force. Convinced that the blacks were more pliable if not more committed to hard work than Guatemalans, the UFCO managers often divided work assignments along ethnic lines much as the meat packers did in Argentina.

However, both West Indians and Guatemalans had to show proper deference toward white managers, and neither group could expect the treatment accorded white employees. Indeed, for all of UFCO's investment in the development of the port with modern cargo handling equipment, electric lighting, a radio station, telephones, and even a country club, the view of this modern wonder could be considerably different from the perspective of black and Latin workers alike. The U.S. journalist Carleton Beals offered that alternative perspective during his visit to Puerto Barrios:

> I often wandered out through the hodge-podge town, built on a pestiferous marsh, reeking with spilled petroleum, out along the twisted paths where are massed in utter promiscuity the atrocious blue and yellow shacks of negroes and Indians and Chinese. Boards and gunny sacking, banana and palm tree leaves, river cane, sheet iron and rags have gone into the making. Picking my way through the slime and excrement and swarms of naked, mud-smeared children. . . . I came out on the walk fronting the foot-high breakwater over which the waves sometimes come flooding into the low shacks, and there saw the curve of the shore and the line of tall taut coconut palms broken by an interminable row of spider-leg piers stretching out to cubbyhole water-closets set about four feet above high tide. This is Puerto Barrios' highest word in esthetics.[8]

Although UFCO provided its labor force with medical treatment for diseases affecting their ability to work, it also left those same workers to live in squalid, disease infested shantytowns. Amidst the alternating images of clean, rigid functionality, and the utter squalor created by United Fruit, Guatemalans and West Indians had to come to grips with the new social reality it defined—an environment in which the importance of family, friendship, and community was secondary to the individual's position in the rationalized process of production. In their attempt to adapt to that reality, workers faced serious conflicts with the fruit company.

UFCO's close relationship with dictator Manuel Estrada Cabrera ensured it a free hand in shaping the work environment of its operations in Guatemala—an arrangement that would persist under the dictator's successors. The military garrison stationed in the heart of Puerto Barrios clearly symbolized the government's role in United Fruit's labor affairs.

Free to determine work conditions, and confident of state support in case of labor unrest, the company employed task or wage systems depending on the background of the workers. Guatemalan peasants, generally unaccustomed to the disciplines of wage labor, and likely to wander away after receiving a day's wages, were paid only when they completed a specific task. Jamaicans, who were more familiar with wage labor, received wages for their work on the docks. In both cases the company kept a minimum number of full-time employees summoning most workers on an as needed basis. This meant a highly irregular work schedule as the company called out field hands to cut bananas non-stop when a steamer approached port, while stevedores responded to a similar signal when the time came to load the fruit on the waiting ship. In addition to uncertain and irregular work schedules, the stevedores also faced an attempt by the company to shift from a wage to a task system. UFCO's attempt to speed up the work process triggered a strike by the dock workers in 1914 that forced the company to abandon the task system. But nine years later a strike with broader goals would prove far less successful.

On February 3, 1923, the dock workers at Puerto Barrios struck, refusing to load bananas and demanding higher pay, as well as housing and medical services. The Guatemalan workers also demanded an end to the preferential treatment they claimed the company gave to Jamaicans. Realizing that the issue of racial preference would limit the appeal of their movement among the predominantly black work force, the Guatemalans soon abandoned this last item. Meanwhile, the stevedores successfully blocked the company's use of scab laborers. They then seized a train and headed into the countryside to rally support among farm workers. With their numbers swelled to over 1,000, the strikers occupied the company town of Quirigua in the interior. The farm workers there added a new item to the stevedores' agenda. Harkening back to a time when, as self-sufficient peasants they worked their own land, the laborers explained to a local military commander that they had no intention of returning the company's farms or other land because they were its rightful owners. At the same time, the dock workers had further broadened the ideological base of their actions.

In petitions to the Guatemalan president and the U.S. minister, the UFCO workers complained that Estrada Cabrera had violated the constitutions of both countries. He had ceded control over railways, shipping, and the banana industry to a single foreign company, jeopardizing the national interests of Guatemala and violating U.S. laws against restraint of trade. At the same time, the workers assured the U.S. ambassador that they welcomed any foreign company willing to promote Guatemala's economic growth and urged him to invite other U.S. firms to compete with UFCO in their country. The fruit company's workers had wisely broadened the scope of their action, casting it in terms of Guatemalan nationalism and anti-imperialism. This strategy won support in the local press and even among some government officials, but the strike ended in failure after six weeks of government mediation. The frutera had refused to yield to the workers' demands and its enormous influence ensured the Guatemalan government's cooperation.[9] Just to the south in Honduras, however, banana workers enjoyed broader support and would experience greater success in their efforts.

In Honduras, the fruit companies destabilized national politics as they chose sides in domestic political contests to secure favorable treatment for their enterprises. In this volatile political environment, local *caudillos* or power brokers made the companies targets for extortion to enrich themselves and secure concessions from the national government. This turbulent situation created considerable opportunity for maneuvering for the labor movement on the banana coast. Striking workers also benefited from alliances with small planters and merchants who found themselves at the mercy of the increasingly powerful fruteras.

A classic instance of such cooperation occurred in 1920 when more than a thousand striking banana workers and a local planter, Jacobo Munguía, seized the port of La Ceiba. For the workers who won a wage increase from Standard Fruit the strike represented their attempt to come to grips with their position as full-time wage laborers. Munguía and other planters joined the strike in an unsuccessful attempt to preserve their positions as small independent growers. Four years later, when stevedores at two ports controlled by United Fruit struck, they enjoyed the support of local merchants, resentful of United Fruit's refusal to redeem company scrip spent by workers in local stores. In all of these actions, the workers also counted on the tacit and sometimes active support of local officials and politicians, sensitive to the fluid political situation in Honduras.

Workers cast these activities not simply in a labor versus management context; they also made it clear that they were engaged in an anti-American campaign. In response to the fruteras' use of U.S. naval forces to discourage labor protests, workers countered with threats to murder Americans, leaving many of the fruteras' U.S. employees in constant fear for their lives. Henry F. Plummer, a stockholder in United Fruit who visited the coast in 1924, reported that "the feeling of the natives against the Americans on the north coast was exceedingly bitter, largely because of the conduct of the Americans and their attitudes."[10]

In the case of Honduras, the reshaping of the banana coast had created clashes with workers, growers and merchants who had joined in an anti-American crusade by the mid-1920s.[11] In Cuba a similar alliance had begun to emerge in the sugar industry.

Through the First World War, U.S. sugar companies in Cuba emphasized increasing production. However, the post-war collapse of sugar prices compelled American managers to dramatically increase efficiency. They imported millions of dollars of new, labor-saving grinding and cane handling equipment. The companies also improved performance with the increased use of electric power and by employing more chemists and technicians to oversee and manage their mills. These innovations enabled mills to extract more sugar from the cane, and reduced the number of days required for the harvest.

For Cuban mill workers these changes meant an increasingly impersonal work place where they had less and less control over the work process. Worker resistance to this transformation triggered a strike in the mills in 1924. Union recognition lay at the heart of the struggle between the workers and the companies. As American business interests readily acknowledged, union recognition would mean greater worker control over the production process—a prospect they absolutely rejected. The strike suffered from a number of problems including a lack of strong support from the professionals in the mills. Through their organization, the National Sugar Industry Association, the Cuban white-collar employees acknowledged their mutual interests with the workers but they refused to join the strike, and rejected the strike's goals as too radical. Yet a common nationalist theme already ran through working and middle class concerns—a theme that had deep historical roots in Cuba.

Under colonial rule native-born Cubans not only had few real political rights, but they also found themselves shunted aside by Spaniards in the economic arena. The Americans who came to the island after 1898 repeated and expanded that pattern of discrimination and displacement. U.S. sugar companies had convinced the Cuban government to permit the use of immigrant workers in the industry with the result that thousands of Jamaicans had displaced Cubans in the cane fields. At the same time Spaniards, Chinese, and other immigrants competed with Cubans for work in the mills. Ramón Hernández Reynaldo, a Cuban sugar worker, recalled in later years that when he arrived seeking work at a sugar mill,

> those working in the mill house were English . . . Those in the boiler house were all Chinese. And those on the sugar floor were Spanish. In maintenance, they were also Spanish, there were no Cubans.
>
> In the fields they were Haitians. There were only a few Cubans because the *colonos* [farmers] say that the Haitians were better for the business of cutting the cane because Cubans take Saturdays off.[12]

Even many white-collar employees found themselves fired or demoted and replaced by or subordinated to Americans. In a letter to Gerard Smith, manager of the Cuban Cane Sugar Company, Cuban white-collar employees complained that:

> You should know that between twenty and twenty-five thousand families or perhaps more depend for a living on the work in the mills . . . [W]ith the less than clever exclusive system that you and other American milling companies go about substituting [Cuban] engineers, administrators, doctors, nurses, chemists, plant and office managers, typists etc. etc. with Americans[, you are] decreeing hunger and misery in that multitude of Cuban homes . . .[13]

Treated as strangers in their own land, Cuban workers and middle class professionals established common ground on the issue of their treatment by American companies. Even the Cuban Communist Party deviated from its traditionally internationalist line that condemned capitalism per se, to define the problem in Cuba as one of foreign capital ignoring the interests of the Cuban working and middle classes.[14] Any such alliance of the middle and working classes would represent a serious threat to U.S. business and the whole concept of capitalist development. Such a threat had already taken shape in Mexico.

Despite the assertion of worker and peasant rights, and the strong nationalistic tone of the 1917 Mexican Constitution, the popular classes soon grew disenchanted with the constitution and the revolutionary elite who drafted it. Part of the disenchantment stemmed from the failure of the government to create enabling legislation to enforce the constitution's labor provisions. The revolutionary elite's efforts to accommodate U.S. investors added to that discontent.

Mexico's new rulers found little time to enjoy their newly won power. The new government faced overt hostility from both American business and the U.S. government. American bankers had formed the International Committee of Bankers on Mexico in 1918 to reach an agreement with the new regime on the enormous foreign debt incurred by the Díaz regime. The committee's close links to corporations such as American Smelting and Refining made it the leading private organization asserting U.S. investors' rights in Mexico.[15] Operating in close cooperation with the U.S. State Department, these two powerful U.S. institutions made it abundantly clear to the Mexican government that until it guaranteed the safety of U.S. investments in Mexico, there would be neither new loans nor diplomatic recognition. By 1924 these external pressures convinced President Alvaro Obregón to offer the necessary guarantees to U.S. business. In addition to external pressures, the revolutionary elite sincerely wished to create a viable working relationship with U.S. business, seeing it as a vital part of their plans for Mexican development. The elite anticipated a large albeit regulated role for American business in Mexico's future. As they attempted to forge that new relationship, both sides faced a serious threat from popular protesters.

The revolution had not merely articulated worker rights in the Constitution of 1917, it created local democratic movements committed to defending those rights. The residents of local towns could once again elect mayors who had for decades been appointed by the central government. Locally elected governments demonstrated considerable sympathy for protests by workers and middle class groups against U.S. businesses, and they had far more room for maneuver than they had ever previously enjoyed. For U.S. companies, increased popular militancy compounded the problems they already faced in the 1920s.

The combatants in the Mexican Revolution had inflicted tremendous damage on U.S. companies. The contending armies had destroyed railway tracks, driven off workers, confiscated property, and imposed special war taxes. Severe economic losses combined with uncertainty about the policies the new government would pursue towards foreign investment, drove many small companies out of Mexico. In agriculture, large numbers of

U.S. investors lost their lands as the Mexican government sought to restore national control in that vital segment of the economy. Faced with declining oil reserves in Mexico, U.S. petroleum companies failed to reinvest in their operations. But for many large U.S. companies, Mexico's economic problems and social unrest created opportunities. American Smelting and Refining used this period to absorb failing competitors and upgrade its operations. G.E.'s American and Foreign Power Company entered Mexico at this time, acquiring much of the electrical power net outside Mexico City. These companies made new investments to expand output, and to deal with problems of labor unrest.

The technology U.S. companies now installed in Mexico had substantial labor displacing capabilities. With these innovations, American managers could reduce labor costs, and create a smaller, better trained labor force. To retain that core of workers, the companies introduced a variety of improvements including better housing, athletic programs, safety precautions, and anti-drinking campaigns. Managers expected that these new "Americanized" workers would prove far less susceptible to appeals from radical labor organizers. As a Phelps Dodge manager explained in 1927,

[T]he general policy has been to adopt any device or practice which will break even on cost and do away with men. In other words the Company should be operated with the fewest number of men possible. Gradually, as jobs are combined, we will have a better, higher paid, and more satisfied organization.[16]

But these efforts fell far short of expectations.

Despite U.S. efforts to create a smaller, more manageable work force, the 1920s proved to be a period of acute labor turbulence in Mexico. These problems arose in part because U.S. managers, who still viewed Mexican workers as inherently inferior, often gave minimal effort to industrial welfare programs. Furthermore, the absence of a national labor relations system precluded mediation as a viable option for resolving conflicts. But most importantly, the agenda of much of the working class represented a direct threat to U.S. enterprise, and to the Mexican elite's vision of national development.

Between 1923 and 1925 worker protests erupted into strikes and plant seizures at power stations and oil facilities in Tampico. Although wages and hours comprised a portion of the workers' agenda, they also made more radical demands including control over hiring and firing and a variety of other management activities. Drawing on the anarchosyndicalist tradition in the Mexican labor movement, workers envisioned a just society as comprised of small, self-sustaining communities of workers and peasants. Mexican workers in effect attempted to take back control of the work place from corporate management. Middle class support for the workers added to the seriousness of that challenge.[17]

The revolution and the continued intensification of U.S. investment had distinctly negative effects on Mexican professionals and small businesspeople. The economic devastation of the revolution drove hundreds of thousands of small businesses into bankruptcy. And despite the strong nationalist tone of the revolution, few U.S. companies offered significant new employment opportunities to Mexican professionals. Under these conditions, middle class Mexicans frequently made common cause with workers in their struggles against American business. In the towns or *municipios*, small businesspeople joined workers in protests. In the industrial work place such as the Huasteca Petroleum Company, engineers and accountants joined and often led workers' unions. In light of the recent revolutionary struggle, these groups espoused a powerful nationalist argument, wherein they asserted that they, and not the Mexican government, were struggling to protect national interests against foreign domination. These social alliances and arguments enhanced the power of a labor movement that threatened to seize control of the work place from capitalists. In the midst of this intense struggle, the Great Depression crippled the ability of the Mexican government and U.S. business to accommodate these groups. Plummeting government revenues and corporate incomes threatened to destroy any attempts at accommodation. The consequences of economic collapse would soon become frighteningly apparent throughout Latin America.

THE GREAT CRASH

The prosperity of the 1920s rested on a fragile new international financial order. The precarious state of international financial institutions derived in large measure from the condition of Germany, the most important national economy in Europe. In the years immediately after the war Germany suffered from hyperinflation which wiped out its domestic capital markets while the country also struggled to pay $33 billion in war reparations. Under these conditions Germany had to borrow heavily in the United States to finance its post-war recovery and make reparation payments. In 1928 alone, Germans accounted for half of the world's international borrowing. Nor was Germany the only heavy debtor dependent on U.S. loans.

During the 1920s, Latin American governments had joined with U.S. banks and investment houses in a frenzy of borrowing that reached the $1.5 billion mark. Many of those loans helped finance current account spending by governments, such as covering government payrolls. Such expenditures failed to contribute to the long-term growth of national economies. In turn, these relationships made Europe and Latin America heavily dependent on continued financing from the United States.[18]

When the New York stock market speculation collapsed in October 1929, it not only wiped out billions in corporate capital and middle class savings, it also severed the credit life line from U.S. banks to the German economy. As two of the world's most important economies collapsed, the effects reverberated around the world. Between 1929 and 1932, world trade fell by 60 percent, industrial production in the United States–which accounted for 42 percent of world output–declined by one-third. Prices for wheat fell by 66 percent while the prices of other primary products such as sugar, coffee, and copper went into similar free falls. International lending dropped by 90 percent between 1929 and 1932. The collapse of the global market for primary products and the evaporation of international lending struck with particular severity in Latin America.[19]

Although countries like Argentina and Mexico had made considerable progress toward industrialization by the end of the 1920s, the export of primary products continued to underpin all economies in the region. Those critical sectors had already shown signs of weakness in the late 1920s as the flood of such products on the world market began to depress prices. With the onset of the Great Depression, those prices fell sharply. The value of exports from most Latin American countries dropped by 50 percent or more between 1928 and 1932. Such price declines devastated economies where exports generated between 30 and 50 percent of gross domestic product (GDP).[20]

While the severity of the depression varied from country to country depending on the degree of decline in export prices and volumes, all Latin American countries shared in the increased burden of debt financing. As economic disaster spread across the U.S. economy, U.S. banks limited their credit extensions to bridge loans which simply allowed Latin American governments to make payments on existing loans. By 1931 even that trickle had dried up and countries in the area faced the nearly impossible task of servicing huge debts with rapidly falling export revenues.

Chile became a prime example of the impossible situation the Latin American economies now faced. During the 1920s Chile had borrowed $1.76 billion in the U.S. By 1930 the annual service on its foreign debt had reached nearly $400 million. In the face of plummeting export revenues, the country simply could not earn the dollars required to pay its debt, and Chile defaulted in 1931.[21] In fact, one nation after another defaulted on its foreign debt. No Latin American country repudiated its debt, and many attempted to make at least some payments. But the drying up of the credit stream and the mounting number of defaults signaled the effective collapse of the international credit system. Adding to the disaster, the severe loss of foreign exchange rapidly drained gold reserves in these countries to pay for imports. To staunch this financial hemorrhage, governments placed limits on imports and imposed restrictions on the exchange of local currency for gold.

The Depression and attempts to cope with it effectively dismantled the open economic systems created by Liberal regimes over the previous half century. Internally, the Depression struck most severely in urban areas— the main links between the world economy and the export sectors of the domestic economy such as mining and commercial agriculture. In Mexico, for example, employment in the mining sector fell by 50 percent and unemployment rose sharply in urban areas as well. While subsistence agriculture protected peasants from the worst effects of the Depression, that was little comfort to the unemployed and often militant workers in the urban and export sectors. For the middle class, the Great Depression meant austerity programs, unpaid government bureaucrats, corporate salary cuts, and the disappearance of imported consumer goods from store shelves.[22] Meanwhile, the U.S. corporate leaders who had promised to drive Latin America into a new unparalleled era of growth and prosperity were themselves reeling from the effects of the Great Depression.

U.S. mining companies suffered severely from the sharp decline in industrial output in the United States. With automobile production dropping by 50 percent between 1929 and 1931 and the output of electrical products suffering similar slumps, the demand for copper and iron ores nosedived. The Phelps Dodge Corporation shut down its operations in Mexico and disbanded its work force. Although the company would later reopen its mines, dozens of other U.S. mining companies in Mexico closed for good. In Chile, the Kennecott and Anaconda companies–after investing over $200 million in the development of Chilean copper deposits–saw the value of their ouput fall from $111 million in 1929 to $11 million in 1932. For American and Foreign Power (AFP), the Depression knocked the bottom out of the consumer market for electricity and electrical products, while foreign exchange controls in Latin America severely impaired the company's ability to remit profits to the United States. The company's net revenues fell seventeen percent between 1930 and 1931. With a dramatic drop in income, AFP struggled with the burden of debt it had assumed to build its impressive power network.[23]

U.S. sugar and banana companies also suffered sharp declines in profitability and resorted to cutting output, reducing their work forces, and cutting the hours and wages of the laborers who remained. Throughout Latin America, U.S. corporations retrenched by reducing investments, output, and wages. The American promise of perpetual prosperity had disintegrated in a few short years. For millions of Latin Americans it seemed clear that their elites and U.S. business leaders had pursued a course to enrich themselves, while leading Latin America down the road to disaster.

In Central America, the American fruteras had successfully confronted worker protests of the 1920s largely through a combination of their own resources, influence over local governments and, in extreme cases, direct intervention by the U.S. government. But the Depression triggered a series of challenges to all of these options. In the early months of 1932, banana workers across the north coast of Honduras struck against the Standard and United Fruit Companies. These strikes represented the most serious threat yet to the power and influence of the fruit companies. Workers reacted against reductions in hours and wages imposed by the companies in response to the Depression. The workers enjoyed assistance from recently organized leftist political and labor movements in Honduras. In addition, local planters and merchants threw their support to the strikers as a means of protesting the fruteras' monopolistic practices. Yet the fruit companies, particularly United Fruit, enjoyed their own advantages in responding to this new threat. Samuel Zemurray, owner of the Cuyamel Fruit Company, sold his company to UFCO in 1929. Then, in a series of stock maneuvers, he seized control of his one-time rival in 1930, emerging as the president of a new and more powerful United Fruit Company. The new United Fruit used its now uncontested influence within the Honduran government, and its own security forces to crush the wave of strikes sweeping across its facilities. But if UFCO had defeated the popular uprising on the north coast, it was also clear that it had faced the greatest challenge of its existence in Central America up to that time. Similar challenges to large U.S. corporate interests had also erupted in Peru and Chile.

POPULISM

Like many of his counterparts in Latin America, President Augusto Leguía (1919–1930) of Peru fell victim to the effects of the Depression, and was toppled by a military coup in August 1930. Leguía's fall triggered a wave of protests against his dictatorial rule and his ardently pro-American policies. By September, the Cerro de Pasco Corporation confronted a wave of strikes throughout its mining camps in the Andean highlands. Those strikes enjoyed the support of local merchants as well as officials from municipal governments and national government officials who perceived a common nationalist agenda in their protests against the giant U.S. corporation. As one American diplomat noted,

> There is a general feeling on the part of all Peruvians that the Company has enormous resources which have accrued to it during the recent years as a result of the exploitation of the natural resources of Peru and that, in spite of general unsatisfactory business conditions in the world. A large share of these resources, they feel, belong to the Peruvian nation and should be distributed to Peruvian workmen in the form of higher wages and better living conditions.[24]

After failed attempts by the company to negotiate a settlement, the workers organized a congress in the highland city of Oroya, under the aegis of Peru's emerging Communist Party. The Communists, however, rejected the alliance of middle and working class interests, and a confrontation between workers and soldiers provided the necessary rationale for the Peruvian government to concede to the company's demand that it crush the uprising. The suppression of the strike did not ensure tranquility for U.S. companies. In the months that followed, ITT's female telephone operators in Lima, the Grace Company's clerks in the south of the country, and IPC's oil workers in the north all launched strikes that frequently ended in violent repression. Much like their counterparts in Mexico, the Peruvian protesters formed a nationalist coalition against U.S. interests that challenged the very principle of corporate control of the work place. In the case of Peru those protests assumed the form of a national political movement.

In founding the Alianza Popular Revolucionaria Peruana (APRA)in 1924, Víctor Raúl Haya de la Torre gave voice to much of the popular discontent which erupted after the fall of Augusto Leguía. Indeed, in Haya, the eldest son of Edmundo Haya, the failed entrepreneur and newspaper editor from Trujillo (discussed in Chapter 2), can be found the roots of much of the populist discontent sweeping Peru and other Latin American nations at this time. Haya had witnessed the struggles of his father, and those of other small businesspeople and farmers in the Chicama Valley as large sugar companies, including that owned by the Grace family, came to dominate the region. Through APRA, Haya de la Torre enunciated an anti-imperialist, nationalistic program dedicated to the defense of middle and working class interests. Living in exile at the time of the dictator's demise, Haya de la Torre returned to his homeland in 1931 to campaign for president amidst growing social and economic unrest.

In the face of a rising wave of discontent in Peru, Julian Smith, an assistant U.S. commercial attaché in Lima, prescribed the following solution:

> [T]he masses have not the proper respect for law and order and it will take fear alone to inspire this. It is further generally believed that the time is soon coming when such action will be necessary and that the result cannot be obtained by a few shots in the air followed by a few scattered casualties, but only by a cold blooded slaughter with machine-guns. This is a general belief among the better element of Peruvians and foreigners alike.[25]

Smith's proposal for a violent restoration of social order was soon carried out with tragic consequences. After Haya's defeat by Luis Sánchez Cerro, the military officer who had overthrown Leguía, APRA launched an armed uprising that the military brutally crushed. Yet even after APRA's defeat, Sánchez Cerro felt compelled to assume a nationalist/populist stance towards U.S. business by imposing additional taxes and requiring increased national representation in the companies' management cadres. But these political and policy attacks on American business paled in comparison to the armed assaults on U.S. business occurring in Nicaragua.

The ongoing power struggle between Nicaraguan Liberals and Conservatives since the fall of José Santos Zelaya erupted into armed conflict in 1927. Fearing damage to its business interests and influence in the country, the U.S. government soon mediated a compromise allowing the Liberals to return to power in the next presidential election. But one Liberal commander, Augusto Sandino, refused to accept the U.S. brokered deal which essentially preserved the status quo, particularly the dominant influence of the United States in Nicaraguan national affairs.

In numerous messages and manifestos, Sandino clearly outlined the social basis of his movement and defined its enemies. In an interview with the U.S. journalist Carleton Beals, he asserted that "Our army is . . . composed of workers and peasants who love their country." In a message to workers he declared, "The working class of all Latin America today suffers a double exploitation, that of imperialism, mainly that of the Yankee, and that of the national capitalists and exploiters, who in their eagerness to obtain the favors of the insatiable invader are constantly intensifying the destruction of the revolutionary movement. . . ." Finally, in a letter to President Herbert Hoover, who as an engineer had once worked at a Nicaraguan mine, he declared, "[Y]ou owe us the peace lost in our society since 1909, when Wall Street bankers introduced the corrupting vice of the dollar in Nicaragua. For every thousand dollars that the Yankee bankers have introduced into my country, a Nicaraguan has died, and our mothers, sisters, wives and sons have shed tears of sorrow."[26]

Sandino's denunciation of U.S. domination touched a responsive chord among many Nicaraguans, especially workers in American companies. His armed assaults on leading symbols of the U.S. corporate presence such as the La Luz and Los Angels Mining Company and the Bragmans Bluff Company (a Standard Fruit subsidiary) drew workers in these enterprises into the ranks of his rebel army. For the laborers in U.S. businesses, Sandino's nationalist campaign gave vent to their animosity toward the rigors of industrial labor, low wages, and miserable working conditions which they identified with corporate America. That popular base of support allowed Sandino's forces to battle thousands of U.S. marines to a standstill. But in 1934, Anastasio Somoza, head of the U.S. trained Nicaraguan National Guard, arranged Sandino's assassination, crushed the remainder of the rebel forces, and eventually imposed a pro-American dictatorship. Yet at the very time that Somoza was salvaging U.S. interests in Nicaragua, events in the United States and Cuba forced the American government to reshape its policies toward Latin America.

THE GOOD NEIGHBOR

Since 1896 the Republican Party had dominated national politics with the support of large corporations. But by the end of World War I, several different forces began to undermine that coalition. Capital-intensive companies with strong competitive positions in international markets developed policies distinguishing them from labor-intensive, domestically oriented firms. Corporate giants such as Standard Oil of New Jersey and General Electric espoused industrial welfare labor policies and internationalist trade policies in contrast to steel and textile companies, which stressed antiunion and protectionist programs. These differences within the corporate community took on the dimensions of a life and death struggle as the Great Depression threatened to destroy the U.S. economy. With Franklin Roosevelt's election in 1932, high-tech firms and their allies among international financial houses began to forge an alliance with the Democratic Party and labor unions that would dominate the U.S. political scene for the next three decades. The new coalition's internationalist economic policies would quickly take shape because of the challenges facing the United States in Latin America.[27]

Early in his first administration Roosevelt addressed the collapse of international trade with federal initiatives. He created the second Export Import Bank to provide federal funds designed to assist foreign, especially Latin American, nations' trade with the United States.[28] The president also secured Congressional approval of a reciprocal trade agreement bill that gave the executive considerable leeway to lower U.S. tariffs as a part of trade negotiations with other nations. But even as he sought to revive international economic activity between the United States and Latin America, events in Cuba brought home to Roosevelt the mounting danger to U.S. companies from nationalist populist movements.

Collapsing prices caused sugar companies in Cuba to reduce their work forces and slash wages. With even the mightiest of New York financial institutions battered by the global crisis, Cuban dictator Gerardo Machado (1925–1933) could no longer turn to U.S. banks such as Chase and J.P. Morgan to salvage the economy and his government. Machado's resignation triggered a broadbased popular rebellion with strong anti-American elements. Sugar workers seized dozens of American owned mills and set up workers' committees to run them. After failed negotiations, American and Foreign Power's workers occupied its plants and began to operate the company on their own. The white-collar employees of the U.S. companies gave strong backing to these actions. An alliance of working and middle class groups objected to loss of control in the work place due to U.S. scientific management methods, displacement of Cubans from jobs in favor of Americans, and gave vent to longstanding national resentment over U.S. domination of the island. This same type of social alliance threatened U.S. interests throughout Latin America. The new Roosevelt administration could not afford to ignore such a challenge.

Ultimately, in dealing with the Cuban crisis Roosevelt refused to use the traditional method of solving such problems in Central America and the Caribbean—direct military intervention. But the U.S. president had not abandoned the use of American power to achieve national goals in the region, particularly the protection of U.S. business interests. In Cuba, the administration sent warships to cruise off the coast while denying diplomatic recognition to the reformist government of President Ramón Grau San Martín (1933–34, 1944–48). Roosevelt, by rejecting diplomatic and therefore economic ties with Cuba, sent the unmistakable message that Grau's tolerance for radical nationalism would doom his regime. In April 1933, Sumner Welles, the newly appointed ambassador, personally carried that warning to Cuba. Cubans no doubt took note of the message and the fact that Wells arrived in Havana harbor aboard a United Fruit passenger liner. The new ambassador, along with leading U.S. businessmen, soon turned to the head of the Cuban military, Fulgencio Batista, for solutions to labor problems paralyzing U.S. companies. In turn, Batista became convinced that the U.S. diplomatic and economic boycotts would end only when Grau was disposed of. He demanded and received Grau's resignation on February 14, 1934, hours after the president had ordered the government to intervene in the AFP properties in support of striking electrical workers.

In the aftermath of these events, Batista established himself as the most important political figure in Cuba for the next quarter of a century. Batista built that dominant position in part by using the military to crush the upheavals sweeping the island and by ensuring the security of U.S. interests. But Batista did not simply return to the past. While rejecting the radical goals of worker control and Cuban economic sovereignty, he did support better wages for unionized workers, and improved opportunities for the Cuban middle class in U.S. corporations. Batista's actions represented one attempt on the Latin American side to reach a new accommodation with the United States in the midst of nationalist populist upheavals. Meanwhile, the Roosevelt administration, having rejected overt intervention, took additional steps to adjust to new Latin American realities.

In 1930, a military coup in Brazil brought to power Getúlio Vargas who had lost the recent presidential election. Although Vargas's early career marked him as a very traditional Brazilian politician, he would use the opportunity created by the 1930 coup to fashion a regime reflective of the new trends in popular politics and nationalist economic programs designed to enhance the role of the state in the economy, promote industrialization, and limit the role of foreign corporations. The Brazilian state took a very direct role in the industrialization process, evidenced by the creation of the National Motor Factory to produce trucks and the Volta Redonda steel mill, among other things. Anxious to demonstrate its acceptance of the new populist nationalist trends in the region, the Roosevelt administration agreed to help finance the steel mill after private U.S. steel companies refused to become involved. But a far more serious challenge to U.S. interests had already emerged in Mexico.

In March 1938, Mexican President Lázaro Cárdenas ordered the nationalization of U.S. oil companies. This president's actions represented more than a sudden nationalist challenge. Mexican oil workers and white-collar employees had confronted the American companies with requirements for union involvement in management which could ultimately give control of the corporations to the unions. Although the initial American response included a sharp diplomatic rebuke and a cutoff of U.S. government purchases of Mexican silver, in the long run the Roosevelt administration took a conciliatory approach. Eventually, the oil companies would have to abandon their greatly inflated claims about the value of their properties and accept relatively small amounts of compensation.

The rather subdued response of the U.S. government represented in part a realization that the Cárdenas regime's action enjoyed enormous popular support in Mexico and that an aggressive U.S. reaction might pressure the Mexican government to seek the assistance of U.S. competitors such as Germany and Japan in running its oil industry. But more importantly, the U.S. government recognized that Cárdenas represented far more of an ally than an enemy of U.S. business. Cárdenas acted in part to avoid more radical action by the oil companies' workers and employees. He had no intention of allowing the workers to take control of the industry. Indeed, in the months that followed, Cárdenas rejected similar attempts to assert worker control in the mining and electrical industries. In fact, because the oil nationalization enhanced the nationalist credentials of the regime, Cárdenas was able to spurn the more extreme demands of the Mexican working and middle classes. That popular base of support allowed the Mexican president to affirm the right of workers and employees to hour and wage concessions, while rejecting their more radical agenda, and laid the groundwork for a continuing alliance with U.S. corporations.

The U.S. government, U.S. businesses, and Latin American elites constructed a new relationship as a result of crises such as those in Cuba and Mexico. In the face of the Great Depression and challenges from nationalist populist movements, the U.S. government assumed a far more assertive role in Latin America. Rather than leaving U.S. business to take the lead in the region, and then intervening aggressively when corporate interests were threatened, the federal government now adopted a proactive role. The Roosevelt administration took direct action to restore Depression-savaged trade levels with the Export Import Bank and reciprocal trade agreements. At the same time it demonstrated a new, more sophisticated approach to exerting pressure in the case of Cuba, and a willingness to work with the new nationalist regimes such as that of Lázaro Cárdenas.

U.S. corporations, with their vital interests threatened by economic depression and nationalist populism, proved far more willing to seek cooperative relations with the federal government. In time they would learn to make their own adjustments to the new reality in Latin America. They would seek to accommodate the demands of the middle class for more and better job opportunities and present themselves as partners with Latin American governments in the process of national development. Those adjustments would allow the companies to continue their penetration and transformation of Latin American societies. Those changes would take place in an era marked by world war, dramatic changes in Latin American economic policies, drastic shifts in the types of U.S. investment, and a resurgence of the radical agenda of the 1930s.

SUMMARY

Even before the Great Depression devastated the Latin American economies, U.S. corporations had triggered mounting popular opposition to their transformational mission. That opposition erupted at all levels of the region's social hierarchy, from members of the elite to workers and peasants. Although they had initially welcomed U.S. corporations, members of the elite often found themselves competing unsuccessfully with U.S. businesses, or frozen out of important economic sectors like petroleum which American companies monopolized. Middle class entrepreneurs also fought losing competitive battles with North American corporate giants, while white-collar employees faced job discrimination from U.S. managers who viewed them as inherently inferior. Middle and working class employees alike resented attempts to Americanize them. Workers reacted against attempts to speed up the work process and other harsh working conditions, while peasants and small farmers in countries like Mexico, Honduras, and Peru faced loss of their land or control of their activities by marketing monopolies such as the one created by United Fruit.

The Great Depression galvanized this array of dissident groups, especially the middle and working classes, into a potent new populist force. APRA in Peru, Cardenismo in Mexico, and the rebels led by Augusto Sandino in Nicaragua emerged as important new political movements enunciating calls for social justice and economic nationalism. The populist message that the elite's open door economic policies and resulting U.S. corporate domination contributed to the Great Depression had enormous appeal in the region. The populists who came to power with an anti-American nationalistic agenda represented a regionwide threat to U.S. business. Even Mexican President Lázaro Cárdenas, who ultimately sought accommodation with the Americans, undertook one of the most dramatic acts of Latin American nationalism when he took over the U.S. petroleum companies.

Facing both the damaging effects of the Great Depression and the mounting threat from Latin American populism, U.S. corporations sought an alliance with their own federal government to protect and rebuild their interests in the region. Under President Franklin Roosevelt the government took a more proactive and cooperative role to protect and advance the Latin American interests of U.S. corporations. While promoting international trade and accommodating nationalists like Lázaro Cárdenas, the Roosevelt administration also made clear in its actions in Cuba that it would not tolerate the more extreme expressions of nationalism and social radicalism that threatened the long-term presence of U.S. corporations in the region. In the decades ahead, Washington and multinational companies would use their alliance to broaden and increase their presence in the region. Along the way, they would pursue their mission to transform Latin America with a new vigor.

CHAPTER FOUR

WAR AND NATIONALISM,
1939–1959

On New Year's Day 1959, Nelson Rockefeller, the newly elected governor of the state of New York, delivered his inaugural address to the state assembly. To many observers, Rockefeller's speech took on an international focus that seemed at odds with the scope of the office he had just been elected to. But that focus was entirely in keeping with Rockefeller's lifelong interest and experience in Latin America. As one of the principal heirs to the Rockefeller/Standard Oil fortune, Nelson had taken an interest in the family's oil operations in Latin America. Visiting Standard's operations in Venezuela in the spring of 1937, shortly after a major oil workers' strike, Rockefeller became convinced that Standard must take a greater interest in the well-being of its workers and the general welfare of the Latin American nations in which the company operated. Otherwise, it would fall victim to the rising tide of nationalism in the region. At the time, Standard's directors ignored the young millionaire's advice, but Nelson soon secured a much larger laboratory where he could test his ideas.

In 1940 President Franklin Roosevelt named Nelson Rockefeller to head the newly created Office of Inter-American Affairs (OIAA). Under Rockefeller the OIAA launched an aggressive cultural offensive in Latin America, using motion pictures, radio, and newspapers to promote a positive image of the United States. Three years later he accepted the post of Assistant Secretary of State for Latin American Affairs. After the war, convinced that the federal government was no longer committed to development programs in Latin America, Rockefeller founded the American International Association for Economic and Social Development, and then a parallel profit-making operation called the International Basic Economy Corporation (IBC) to carry out development ventures in the region.[1]

But even as Rockefeller spoke in Albany on New Year's Day, Fulgencio Batista, a long-time friend of U.S. business, was fleeing Cuba and a young, bearded revolutionary, Fidel Castro, was making a lightening swift march across the island to seize power. Over the next several years, Castro would nationalize a billion dollars of U.S. corporate investment on the island, including the interests of Standard Oil. His revolution launched an era of new radical threats to U.S. business in Latin America, challenging Rockefeller's vision of an enlightened American business community working in harmonious relationship with Latin Americans. These events would leave many to wonder what had gone so terribly wrong in the quarter century since Franklin Roosevelt declared his Good Neighbor policy toward Latin America, and many U.S. corporations had attempted to reform their enterprises and adjust to the new realities of Latin American nationalism.

The twenty years between the outbreak of World War II and Fidel Castro's seizure of power proved to be two of the most challenging decades in the long history of U.S. business in Latin America. The war expanded opportunities for American enterprises as it choked off European investment and launched the U.S. government on a conscious policy of tying the region's economies evermore closely to its own in order to tap their resources for the war effort. Furthermore, American manufacturing enterprises emerged as the fastest growing sector of U.S. investments in the region. Those enterprises launched new, highly successful campaigns to promote consumerism. U.S. manufacturers also built a network of connections to local suppliers for their factories and retailers who marketed their brand name products. In this process U.S. corporations became more influential and involved in Latin American societies than ever before. These trends, however, also gave new energy to the populist initiatives of the 1930s.

From Venezuela to Chile, political movements came to power with the expressed intention of challenging the American hold on their economies. The populist challenges of the 1930s became the government policies of the 1940s and 1950s. In the midst of these countervailing forces, many U.S. companies pressed ahead with programs of reform seeking to provide their workers with better housing, education, and health services. Yet underlying these reforms there remained the U.S. conviction that Latin Americans lacked the intelligence, ambition, and discipline to develop their own societies. In the end, populist policies and renewed efforts at corporate reform had done little to assuage nationalist sentiments or solve basic problems of poverty and social injustice. Those failures would open the door to far more radical reactions toward American enterprise and culture.

CORPORATIONS, FOUNDATIONS, AND THE STATE

The fact that the United States could expand its dominance of Latin American economies resulted in part from the force of circumstances. The United States had already established itself as the single most important international trading partner and source of foreign investment in Latin American countries. World War II reinforced that position as the United States remained free of invading armies and blockades even after it entered the war as a belligerent. Those factors in themselves ensured that the U.S. position in Latin America would benefit from the war. But the United States government would not simply rely on circumstances to enhance its economic influence in the Southern Hemisphere. The Roosevelt administration had already launched a series of efforts to revive trade and investment during the Great Depression. The U.S. government would greatly expand those efforts to ensure control of Latin American resources during the war and then sought continued American domination in the post-war era.

The outbreak of the war in Europe gave fresh energy to efforts such as the Export Import Bank and the enhanced power of the president to modify tariffs, and prompted new attempts by the U.S. government to strengthen trade and investment ties with Latin America. Anxious to cushion the blow of the war on Latin America's international trade and to strengthen U.S. economic ties to the region, Congress in 1940 agreed to triple the lending authority of the Exim Bank. The bank's activities moved beyond simply financing international trade to promoting new areas of economic activity. The most notable example of this came in 1940 when the bank helped finance the building of a steel mill by the Brazilian government. Over the next several years, the federal government would sign exclusive purchase agreements for a number of strategic materials produced in Latin America, make resources available to expand their output, and encourage the development of new export products. These agreements encouraged the rapid growth of Latin American exports and guaranteed price levels for producers.[2] Efforts to expand U.S. influence in Latin America went far beyond these purely economic initiatives, however.

In 1940 President Roosevelt created what soon became the Office of Inter-American Affairs (OIAA) to serve as a coordinating center for policy matters affecting Latin America. More specifically, the agency became the focal point of government efforts to expand communication links, technical assistance, and propaganda in the Southern Hemisphere. The OIAA's film section not only succeeded in censoring commercial movies containing elements potentially offensive to Latin Americans, it also promoted the development of films with themes of inter-American solidarity. Its press office provided copy and photos stressing the same objective to news services for distribution throughout Latin America. Paralleling the efforts in film, the radio section developed close ties with the broadcast industry and expanded U.S. programming available throughout the region.[3] The close cooperation between business and government in the operations of the OIAA reflected in part the very strong personal ties binding these two segments of U.S. society together.

The OIAA's policies reflected the views of its director, Nelson Rockefeller. Rockefeller envisioned an alliance of business and government to ensure private sector development of Latin America while at the same time accommodating the nationalistic concerns of the region's people. While Rockefeller's dedication to Latin America was somewhat exceptional, many international executives duplicated his dual business-government career both before and after the New Deal. Will Clayton of Anderson Clayton, one of the largest dealers in Latin American primary products, served as Assistant Secretary of State for Economic Affairs in the Roosevelt administration.[4] Numerous other representatives of large U.S. corporations would join them in key positions in the federal government after the war. During the Eisenhower administration, John Foster and Allen Dulles, who had both served as attorneys for the United Fruit Company or its subsidiaries, held the posts of Secretary of State and Director of Central Intelligence, respectively. By this time, U.S. business developed yet another allied institution to assist it in overseas operations.

The American missionary movement which had conveyed not only Christian, but also U.S. values to Latin America early in the twentieth century, suffered severe setbacks during the Depression years as sources of financial support dried up. However, by that time, private foundations had emerged as equally useful institutions in creating a favorable environment for U.S. business overseas.

Large private foundations provided a uniquely American merger of business and religious interests. The most striking example of that merger resulted from the work of the Reverend Frederick Gates, the Baptist minister who so readily perceived and promoted the mutual interests of Protestant missionaries and U.S. businessmen overseas. Gates had enormous influence over John D. Rockefeller, Nelson's father, convincing him that corporate philanthropy could spread the message of Christianity, promote human welfare, and serve the needs of modern corporations. The Rockefeller fortune would fund missionary work as well as medical research and services. The family's philanthropic activities took institutionalized form with the creation of the Rockefeller Foundation in 1913. The foundation and others like it would pursue a wide range of programs beneficial to business interests.

The creation of the Rockefeller Foundation represented a new and far more direct effort by business leaders to shape U.S. society into an environment fully compatible with the interests of large corporations. Through these organizations, magnates like the Rockefellers and later the Fords would promote a social philosophy stressing the implementation of rationalized, efficient policies to alleviate the more extreme degrees of poverty and suffering. In turn the foundations would attempt to reward individualistic and competitive values among workers by ensuring moderate, gradual reform within the larger structures of capitalist society. The foundations gave expression to this philosophy through a variety of programs designed to reform public education and public health.[5]

By the end of the Second World War both the Rockefeller and Ford Foundations had extended these policy initiatives to Latin America. Much like earlier domestic programs funded by these foundations, the overseas initiatives included health and education. But far more ambitious goals and programs were attached to their international endeavors. For Latin America as well as other Third World areas, foundation executives crafted a program of economic and social engineering designed to achieve capitalist development with a major role assigned to U.S. corporations in that process. To implement that vision, the foundations promoted a wide array of programs, including assistance to Latin American universities to train an elite cadre imbued with the U.S. developmentalist philosophy. They also launched agricultural assistance programs to expand food output and lower food costs for an expanding proletariat, and technical assistance programs to relieve developmental bottlenecks. The numerous foundation officials and academics who ardently supported these programs optimistically looked to a future in which a new, modern Latin American elite would work hand and glove with American corporate leaders to guide the capitalist development of the region. The foundations' influence even extended to U.S. foreign policy.

By the end of the 1930s, the Rockefeller and Ford Foundations became major financial contributors to the Council on Foreign Relations. The Council, while technically a private non-profit organization, exercised an increasing role in conveying corporate views on foreign policy to the federal government, and in directly influencing that policy. In 1939 the Rockefeller Foundation began funding a series of studies by the Council which examined long-term problems related to the war and the post-war world. Those studies concluded that U.S. corporations must play a central role in securing raw materials overseas in order to ensure the continued prosperity of the United States. Given the close links between the foundations and the federal government, those views would carry substantial weight in the policy making circles of the federal government. That became apparent in the 1952 report by the President's Materials Policy Commission that repeated almost verbatim the arguments of the Council's studies. The Commission stated that the country now depended heavily on imported raw materials and that the U.S. government needed to foster overseas investment in such materials by American corporations. A 1958 article in the Council's journal *Foreign Relations* summarized these findings. The article argued that "our purpose should be to encourage the expansion of low-cost production [of raw materials] and to make sure that neither nationalistic policies nor Communist influence deny American industries access on reasonable terms to the basic materials necessary to the continued growth of the American economy."[6]

Investments by U.S. corporations would also ensure improved economic conditions for people around the globe, but only if U.S. companies could operate in a non-threatening, capitalist oriented international environment. Such conclusions strongly suggested the need for a concerted effort by the public sector to ward off nationalist and communist threats to corporate endeavors overseas. Given the close links between the foundations and the federal government, these views would carry substantial weight in the policy making circles of the U.S. government. That became apparent in the 1952 report by the President's Materials Policy Commission which repeated almost verbatim the arguments of the Council on Foreign Relations. The Commission stated that the country now depended heavily on imported raw materials and that the U.S. government needed to foster overseas investment in such materials by American corporations.[7]

The direct influence of the foundations on U.S. foreign policy is perhaps even more strikingly revealed by the fact that between 1952 and 1977, three different trustees or officers of the Rockefeller Foundation (John Foster Dulles, Dean Rusk, and Cyrus Vance) occupied the position of Secretary of State. At the same time officials of the Ford Foundation have also occupied critical foreign policy positions, such as McGeorge Bundy who served as President John F. Kennedy's national security advisor. Such links offer just one basic example of the way in which corporate leaders, their foundations, and U.S. government officials formed a cooperative and interrelated community which shaped U.S. policy toward Latin America in the years during and after the Second World War. Further evidence of that relationship can be seen in the policies actually pursued by the U.S. government.[8]

In the midst of implementing policies designed to lift the Western Hemisphere out of the Depression and support the war effort, the Roosevelt administration made clear that those goals were to be accomplished largely through the promotion of U.S. business interests. For example, the Exim Bank had made it clear that it would not loan money to Mexico unless it settled the claims against it by the expropriated U.S. oil companies. The decidedly pro-business orientation of the Roosevelt administration's Latin American policies carried over into the postwar decades.

Under the Truman and Eisenhower presidencies, the U.S. government continued to pursue a series of mutually compatible goals in Latin America. U.S. officials sought to promote a capitalist model of economic development for the region based on a cooperative effort among U.S. companies and the U.S. and Latin American governments. At the same time they recognized the need for greater sensitivity to Latin American nationalism. U.S. government officials would seek to frustrate perceived threats to their policies which ranged from Marxist political movements to protectionist economic policies. To achieve these ends, the U.S. government sought to add to the existing foreign policy instruments at its disposal. Those additions included new federal entities such as its principal foreign aid organization, the Agency for International Development (AID), as well as new multilateral lending agencies, including the World Bank and the International Monetary Fund (IMF), in which the United States played a dominant role. The functions of these agencies varied from the technology transfer programs of AID to large-scale infrastructure projects financed by the World Bank to debt management and currency stabilization initiatives of the IMF. In addition, these administrations called upon another faction of the New Deal alliance—the labor movement—to assist in promoting U.S. business in Latin America.

In 1951 the Central Intelligence Agency funneled money through the American Federation of Labor to found the Organización Regional Interamericana de Trabajadores (ORIT) in Mexico City. Under the leadership of Serafino Romualdi, an AFL representative and CIA operative, ORIT challenged the Confederación de Trabajadores de America Latina (CTAL), a regional labor federation led by the Mexican labor activist Lombardo Toledano. With the assistance of the AFL and its president George Meany, ORIT would create U.S. style labor unions focused on economic issues, and avoid more radical demands for worker control of industry. In effect they would create a pro-business labor movement in Latin America, which would accept the principle of a labor management partnership that lay at the heart of the capitalist reforms promoted by Nelson Rockefeller and other U.S. business leaders.[9]

By the end of the Second World War, the U.S. corporate experience in Latin America had become a far more complex undertaking than the free-wheeling entrepreneurial activities in the period prior to the Great Depression. In the earlier era, U.S. corporations had launched vast investment projects with little regard for the concerns of the host society or the policies of their own government. These selfish policies had ended in an eruption of populist nationalism in Latin America and the economic disaster of the Great Depression. But after the Second World War, an alliance of business, government, foundations, and organized labor pursued policies designed to defend and expand U.S. corporate interests in Latin America.

The Great Depression triggered a collapse in the value of U.S. direct investments in Latin America which had totaled $3.7 billion in 1929. By 1940 those investments had stabilized and even rebounded slightly, reaching $3 billion. Over the next two decades the effects of war and the policies of the government business alliance launched a new era of heady growth in U.S. investments, with the total reaching $8.3 billion in 1960. Much of that growth occurred in the traditional extractive sectors of petroleum and mining. After the war, utilities–which had represented the largest single investment area in 1940–had stagnated, and U.S. investment in agriculture, once a key sector, had collapsed. On the other hand, manufacturing became the fastest growing area of U.S. investment.[10]

In addition to the above developments in the direct investment sector, U.S. financial ties to the region had undergone considerable change as well. By 1934 Latin American countries had defaulted on over $1 billion in loans from U.S. banks. During the 1930s and 1940s the holders of the bonds representing these loans and Latin American governments worked out debt repayment agreements, dramatically lowering the total debt by means of reduced interest rates and other mechanisms. However, the haunting memory of the collapse in debt servicing precluded significant lending to governments in the region by U.S. banks in the years after the war. Here, the U.S. government stepped in to fill an important part of the financing gap. Between 1948 and 1955 the U.S. government provided Latin American countries with over $250 million in direct aid in the form of technical assistance and other programs, and loaned the region more than $1.5 billion, much of it channeled through multilateral agencies such as the World Bank.[11] Yet the rapid growth in U.S. enterprise and the expanded role of the U.S. government in the development process hardly ensured a harmonious relationship between Latin Americans and U.S. business interests. Stresses in that relationship had begun to mount even as the war promoted renewed growth in the area's export economies.

ECONOMIC NATIONALISM

Despite the efforts of the Roosevelt administration to promote inter-American solidarity, both before and during the war, Latin Americans did not readily embrace the concept of the Good Neighbor. They quickly recognized that U.S. efforts to promote economic growth in the region served to reinforce past patterns of dependence on primary product exports, which had heightened the vulnerability of their economies to the Great Depression. Furthermore, it was clear that U.S. programs were designed to retain and expand the dominant position of American corporations in local economies. U.S. officials were loath to promote economic programs which competed with or infringed upon U.S. corporate interests, and even wartime policies such as the purchase agreements for raw materials did not necessarily operate to the exclusive benefit of Latin American countries. Latin Americans objected to the fact that prices set under the agreements often represented lower prices than would have prevailed in the free market, and that in many cases the profits from the fixed prices went directly to large U.S. corporations which dominated much of the export sector. Adding to these concerns was the indifference of Americans toward the hardship endured by Latin Americans whose incomes were being eaten away by rising inflation. Although the new corporate–government alliance professed to be pursuing policies that represented a pragmatic nonideological solution to problems of Latin American development, in fact their plans were strongly biased in favor of promoting U.S. business. American policy makers and business leaders not only vigorously discouraged socialist policies, they opposed even modest efforts at protectionism to encourage domestic industrialization. These sharp differences between Latin Americans and the U.S. business–government alliance gave additional momentum to the populist movements that surged to the forefront of national politics during the 1930s.

After 1939, the U.S. promoted Latin America's continued dependence on raw material exports, expanded the role of U.S. business in the region, and ensured the adoption of an American model of development. These initiatives gave new momentum to Latin American populist movements begun in the 1930s. Furthermore, in the years after the war, populist movements contained more than a critique of foreign business as a basis for planning the future. Latin American governments imposed tariffs and exchange controls to avoid exhaustion of foreign exchange reserves, evidence of being forced to assume a much larger role in respective national economies by the Great Depression. Governments also directly intervened in the domestic economy in an attempt to restart the process of growth. Argentina provides a major example of such efforts.

The ambitious Colonel Juan Perón recognized an extraordinary opportunity for advancement as a member of the military regime ruling Argentina during the Second World War. In the rapidly expanding working class of Buenos Aires Perón saw a new national power base. Handling labor matters for the military regime, Perón intervened in a general strike launched by meat workers in September 1943, and negotiated an end to the strike. Perón quickly established himself as a friend of the workers, securing wage hikes and welfare benefits, as well as union recognition for many of them. At the same time he worked to purge the unions of leftist leaders who would challenge his personal leadership of the labor movement. Perón used this base of support to win the 1946 presidential election.

As the democratically elected president of Argentina, Perón not only continued his pro-labor policies, he also pursued a strident economic nationalism. Perón nationalized several foreign-owned interests, most notably the nation's British controlled railways. He also seized nearly forty percent of American and Foreign Power's electric network in Argentina. In addition, he created a number of state-owned companies in areas as diverse as steel, shipping, and insurance.[12]

Meanwhile, Getúlio Vargas, Brazil's populist president who was handed the presidency by a military junta following a coup in 1930, continued to pursue similar policies. In 1945 Vargas issued an antimonopoly decree that restricted the role of foreign companies within the national economy. Although the military ousted Vargas later that same year, he would win election to the presidency in 1950. In his new term of office, Vargas not only denounced high levels of profit repatriation by foreign companies, he also launched what became the state oil company, Petrobras.

During his administration, Vargas did not neglect the populist side of the political spectrum. In 1943 he initiated a new labor code that legalized and codified unionization throughout the country, while subjecting unions to tight control by the central government at the same time. Over the years he also demonstrated his populist leanings with policies to improve urban education, to create a social security system, and to increase the minimum wage.

The presidencies of Vargas and Perón offered clear examples of the important new trends in Latin America by the end of World War II. After the war, many of these ad hoc policies received intellectual support and direction from the United Nation's Economic Commission for Latin America

(ECLA). Under the leadership of its executive secretary Raúl Prebisch, an Argentine economist, ECLA developed a powerful argument for using protectionist policies to promote industrialization. ECLA studies argued that, with rare exceptions, such as the recent period of war driven demand, unequal international terms of trade functioned to the detriment of countries that relied on primary product exports. Simply put, Latin American countries were, as a rule, trading low-priced raw materials for high-priced industrial goods. These unequal exchanges drained capital from the region and would continue to frustrate attempts to achieve economic development. To break this cycle of underdevelopment, Prebisch argued for a policy of import substitution industrialization (ISI). Under this plan, governments would raise tariffs on imported consumer goods to prohibitive levels and pursue domestic policies designed to encourage the development of local industries that would produce previously imported consumer goods. This policy would ultimately encourage industrialization in capital goods sectors like steel, which would in turn provide inputs for consumer goods industries.[13]

ECLA's development strategy now provided the nationalist populist cause with a coherent economic philosophy to offer as an alternative to Liberal policies. An increasing number of governments adopted strategies that deviated radically from the internationalist policies installed by the old Liberal elite. These new regimes launched initiatives to more tightly control the operation of foreign corporations, nationalize key sectors of the economy such as transportation and utilities, and expand protectionist policies to promote industrialization at the expense of foreign imports. Furthermore, they adopted social welfare policies to address some of the most urgent needs of the middle and working classes. Nor were such policies restricted solely to regimes that can be defined as populist. Conservative administrations in Peru imposed higher taxes on the Cerro de Pasco Corporation and enforced domestic price controls on petroleum products causing serious problems for the Rockefellers' International Petroleum Corporation. In 1943, a military regime in Venezuela forced the oil companies to surrender half of their profits to the government, and establish more generous wage and benefit terms for their workers. The mobilized popular classes of Latin America were forcing regimes of every political stripe to adopt at least some elements of the nationalist populist agenda of the 1930s.[14]

THE CORPORATE RESPONSE

Inevitably, the postwar surge in Latin American economic nationalism had enormous impact upon U.S. businesses. Mining and oil companies would face heavier taxation and limits on their operations. Utilities would encounter serious problems due to foreign exchange controls, limits on profit repatriation, government control of rates, and a growing sentiment throughout the region that utilities should be owned and operated by the state. U.S. enterprises also had to deal with nationalistic and progressive social policies requiring greater national representation at all levels of their work force, and greater benefits for workers and white-collar employees. Company responses would include resistance and accommodation to the demands placed upon them by host countries. And more often than not those responses came not merely from corporate headquarters, but from the various elements of the business-government alliance which was firmly in place by the end of World War II.

Yet the outcomes for U.S. business in this complex interaction were by no means uniform. Many mining companies managed to prosper and expand under these conditions. Petroleum companies, especially Standard Oil, undertook massive expansion programs and enjoyed excellent profits during these years. Some of the nationalist policies actually spurred the growth of U.S. investment in manufacturing, making it the fastest growing sector of U.S. investment in Latin America.

On the other hand, U.S. businessmen considered the new environment in the region a source of constant problems, and many corporations suffered sharp setbacks—especially the utility companies. By the end of the 1950s, American and Foreign Power Company, the leading U.S. corporate investor in Latin America in the early 1930s, was on the verge of surrendering control of the vast international power grid it had built in the Western Hemisphere over the previous four decades.[15] As the radically different outcomes for Standard Oil and American and Foreign Power suggest, a variety of factors including state and corporate policies and international economic forces as well as political factors played important roles in determining the winners and losers in the new Latin American environment. The story of Standard Oil's success in Venezuela offers insight into the complex interaction of those forces.

The world oil market endured a series of sharp cyclical changes between the 1920s and 1960s which directly influenced the behavior of Standard Oil in Latin America in general and Venezuela in particular. From rising prices and demand in the 1920s, the global oil market slipped into depression with the rest of the world in the 1930s, only to enjoy war-driven resurgence during the 1940s and early 1950s, and then another down cycle by the mid-1950s. Standard Oil reacted to the upward cycle of the 1920s by buying out the Creole Oil Company in 1928, and the Pan American Oil

Company in 1932. In expanding its interests in Venezuela, Standard responded to both a buoyant world oil market and the fact that by 1928 Venezuela had replaced Mexico as the leading oil exporting country in the world. The wisdom of those investments seemed highly questionable in the decade that followed as the Great Depression battered petroleum prices. When the Second World War resuscitated the world oil market, it created both prosperity and new problems for the company in Venezuela.[16]

Venezuela's longtime dictator Juan Vicente Gómez, who died in 1935, was replaced by a series of military rulers who seemed likely to continue his generous treatment of foreign oil companies. However, the rising tide of economic nationalism in Venezuela, and the war driven prosperity of the industry prompted the government of military strongman Isaias Medina to announce its intention to revise the oil companies' concessions. The Venezuelan government's efforts to write concessions with flexible provisions ran directly contrary to Standard Oil's view that such concessions were and should remain immutable. The U. S. government, concerned about meeting wartime demands for oil and remembering the Mexican expropriation, pressured the company to negotiate with the Medina regime. Standard executives finally agreed to enter into negotiations leading to a new petroleum law in 1943. The new law overhauled concessions, and dramatically altered the tax levels imposed on the company. The increased taxes and royalty payments established the principle that the government and the company would divide the corporation's profits equally, a concept that soon became the standard for international petroleum companies operating in Third World countries.

Standard's acceptance of changed concession rules and higher taxes stemmed not merely from U.S. government pressure and a changed attitude among its executives. It also reflected the fact that the company stood to profit from these new arrangements. The new concession rules actually extended the life of oil concessions and, under wartime conditions, both production and profits would grow rapidly. By 1948, taxes per barrel had increased by 150 percent but profit per barrel was up by nearly 400 percent. The returns to Venezuela proved equally impressive as production more than doubled and government oil revenues quadrupled.[17] Thus, the world oil market's rebound enabled Standard to accept a drastic revision of tax and concession policies, and still see its profits rise dramatically. But the demands from Venezuela were not focused solely on the issues of concessions and taxes.

Much like their brethren in Mexico, Venezuelan workers found the coming of the petroleum multinationals to be a mixed blessing. Although the oil companies paid wages far above those available elsewhere in Venezuela, they received far lower compensation than U.S. workers, who also dominated the skilled positions in the oil fields. Venezuelans endured miserable working conditions and an absence of significant benefits. One worker in 1936 made very clear the conditions which would soon drive them to strike:

> We oil workers are conscious of what we ask for, first because we are hungry; second because our homes are shacks that could best serve as garbage dumps; third because our exploiters enjoy every comfort and opportunity, their children sleep in cribs, they go to secondary school or have special tutors in their home, they have recreational centers, while our children sleep on straw mats and lack even medical care; and finally, we can't send them to school so they can become informed and free citizens.[18]

The economic downturn of the 1930s caused many skilled American workers to return to the United States and allowed Venezuelans to occupy an increasing number of skilled positions. Furthermore, workers soon exploited a gap in the authoritarian political structure created by Gómez's death. In December 1936 the oil workers, aided by elements of the middle class, shut down much of the industry demanding union recognition and a closed shop along with improved economic benefits. The strike quickly assumed far greater significance than the workers' basic economic demands. As the Caracas daily *La Voz del Pueblo* asserted:

> The triumph or failure of the oil workers will be the triumph or failure of the Venezuelan labor movement. Their struggle is the struggle of all workers of Venezuela. At their side, in sympathy and action, all the people must stand, because this group of men in the land of Zulia [oil extraction region] are confronting the oil companies, because they are defending in reality, the sovereignty and the dignity of our fatherland in the face of the foreign exploiter.[19]

By mid-January, the government had forced the workers to return to work in exchange for a few minor wage concessions. But both Standard Oil and the government eventually recognized the necessity of further accommodating the workers in order to avoid future confrontations and to curtail the widespread influence of Communist organizers within the labor movement. In the years immediately following the strike, Standard commenced a massive housing program for its workers, initiated new educational programs for workers and their children, and even began teaching Spanish to its English-speaking employees. The company also accepted the government's mandated profit sharing plan which substantially increased the earnings of the oil workers. Through these policies the government and the company hoped to maintain labor peace, and wean the workers away from the more radical demands of the Marxists for worker control of the industry. At least initially, their efforts to diminish leftist influence were a failure.

During the war, Communist influence continued to grow within the rapidly expanding oil workers' unions where leftists competed successfully with the more moderate Acción Democrática (AD) unions. However, in 1944 President Isaias Medina dissolved all ninety-three Communist-controlled unions on the grounds that their professed affiliation with a political party violated the national labor code.

The AD labor movement also benefited from a military coup in 1945 that installed an AD government. The new regime remained faithful to the nationalist, reformist goals of its middle and working class constituencies. In 1946 the government oversaw the negotiation of a new labor agreement with the oil companies that increased base pay; added overtime and sick pay, bonuses, and vacation time; and provided a wide array of other benefits. The agreement offered convincing evidence that the AD's stance on labor issues, emphasizing economic issues versus worker control, could bring large and immediate benefits to workers. The continuing increase in government oil revenues also allowed the AD to extend similar benefits to other parts of the working and middle classes by subsidizing food prices, lowering rents and electric rates, and expanding social security benefits.

In turn, Standard and the other oil companies improved worker grievance procedures and placed a greater number of Venezuelans in positions of authority. Although the AD's tenure proved brief as a military coup ousted it from power in 1948, the party and Standard had established a modus vivendi that survived for the next several decades. Under the Medina and AD regimes, the government and the company successfully developed formulas to increase revenues for the state and the company, and to pursue policies that defused the more radical demands of the working class by offering increased mateial benefits as an alternative to labor's demand for increased control in the work place.

The Standard Oil experience in Venezuela during the 1940s was fairly unique for U.S. corporations in this period. First, the highly favorable conditions in the international oil market made it possible for the company to accommodate both the Venezuelan government and popular forces, and still increase its own profits. Second, it found a partner in Acción

Democrática whose nationalist reformist goals could be accommodated within the new philosophy developing among U.S. corporations doing business in Latin America. They sought progressive reforms in labor policies to create healthier, better educated, and more contented blue and white-collar workers as a way of undercutting the appeal of populist and more radical political movements. Indeed, a key player in Standard Oil, Nelson Rockefeller, was one of the principal architects of that policy. However, even Standard was not consistent in its adherence to a policy of accommodation toward nationalist populist forces in the rest of Latin America.[20]

Standard had first established a serious presence in South America through the activities of its IPC subsidiary in Peru. After the Great Depression struck, the company became embroiled in controversy with the Peruvian government over its labor policies. During the early 1950s conflict with the government erupted again, but this time it focused on the issue of IPC's prices and profits. Despite the nationalist agenda of the populist movements of the 1930s, two large U.S. corporations, Cerro de Pasco and IPC, still dominated Peru's economy in the 1950s. They became the targets of increasing nationalist animosity which focused on the Standard Oil subsidiary. IPC's vulnerability largely stemmed from the changing role of oil in the Peruvian economy.

Prior to the entry of the United States into World War II, Peru had exported 70 percent of its oil production. However, stagnant production levels and increasing domestic consumption reduced that figure to 50 percent. During the early 1950s IPC became embroiled in growing public controversies over its insistence that the Peruvian government raise domestic fuel prices and a questionable 1922 agreement granting it ownership of the La Brea and Parinas oil fields. Rather than taking a conciliatory approach to growing public resentment, IPC took a more combative stance.

In 1951 the oil company informed the government that without a price increase, it would have to reduce its activities and lay off workers. The implied threat was simple—falling output would force Peru to import oil at higher prices than those paid for the domestic product. In fact, IPC proceeded to halt its exploration work and laid off more than 1,000 workers. After a change of regimes, the government reached an agreement that raised prices on all petroleum products in return for increased reinvestment by the company, and the rehiring of workers. The virtual surrender to IPC touched off a firestorm of public protest that finally forced the government to submit legislation calling for the state's acquisition of IPC's assets by the end of the century. The legislation was never enacted, but the public furor began to subside. However, IPC had reinforced its reputation as a rapacious U.S. corporation exploiting the Peruvian people and intimidating its government into agreements that ignored the national interest. Before the end of the 1960s, its actions would come back to haunt the company. Meanwhile, IPC's counterpart in the mining sector had experienced serious problems of its own.[21]

The mining industry, particularly copper, had benefited from some of the same conditions which spurred profitability in the oil industry during and after the war. Stockpiling in anticipation of wartime needs helped boost world output of mining products in the years before the war, and those levels remained high during the early years of the war. The end of the war and price controls sent prices soaring. Copper, for example, doubled in price between 1945 and 1951. Yet these highly favorable market conditions did not immediately translate into profitable operations for Cerro de Pasco, the largest U. S. corporation in Peru.

Even as world market prices for copper were soaring after the war, Cerro de Pasco's output was declining due to the diminishing quality of the company's ore deposit. Furthermore, the Peruvian tax system proved a significant disincentive to increase production because export taxes based on the price of metals increased the tax burden substantially as metals prices soared. Significant efforts to reverse the company's problems came only after the issuance of a new mining code in 1950. General Manuel Odría's government, installed in 1948, was highly favorable to foreign business. The new code shifted the tax base from prices to profits, established depletion allowances, and provided the government with broad discretion to waive taxes on the profits of new ventures. The new code had the intended effect of encouraging large new investments in open pit mining, which had considerably lower unit costs than the traditional underground methods. Cerro de Pasco took advantage of this opportunity in the mid-1950s by creating an open pit mine at its operations in the town of Cerro de Pasco. In addition, the company joined a consortium known as the Southern Peru Copper Corporation (SPCC) headed by the American Smelting and Refining Company to develop an open pit copper mine at Toquepala near the Chilean border.

The favorable tax terms of the mining code encouraged mining giants like ASARCO, Cerro de Pasco, and Phelps Dodge to invest $100 million in Toquepala beginning in 1956, but that was only half of the cost of the project. The U.S. government provided the other half in the form of a loan by the Exim bank. For U.S. business and government leaders, the SPCC represented precisely the kind of partnership between the U.S. government, American business, and a Latin American regime that lay at the heart of the American model for development of the region. In 1960, open pit mines produced seventy-five percent of Peru's copper, and total mineral output in the country had more than doubled from a decade earlier. Yet these dramatic changes had not come about without substantial conflict with the Peruvians most involved in the industry—the mine workers.

In 1945 José Luis Bustamante (1945–1948) won election to the Peruvian presidency with the support of Haya de la Torre and APRA. In return, the Bustamante administration helped enact labor legislation that not only legalized unions for the first time since 1930, but also set out a series of regulations regarding the hiring of workers, compensations for dismissal, and payments to be made for holidays. The new labor laws created a far more positive environment for union activity in the mining district. The Cerro de Pasco Corporation recognized the new reality, forming a Department of Industrial Relations and engaging in its first collective wage negotiations with the unions. The new opportunities for labor militancy helped boost wages for workers by more than 100 percent between 1945 and 1949. But this springtime for labor ended with the ouster of Bustamante and the installation of Manuel Odría (1948–1956).

The pro-business Odría regime proved far less sympathetic to labor, but despite its periodic use of force against workers, there was no going back to the conditions of the 1930s. Unions now formed a permanent part of the mining community. In the decade and a half after the war, APRA and the Communist Party competed for influence in the labor movement with the power of each waxing and waning in response to political developments. The Bustamante regime and its labor legislation gave APRA the dominant position. Under Odría, the Communists replaced APRA. Then APRA achieved ascendancy once again between 1956 and 1961. As political parties competed to represent the mine workers in the government, they created considerable space for the workers themselves to act in pursuit of their own goals even as the corporation attempted to shape them into a "modern work force."

After 1950 as the Cerro de Pasco Corporation invested in new technologies and open pit mining in order to improve productivity, it sought to create a labor force compatible with these modernized operations. The company redoubled past efforts to create a more stable labor force with a higher percentage of workers who remained permanently with the firm, rather than shifting between the mines and their lives as peasants. The company offered bonuses and other incentives to keep workers on permanently, and provided additional training programs to raise their skill levels. The company now described itself as a great family, instituting programs to instill in workers the proper values of individual initiative and respect for the company. At the same time, despite the labor legislation of 1945, the establishment of regularized labor negotiations, and industrial welfare programs, the company still oversaw a militant and restless work force.

Labor conflicts arose in part from specific economic issues such as layoffs and speedups. But conflicts were sometimes provoked by American managers' perceptions of the Peruvian working class. At the end of 1958 the Cerro de Pasco Corporation began construction of a new seventeen-bed hospital at its Goyllarisquisga mine site. The hospital formed part of the company's network of medical facilities serving its work force and their families. But, Cerro's managers still attributed the health problems of workers' families to "ignorance, fear and superstition" on the part of workers and their wives. Pointing to the high mortality rate among workers' children, the company management concluded that, "Ignorance, carelessness and the strange belief expressed in the phrase 'one dead baby, one more angel' are the reasons underlying a still disproportionately high mortality rate."[22]

If technology had changed significantly at Cerro de Pasco, American attitudes had not. As a result, relations between the company and its workers remained highly volatile and even violent. Such attitudes persisted even at the SPCC's new open pit mine at Toquepala. On the one hand, managers complimented the Peruvian worker's willingness to learn how to operate new machinery, but they detected a child-like simplicity in his enthusiasm:

> In fact, his eagerness to push buttons and move levers that will make machines run and do things is so intense that he has to be restrained until he can be properly trained. . . . And admirable though this quality [of enthusiasm] may be, the danger for instance of running a 25-ton truck over a bank makes managers insist that workers only run equipment after they have had thorough training. . . .[23]

As a result of these attitudes, a culture of terror, much like that which prevailed in Central American banana camps in the 1920s and 30s pervaded the Peruvian mining region. Even trivial events could lead to the eruption of violence between the workers and the company as illustrated by an event in the town of Cerro de Pasco in 1958:

> [A]t a certain moment the rumor was going around that supervisor O. had struck the miner B. with a stick . . . A little later about 100 workers gathered around the Lourdes office. It was now been [sic] shouted that O. had shot B. When O's assistant D. tried to explain

what really happened (B. jokingly attacked O. who defended himself), he was met by a hail of stones. After a quarter of an hour a crowd of over 1000 men were present demanding "away with O." and "away with D." Delegation after delegation entered T's office (the assistant supervisor), demanding concessions which T., out of fear agreed to. When the secretary-general of the union tried to calm the crowd he too was greeted with stones. He proposed the compromise that O. and D. would sign written resignations to the company. The crowd screamed "and Y. also" whereupon Y. also signed. A large number of women and children had also joined the crowd. Feelings ran so high that the building was forcibly entered: the fleeing staff members were pursued. . . .[24]

At other times those violent confrontations had specific economic and social goals.

Even before the labor legislation of 1945, workers successfully resisted attempts by the company to lengthen the work day and speed up the labor process. When wage increases failed to keep pace with the rising cost of living, they struck out in the town of Cerro de Pasco attacking company property and killing the mayor. Protests erupted again in the same town in 1956, when the company bought up most of the municipality and began demolishing it to make way for its open pit mine. When the company cut 2,500 workers from its labor force of 31,000 in 1958, trouble struck once again in Cerro de Pasco, with workers attacking corporate owned property. During the 1950s workers resisted attempts to restructure the labor force into a modern proletariat through a series of strike actions. Much like IPC's conflict with the government, those events would come back to haunt the company in the future. Meanwhile, U.S. mining companies in Chile were making their own efforts to accommodate themselves to the new realities of Latin America.[25]

Much as in Peru, the outbreak of the war produced favorable conditions for the U.S. copper companies, Anaconda and Kennecott—the heirs to the great Guggenheim mining initiatives in Chile earlier in the century. Purchasing agreements and controlled prices well above Depression era levels provided a secure and profitable working environment for the companies. However, Chileans did not take kindly to the fixed prices imposed by the U.S. government. In later years, critics of the arrangement would argue that it cost the country anywhere from $100 to $500 million that could have been earned under free market conditions. Furthermore, when the Korean War erupted in 1950, Washington again fixed prices, this time in cooperation with the copper companies, but without even consulting the Chilean government. In 1951 Chilean protests brought an increase in the fixed price and permission for the country to sell 20 percent of its output on the free market. However, U.S. actions had reawakened the nationalist animosities of the 1930s and they would continue to grow in the postwar period.

Chileans of every political stripe became convinced of the applicability of the Prebisch model to their own country. Statistics clearly indicated that Chile's terms of trade had declined precipitously between 1938 and 1948. Such figures and the experience of U.S. price fixing convinced most Chileans that American control of the strategic copper industry made the nation dependent on large U.S. corporations. Chileans also believed that those companies returned only a fraction of the revenues the Chilean government needed to fund its social policies and promote industrialization. In an effort to secure a larger share of the copper wealth, the government created a state sales monopoly in 1952. But the government's inexperience in the world copper market doomed the effort.

In light of the failure of the sales monopoly, conservative political forces promoted a free market approach to the problems of the copper industry. Under the Nuevo Trato or New Deal approved by the government in 1955 the copper companies enjoyed lower income tax rates. The new tax structure provided a sliding rate with the lower rates available to the companies if they increased production. But the New Deal not only failed to promote an increase in copper output, it also heralded a new wave of social upheaval directed against American companies and the conservative policies of the Chilean government.

The failure to increase output stemmed, in part, from the fact that for multinational copper companies, Chile comprised only one portion of their operations. Anaconda and Kennecott had both integrated vertically into areas such as wire and brass manufacture and sought to reduce their risk by operating mines not only in Chile but the U.S. and Africa as well. Given this drive at sectoral and geographical diversification, the companies had strong incentives to devote their resources to purposes other than increased production in Chile, despite the incentive of lower taxes. The Nuevo Trato offered limited incentives because even before its enactment the companies enjoyed excellent profit levels due to high copper prices. Yet prosperity for the companies did not guarantee them labor peace in their mining camps.

Anaconda and Kennecott continued and expanded the Guggenheims' efforts to employ industrial welfare programs in their Chilean mines. At Chuquicamata, Anaconda built new and upgraded worker housing, provided free schooling for workers' children, and offered scholarships for some of the children to attend trade or technical schools. Anaconda provided its workers rent-free housing and controlled company store prices. The mining camp even sported an employee orchestra and choir that performed works such as Handel's *Messiah*. Not only did the companies continue to provide housing, utilities, medical clinics, schools, and sports teams, they also sought to shape an entire community of workers, their spouses and children into a stable, motivated and skilled laboring community to support the corporate enterprises. The companies encouraged marriage among workers and their partners. A company advocate proudly noted in 1957 that the percentage of married workers had increased from fifty-five to sixty-three percent since 1948. Indeed the company promoted the ideal of the working husband supported by a spouse who would manage the domestic sphere of their relationship, and train children to assume those same gender specific roles as adults. Company executives described these efforts as the policies of a corporation that constituted a concerned and caring family in which managers and their white- and blue-collar workers each had important and cooperative roles to play. But despite high pay and an array of company policies, copper workers remained leaders in a growing and increasingly militant national labor movement in Chile.

The fact that copper workers refused to become obedient and loyal members of the corporate family stemmed from at least two factors. First, for all their progressive policies, the American copper companies maintained a national origin biased hierarchy within their corporate structures. Chileans could secure some blue- and white-collar positions, but the top positions in the white-collar labor force and of course all significant management positions remained the exclusive preserve of Americans. Americans received better pay, accommodations and services, and they expected and enforced continued deference from their Chilean work force. At the El Teniente mine, Kennecott divided housing into four categories ranging from the A class of single family dwellings for the top American mangers to D class, five-story apartment buildings for manual laborers.

Eduardo Pérez went to work for the El Teniente mine in the 1940s. Pérez seemed to become the ideal, upwardly mobile worker that the U.S. companies sought to create. He earned promotions to several skilled positions and became a star on the company soccer team. Yet Pérez also served as a union leader and became a member of the Socialist Party. Pérez explained the continuing distance which separated the Chilean workers from their American bosses this way:

> [I]n cultural and social life the *gringos* lived in a form very distinct [from the workers] which made many people dislike the *gringos*. . . .

[I]f you even looked at the *gringo* camp they would haul you up to *Bienestar* [personnel department] to be disciplined, and if you went near it or tried to enter, they would fire you.[26]

Those continuing distinctions between the status of Chileans and Americans served to undermine the "familial" bonds which U.S. managers sought to forge within the copper companies. In addition, while copper workers received substantial pay increases, they suffered from the relentless erosion of inflation which angered and mobilized the entire organized sector of the Chilean working class.[27]

The triumph of the center left Popular Front created a positive environment for the mobilization of the working class. Between 1938 and 1945 the number of unions in Chile increased from 932 to 1,581, and the number of unionized workers rose from 125,000 to 230,000. The Popular Front also took a pro-labor stance in strikes, putting its support behind wage increases and other economic benefits. However, the Chilean middle class emerged as the principal beneficiaries of the Popular Front government and its immediate successors. The growing revenues from the copper industry helped fund better housing and schools as well as social security benefits for the middle class. For the vast majority of Chilean workers, higher copper taxes and prices produced an era of increasing poverty and mounting unrest.

In the immediate postwar years conflict between the Socialists and Communists weakened the labor movement. A 1948 law banning the Communist Party delivered another blow to the militant workers. But despite these setbacks, workers continued to organize and strike as inflation eroded their standard of living. The average annual number of strikes shot up from 85 between 1939 and 1946 to 205 a year between 1952 and 1958 as annual inflation soared to 36 percent. Then, in the very same year in which the government granted a massive tax reduction to the copper companies under the Nuevo Trato or New Deal, it reduced workers' incomes when it imposed a rigorous anti-inflation program that drastically reduced government subsidies for public services such as potable water and transportation, and suspended automatic wage adjustments for inflation. The program would slow inflation but it would also undermine the standard of living for most Chileans.

The government's measures brought a swift response from the working class with the copper workers taking a leading role in a general strike which began on January 9, 1956. The regime of former dictator Carlos Ibáñez, who had been elected president in 1952, declared a state of siege and launched mass arrests of labor leaders, incarcerating many of them in prison camps in the desolate northern desert region. The government successfully broke the strike, but it also had laid the groundwork for an increasing radicalization of Chilean politics and mounting anti-Americanism. Most Chileans soon concluded that the nation's economic problems and the impoverishment of the Chilean working class derived from the same source—the continued domination by U.S. companies of the country's economic life.[28] Economic conditions and government policies also triggered a rapid penetration of Latin America's manufacturing sector by U.S. companies.

NEW ENTERPRISES

Despite the centuries-long development of economies based on the export of raw materials, the largest Latin American countries had in fact experienced significant industrial development in the first half of the twentieth century. Manufacturing already accounted for 20 percent or more of national income in Mexico, Argentina, and Chile. Despite economic policies geared to encourage foreign imports, the textile, food, and construction material industries had begun to flourish early in the twentieth century. By drastically reducing foreign exchange reserves, the Depression propelled the process of industrialization forward to meet domestic demand for products that Latin American countries could no longer afford to import.

Latin American governments promoted industrialization as a means of insulating their economies from future international shocks. Chile's creation of CORFO (Corporación de Fomento Fabril), a national development agency, is one example of these efforts. The agency helped finance a variety of development projects, including the resuscitation of failing manufacturing industries and assistance in creating new manufacturing operations. In instances where projects were too large for the private sector to undertake, such as the Volta Redonda steel plant in Brazil, the state undertook to develop these industrial endeavors itself.

Government efforts to cope with the impact of the Depression and insulate national economies from future shocks evolved during the 1940s and 1950s into a larger plan that envisioned the growth of manufacturing as the key to national development. ECLA's critical analysis of Latin American economies demonstrated that their comparative disadvantage as exporters of raw materials retarded development. By industrializing, these countries could reduce their dependence on raw materials and their dependence on expensive imported manufactures. Countries like Chile, Argentina, Brazil, and Mexico adopted aggressive programs of import substitution industrialization (ISI). Under these programs individual nations reduced imports, particularly of consumer goods with high import duties, via exchange controls and other devices. While reducing consumer imports, they used agencies like CORFO to promote the creation or expansion of domestic companies to produce those goods. Despite the dim view most Latin Americans had of American corporations, Latin American programs of industrialization encouraged U.S. involvement.

The ECLA critique of Latin American export economies saw foreign investment in manufacturing as a positive step to solving the problem of export dependence. By investing in the region, foreign manufacturers would lower the region's dependence on foreign imports of manufactured goods, reducing the need to trade cheaper raw materials for more expensive manufactured goods. Foreign manufacturers could provide essential capital and technology, especially as Latin American countries attempted to develop the more complex industries producing intermediate and capital goods such as industrial machinery and machine tools. In manufacturing, U.S. investors whose presence in oil, mining, and utilities brought increasing criticism and government regulations, found themselves welcomed with open arms.

U.S. investments in Latin American manufacturing formed only a small part (8 percent) of total U.S. capital in the region by 1929. Much of that investment was linked to existing raw materials exports such as meatpacking plants in Argentina and sugar mills in Cuba. The risks of direct investment and low tariff barriers made it far more practical for most U.S. manufacturers to exploit the Latin American market by exporting their products to the region. However, those favorable conditions soon underwent dramatic change as the Depression dried up foreign exchange reserves, and local governments raised import duties to reduce the drain on those reserves and to protect their own industries. During the 1930s and 1940s a growing number of U.S. manufacturers found it more profitable to leap over import barriers by setting up plants in Latin America, thus benefiting from those locally imposed import duties that would now protect products they manufactured in Latin America.

By the 1950s, Latin American governments had adopted a positive approach to foreign investment in manufacturing, further accelerating the flow of U.S. capital into the sector. Between 1943 and 1960, U.S. investment in manufacturing soared from $340 million to $1.3 billion. U.S. companies focused particularly on the automobile, chemical, and electrical machinery sectors, concentrating on the production of consumer durable goods such as automobiles and refrigerators. These consumer durables industries with their need to promote consumerism and dependence on local suppliers and retailers would penetrate Latin American societies and economies far more intensely than U.S. mining, petroleum and agricultural companies ever had. In the automobile industry, American companies built upon a history of involvement in Latin America that commenced prior to the Great Depression.

Ford Motor Company led the U.S. automotive giants into Latin America, establishing its first assembly plant in Argentina in 1916, followed by similar operations in Brazil, Chile, and Mexico over the next decade. Ford's initial motive was not to escape high tariffs, but the simple fact that shipping unassembled vehicles lowered transportation costs. At the same time, the labor-intensive assembly process could be carried out in economies with lower wage levels than in the United States. During the 1930s, as General Motors and Chrysler joined Ford in the region, tariffs on assembled vehicles rose steeply, providing a new incentive for developing local assembly operations. Imports of assembled vehicles surged after the war when Latin American countries, rich in U.S. dollars, sought to meet pent up demand from the war. But those conditions quickly changed and a more restrictive climate returned. In 1951 Brazil limited the number of automotive part imports, and then moved to halt the import of parts that were already locally produced. Those actions marked the early stages of the first concerted effort to develop a domestically based automobile manufacturing business in Latin America.

In 1956 the Brazilian government established the Grupo Executivo da Industria Automovilística (GEIA) to promote the development of a local auto industry. Under GEIA content guidelines, 90 percent of each automobile's content was to be domestically manufactured by 1961. GEIA also offered tax incentives and financial assistance to any company willing to manufacture automobiles in Brazil. By 1961 eleven companies were producing 145,000 cars in Brazil. Although Ford, GM, and Chrysler at first limited their participation to the truck industry–thereby losing the initiative to Volkswagen–they too finally joined their competitors in automobile manufacture. Argentina and Mexico, the other two large markets for automobiles in the region, quickly followed the Brazilian example of government programs to develop the local manufacture of automobiles. Meanwhile, the General Electric Company had expanded beyond its role of power generation in Latin America to become a leading manufacturer of electrical equipment.

Like many other U.S. manufacturers, General Electric had begun exporting its wares to Latin America before the end of the nineteenth century.

Although such exports would provide the bulk of its sales in the region until World War II, G.E. established manufacturing plants in Latin America soon after the First World War. That strategic decision profoundly affected the corporation's relationship to Latin American societies. The new relationship became particularly evident in G.E.'s Brazilian operations.

In 1921 G.E. opened its first manufacturing plant in Rio de Janeiro to produce incandescent lamps. Over the next two decades the company broadened its local product lines into producer goods for utilities and manufacturers as well as consumer products such as refrigerators, air conditioners, and radios. Its expanding activities drove the company to integrate itself into Brazilian society to a degree never required by its export activities.

As it took on the manufacture of more complex products, G.E. turned to local industries to supply many of the inputs for those products. To ensure that these components met its standards, G.E provided local manufacturers with technical training and quality control methods, as well as financing. In the process. G.E. became a major force in transmitting important aspects of America's second industrial revolution to Brazil's domestic manufacturers. Its dependence on these suppliers also gave it an intensified interest in the evolution of the country's domestic economy and society. Those same concerns were echoed in the corporation's personnel policies.

G.E. designed a variety of policies to create a stable and efficient work force among its 7,000 Brazilian employees. The corporation's personnel section screened applicants searching for those most likely to remain with the company and adjust to the changes it required of them. G.E. also weighed in against absenteeism by offering bonuses to workers for regular attendance and providing health plans to combat the illnesses which were among the most common excuses for absenteeism. The corporation also provided basic skills training as well as creating an array of social clubs and sports teams designed to give workers the training and values that would be most useful to the company. It went even further for its white-collar employees.

To ensure a steady supply of technical experts, G.E. provided aid to leading Brazilian universities, shaping their curriculums to produce the electrical engineers it needed. The company also offered scholarships to engineering students, and sent many of its Brazilian engineers to the U.S. for additional training. Sensitive to the nationalist movements that began in the 1930s, G.E. began a deliberate program to Brazilianize its white-collar labor force. By 1960, 90 percent of the company's in-country supervisors and technical people were Brazilian. Dr. José de Assis Ribeiro came to personify this strategy. Ribeiro had been trained as an engineer in the United States, and in 1926, a few years after returning to his native Brazil, he joined G.E. operations. Over the next three decades Ribeiro rose through the ranks of the company to become president of its Brazilian subsidiary. For G.E., Ribeiro epitomized the ideal outcome of their policies, a Brazilian who had absorbed the technical training as well as the values required by its corporate culture. The company had similar if less ambitions plans for Brazilian consumers.

Two of the major obstacles to G.E.'s consumer products business were the low incomes of most Brazilians and the lack of consumer credit facilities. After World War II, G.E. created a network of credit that extended from the company through its wholesalers and retailers down to the average consumer. By the 1950s, only 5 percent of G.E.'s consumer products were purchased with cash. The company also worked vigorously to create a consumer society by overcoming consumer resistance to its products.

During the 1930s, G.E. encountered difficulty in selling refrigerators in Brazil. Learning that many Brazilians feared that cold air from the appliances would cause health problems, the company launched a massive public relations campaign. It sent trucks into Brazilian neighborhoods with refrigerators offering to let residents use them on a free trial basis. The company followed this up with a media blitz that extolled the refrigerator's health benefits in preventing food spoilage. The campaigns proved highly successful in promoting the sale of G.E. refrigerators, drawing Brazilians further down the road to a full-blown consumer society. Some of its success derived from another G.E. product—the radio.[29]

The U.S. government's decision to foster the creation of the Radio Corporation of America (see Chapter Two) recognized the power and potential of radio. That confidence was rewarded in Latin America where a mere 1 million radio receivers in 1930 exploded to more than 15 million thirty years later. Radio placed a powerful instrument of information, entertainment, and advertising in millions of Latin American homes. U.S. companies like G.E. responded to that opportunity with an advertising blitz for their products. As Carlos Bacarat, a Brazilian radio broadcaster, explained in 1941, "We have all the bigger sponsors which use radio in the country, amongst them American concerns such as Fort [sic] Motor Company, General Motors, Lever Brothers, Colgate-Palmolive, Westinghouse, Carter Pills, General Electric, and many others, . . ." U.S. companies also created tie-ins with the other powerful American medium—the movies. Aware of Latin Americans's fascination with Hollywood, U.S. broadcasters created programs and commercials featuring film stars. The radio thus served both as a consumer product and a device to promote the spread of consumerism in Latin America.[30] Despite the optimism of U.S. corporate leaders and Latin American national planners about the effects of American manufacturing investment, the process raised serious nationalist and developmental issues in the region.

By the mid-1960s, manufacturing would become the largest single segment of direct U.S. investment in the region, larger even than the substantial capital devoted to petroleum. The manufacturing companies' rapid rise to prominence in Latin America owed much to the region's governments which welcomed them as vital contributors to developmentalist strategies based on industrialization. Yet this success story had a darker side that would become increasingly apparent in the years ahead. By the 1960s critics would argue that Latin American countries had simply swapped dependence on foreign consumer goods for dependence on foreign capital and technology. As Fernando Henrique Cardoso, the noted Brazilian politician and theorist of dependency, explained:

> Latin American industrialization was launched during the Great Depression. . . . However, a development pattern was chosen that depended on increasing amounts of foreign investment in the industrial sector.
>
> In terms of diversification of production, levels of development may seem very high. But both capital flow and economic decisions are controlled from abroad. Even when production and marketing are carried out within the dependent economy, earnings go to swell capital funds available to the central economies. Investment decisions also depend in part on external considerations and pressures. Decisions taken by the parent companies, which only partly reflect the domestic market situation, significantly influence the reinvestment of profits generated in the national system. In certain circumstances, firms can opt to transform their profits into capital for investment in the central economies or in other dependent countries.[31]

Furthermore, U.S. companies frequently competed with or displaced nationally owned firms, prompting strong reactions from Latin American business leaders. And much like their counterparts in the extractive sectors, manufacturing enterprises regularly repatriated profits to the United States, which raised the issue of whether multinationals contributed or drained capital from Latin American economies. Besides structural issues of economic development, there was also serious concern about the Americanization of Latin America. Many Latin Americans expressed grave concern about the penetration by U.S. culture, especially values that stressed material consumption as the ultimate source of human happiness, the essential importance of intense personal competitiveness, and the insistence that relentless social change represented a fundamental good. Although the most radical reactions to these and other issues surrounding U. S. corporations did not erupt until the 1960s and 1970s, warning signs began appearing in Latin America by the mid-1950s.[32]

NATIONALIZATIONS

While mining, manufacturing, and oil companies succeeded in expanding and reaping profits in Latin America despite the new nationalist regulations and challenges from labor, utility companies proved far less successful in overcoming these obstacles. U.S. investment in Latin American utilities in 1954 barely exceeded the level of $1.5 billion attained in 1940. Those figures reflected losses the companies had suffered and a new more cautious policy about investments in the area. Part of the problem for the utilities was that their relation to foreign exchange operations was almost the direct opposite of the mining and oil companies.

While the raw materials enterprises earned dollars with their products and paid many of their expenses in devalued local currencies, utilities had to purchase their equipment with dollars and earn their revenues in local currencies. As a result, the utility companies suffered severely when the Depression inflicted sharp exchange declines on local currencies, and Latin American governments imposed exchange controls. American and Foreign Power (AFP) suffered particularly from these developments that occurred in the years immediately following its largest investments in the region. The company estimated that exchange devaluation cost it $24 million in operating revenue in 1932, $34 million in 1935, and $50 million in 1938. Local governments that frequently blocked the repatriation of funds to the United States to prevent a drain on foreign exchange reserves added to this problem. Other government polices also contributed to AFP's woes.

Sensitive to the populist nationalist agenda now at the center of the political stage in much of Latin America, governments in Argentina, Brazil, Mexico, and Chile began imposing wage increases for workers in the utility companies, while they proved extremely reluctant to grant rate increases to the same firms. Furthermore, the urban working and middle class campaigns against foreign ownership of companies that had such a direct impact on their daily lives, had a visible impact on government policy.

In 1941 the Chilean government seized the Santiago Tramway Company in response to a labor strike. Given its existing difficulties with Chilean exchange rates, AFP then attempted to sell the tramway as well as its parent company the Compañía Chilena de Electricidad to the government. Two years later the company suffered the expropriation of two of its subsidiaries in Argentina. In 1945 the Argentinian government expropriated AFP properties in five provincial cities. Faced with accelerating state takeovers of its assets, the company tried unsuccessfully to sell its remaining facilities to the Argentinian government in 1950. In Mexico, AFP faced increasingly stiff competition from government owned power facilities. In light of difficulties in these markets, the company tried to focus its attention on what appeared to be more positive environments, seeking loans from the Exim Bank as well as local financial institutions to expand its operations in countries like Cuba and Guatemala. Despite continuing success in these markets, the outlook for AFP in Latin America had turned extremely bleak by the end of the 1950s. Within a few short years, the company would begin divesting itself of almost all major assets in the region. Although ITT had a much smaller stake in the area than AFP, it had a very similar experience.

Much like AFP, ITT had engaged in substantial expansion on the eve of the Great Depression, buying telephone companies in Uruguay, Argentina, Chile, and Peru. ITT also suffered from many of the same problems that frustrated the power company such as falling exchange rates, exchange controls, and increased government regulation. In response to these problems, ITT president Sosthenes Behn turned his attention to the domestic market. Soon after the war, he sold ITT's largest operation in Latin America, the River Plate Telephone Company, to the Argentinian government for $95,000,000. This left the Chilean Telephone Company as ITT's largest holding in the region, at one-fifth the size of the River Plate Company. ITT would remain a major player in Latin American telecommunications, but as Sosthenes Behn made clear in a speech in 1952, the corporation had now focused its attention on the more secure U.S. market. Nor were the utility companies the only traditional area of U.S. corporate activity to face serious threats to their survival.[33]

Central Americans would have found it difficult to believe that the New Deal had marked the beginning of a partnership between the U.S. government and corporations to pursue more progressive policies toward Latin America. During the 1930s and 1940s the United Fruit Company had resisted the trend among other large companies to pay higher wages and make at least grudging concessions to local government initiatives on social welfare. Indeed, in Honduras and Guatemala, the company worked hand in glove with the dictators Tiburcio Carías and Jorge Ubico who suppressed any sign of progressive domestic movements that might challenge the company's position or policies. But the company, while ignoring the lessons of the populist nationalist movements of the 1930s, would eventually face far more serious challenges to its interests.

After the aging Honduran dictator Tiburcio Carías (1933–1949) stepped down in 1949, his hand-picked successor initiated a cautious program of liberalization that eventually led to preparations for national elections in 1954. Much as in 1932 the contested national elections created an opening for popular protests against the United Fruit Company. Beginning in early May 1954, labor actions spread across the UFCO and Standard Fruit operations, as 15,000 strikers paralyzed the north coast. Three weeks after the strike began, Standard Fruit reached an agreement with its workers making concessions on wages and benefits. Most importantly, for the first time the company had reached a collective agreement with its workers and given de facto recognition to the workers' right to organize. United Fruit proved far more intransigent.

UFCO refused to negotiate with its workers, and by the time of the Standard settlement, 25,000 striking United Fruit workers had been joined by nearly 4,000 male and female workers who walked out of tobacco and textile plants as well as breweries. Much as in 1932, the workers enjoyed support from local merchants. The nationalistic aspect of their struggle against the powerful U.S. corporation also won them support from middle class groups in the capital, including teachers and small businesspeople. Newspapers in the capital picked up on that perspective reporting that "a high employee of the companies can not understand or conceive that these humble peasants have other hopes than to throw themselves in bed when they return from their exhausting work."[34] The strike dragged on for sixty-six days before UFCO finally made concessions on wages and gave de facto recognition to the workers' right to organize. However, the company largely skirted earlier demands by the workers that they have some control over their work conditions. The modest achievements of the strike in part reflected a shift in the orientation of the UFCO labor movement.

As the strike dragged on, a split developed between radical and conservative elements of the workers. The conservatives, who wanted to limit strike demands to economic issues, received assistance from the government which arrested some of the more radical strike leaders, and from the American Federation of Labor's regional labor organization (ORIT). The Federation's support began with the arrival of ORIT labor organizer Arturo

Jaurequi in mid-June. The ORIT backed union leaders, such as Eladio Ruíz Meléndez, attacked their opponents as Communist agitators whose actions only served to strengthen the hand of United Fruit. Meléndez, in an open letter to one of the radical leaders asked, "What have you and the rest of your comrades done for the workers? Whom do you serve: the workers, or the Tela Railroad Company [UFC subsidiary] and Imperialist Russia? I want to remind you that the fruit company is very grateful to you, for your divisionist tactics...."[35] With the assistance of ORIT and the AFL, the more conservative wing of the strike movement succeeded in reaching a settlement with UFCO. Within a year ORIT helped create a single union for UFCO workers, and at ORIT's urging the company finally created a department of labor relations.

In 1963, the city of Tela, the center of UFCO operations on the Honduran coast, became home to the major Central American training center for the American Institute for Free Labor Development (AIFLD). AIFLD promoted educational and social projects and personified the U.S. vision of development as a cooperative project among labor, business, and government. Its president was none other than J. Peter Grace of W.R. Grace and Company, and its board members included Serafino Romauldi and George Meany, president of the American Federation of Labor. Thus, AIFLD symbolized ORIT's successful creation of a tame labor movement friendly to U.S. business in Honduras and its launching of similar movements throughout the region. But more than that, AIFLD was funded and run by the CIA, which used it as a front for its penetration of the labor movement in Latin America. Just to the north of Honduras, the agency had taken far more drastic measures to stem another threat to U.S. business.[36]

Popular unrest toppled Guatemala's long ruling dictator Jorge Ubico (1931–1944) in 1944, and led to the election of moderate Juan Arévalo as president. Arévalo's reformist leanings found expression principally in rhetoric, but his election did create some space for workers to press for better treatment. Workers at United Fruit's International Railways of Central America organized a union and threatened a strike prompting the company to grant pay increases amounting to $700,000 annually. Also under pressure from its workers, UFCO agreed to a forty-eight hour work week, and to pay time and a half for hours in excess of forty-eight hours.[37]

Arévalo's successor Jacobo Arbenz carried out a series of reforms that challenged both the power of UFCO and the nation's landowning elite. Arbenz used a new agrarian reform law to expropriate 400,000 of the 550,000 acres United Fruit controlled in Guatemala. In addition, he offered support to striking workers at the frutera and its railway subsidiary.

United Fruit was not the only U.S. company to face what it considered unwarranted government interference in its labor relations. The managers of AFP's Guatemalan subsidiary reported in 1953 that as a result of a strike by its employees, the Arbenz government appointed a mediator "who immediately installed himself in the company offices with a staff of technical assistants . . ." When the mediator concluded that the company could afford to grant a 40 percent raise, the company "refused to accede to these exorbitant demands, which it considers entirely unjustified and unreasonable. . . ."[38] The UFCO-controlled railway company also faced the end of its transportation monopoly as Arbenz began building a highway parallel to the railway's route from the capital to the Caribbean coast.

AFP's appeals to the U.S. government and the concerns of the Eisenhower administration that a small country in its traditional sphere of influence might successfully challenge U.S. interests, led to a CIA initiated plot to overthrow the Arbenz regime. The CIA's covert operation forced Arbenz's resignation in June 1954, and the installation of a regime which would restore UFCO's property and its dominant position in the national economy. The managers of AFP's subsidiary reported with some satisfaction that, "The situation in Guatemala has been quiet following the overthrow of the Arbenz Government and the installation of President Carlos Castillo Armas. The change in administration should bring about an improvement in the investment climate in Guatemala."[39]

A young Argentine medical student, Ernesto Ché Guevara, who was visiting Guatemala, witnessed Arbenz's overthrow. As a supporter of the defeated Guatemalan president, Guevara fled to Mexico where he would join the followers of Fidel Castro whose revolutionary government in Cuba would expropriate more than one billion dollars in U.S. investments and trigger a regionwide wave of nationalizations and expropriations of U.S. companies.[40]

SUMMARY

By the time that the CIA toppled Jacobo Arbenz from power, the nationalist populist tide was rapidly ebbing in Latin America. Two months after Arbenz's downfall, Getúlio Vargas committed suicide and one year later the Argentine military forced Juan Perón from power. Despite their demise, these movements could rightly claim to have made significant strides in addressing Latin Americans' resentment toward U.S. corporations and corporate culture. Yet their accomplishments masked serious limitations of these movements and respective policies.

True to their roots in the populist movements of the 1930s, the nationalist populist governments of the 1940s and 1950s retained their power base in the urban middle classes and organized labor. These limits to their support constrained the policy initiatives and political futures of the nationalist populist regimes whose urban focused policies and nationalist aspirations failed to touch Latin American nations' large rural populations. The limitations of the regimes' power and the effective alliance between U.S. corporations, private foundations, and the U.S. government help explain the fact that despite the ardent anti-Americanism of the 1930s, the populist regimes of the 1940s and 1950s actually oversaw a massive increase in the American corporate presence, even in sectors such as mining and petroleum which had been the focus of populist concerns.

Private foundations and the U.S. government worked diligently in the decades after the outbreak of World War II to promote the development of Latin America through private enterprise, and particularly the participation of U.S. companies. Foundations trained Latin American policy makers in U.S. free market development ideas. These institutions also had a direct pro-business influence on U.S. foreign policy. The U.S. government now called upon an array of mechanisms, including its own foreign aid programs and the activities of international agencies like the World Bank, to further the interests of American business in the region. And in cases where it perceived a particularly ominous threat to those interests, the U.S. government turned to the covert operatives of the CIA. Furthermore, U.S. companies had taken on a larger and more complex role in the region as they renewed their attempts to transform Latin Americans into employees and laborers who accepted and emulated the policies and procedures of the modern American work place.

Following the principles of the ECLA developmental model, Latin American governments instituted nationalistic and protectionist policies, which while creating a more difficult operating environment for enterprises like utilities, actually opened the door of opportunity for U.S. manufacturers. As U.S. companies exploited these opportunities in areas such as automobile and electrical equipment manufacture, they became more intensely involved in local economies than mining, petroleum, or agricultural companies had ever been. Most would follow the G.E. example in Brazil by seeking out local suppliers and promoting the adoption of U.S. production standards and work methods among Latin American manufacturers. Depending to a significant degree on local markets, they also extended that transformational effort beyond the work place in a new, more intense, and broader attempt to promote consumerism throughout Latin America. While

U.S. companies enjoyed considerable success in shaping the course of economic development in the region and promoting the spread of consumerism, American corporate influence did not always prompt a positive response from Latin Americans.

During the late 1950s inflation in some of the largest economies such as Argentina, Brazil, and Chile was racing ahead at more than 20 percent annually, devouring the wages and salaries of the working and middle classes. In the midst of overall growth, the disparities between rich and poor were growing increasingly acute. Much as in the 1930s, the internal problems of poverty and income inequality fused with growing nationalist resentment of U.S. corporate domination and their influence on local societies. Once again, Latin Americans attributed their problems of economic underdevelopment to an alliance between their own elites who preserved an inequitable social system and U.S. corporations who dominated key sectors of the economy, drained desperately needed capital from the national economy, and attempted to reshape their work forces in an American image. The growing dissatisfaction with the shortcomings of populism and the continued domination of U.S. corporations fused into a new series of radical political movements which would challenge the principles of U.S. corporate culture and the very presence of American enterprise in Latin America.

CHAPTER FIVE

FROM REVOLUTION
TO NEOLIBERALISM,
1959–1999

In March 1971, Chilean President Salvador Allende met with Tim Dunleavy, a director of International Telephone and Telegraph (ITT), and Benjamin W. Holmes, the head of the local ITT subsidiary, the Chilean Telephone Company (Chiltelco). The meeting between a recently elected Marxist president, who had already moved to nationalize U.S. copper companies, and the executives from the American communications giant proved oddly jovial. The men engaged in a bit of sexist banter comparing Chiltelco's debt to a housewife's inability to stay within her budget. Dunleavy joked: "Mr. President, a telephone [company] is like a woman; no matter how much money you give her, she's always asking for more." Allende further lightened the mood by assuring the executives that he had no desire to nationalize Chiltelco. But, in fact, ITT had launched a secret campaign against Allende long before he became president.

During Allende's unsuccessful earlier bid for the presidency in 1964, ITT had made political donations to one of his opponents. In June 1970 John McCone, an ITT director and former Director of the Central Intelligence Agency, met with Richard Helms, the current head of the Agency, to discuss how ITT might make use of $1 million dollars to prevent Allende's victory in the latest presidential race. After Allende's election, ITT officials continued to meet with leading members of the Nixon administration to discuss steps to prevent Allende from surviving his first six months in office.

In turn, Allende soon abandoned his promise about Chitelco and took operational control of the company in September 1971. In subsequent negotiations with ITT officials, Allende offered $24 million dollars for assets the company valued at $150 million. One year after his jovial meeting with Dunleavy and Holmes, Allende announced he would seek a constitutional amendment to expropriate Chiltelco. The publication of secret ITT documents by U.S. newspaper columnist Jack Anderson exposed the company's campaign against Allende. The Chilean president, now fully aware of ITT's efforts to topple his government declared, "[N]o one can dream we are going to pay even half a cent to this multinational company which was on the verge of plunging Chile into civil war."[1] But the ITT officials would have their revenge. In September 1973, Allende died during a CIA-backed military coup. One year later, Chile's new military dictator, General Augusto Pinochet, awarded $125 million to ITT for Chiltelco. The interaction between Allende and ITT demonstrates the violent swings which occurred in the relationships between U.S. corporations and Latin American countries during the closing decades of the twentieth century.

Between 1959 and 1973, U.S. investment in Latin America exploded, but so did Latin American opposition to the ever-expanding American economic and cultural presence. The leftist governments of Cuba, Peru, and Chile not only denounced the role of U.S. business, they engaged in massive expropriations of U.S. corporations. A wave of military interventions followed on the heels of these events. The new military governments instituted long-term policies to suppress internal political and social dissent while encouraging economic growth. Both military and civilian regimes in this period envisioned a significant role for multinational corporations in their economies. The new right-wing governments forged an alliance with multinationals, holding down wages to make their societies attractive targets for foreign investors, and pursuing economic policies to redistribute income toward the middle and upper classes and increase the size of their domestic consumer markets. U.S. corporations responded to these opportunities with increased investments in the manufacturing sector, accompanied by growing efforts to promote consumerism using the powerful new tool of television. U.S. manufacturers also expanded and intensified the application of scientific management principles in the work place.

This development strategy collapsed in 1982 amid popular protests and an international debt crisis which threatened to destroy Latin American economies as well as leading lenders such as Citibank. In the aftermath of this financial debacle, Latin American governments moved to dismantle a half century of protectionist and nationalist economic policies by rolling back tariffs and other protectionist devices. Many of the new regimes also moved to privatize state corporations created in the wake of the Great Depression, opening major natural resources and public utilities to both domestic and foreign private investment. From the radical nationalist agendas of the 1960s, the pendulum had swung to an aggressive neoliberalism.

Neoliberals advocated a smaller role for the state in the national economy including sharp reductions in social spending, and they proposed to fully open their national economies to the world market by tearing down the protectionist barriers erected since the Great Depression. These policies created an environment strongly reminiscent of the conditions under which U.S. business had rushed into the region at the beginning of the century. As a result, American businesses, with the support and encouragement of local governments, launched their most intense efforts ever to transform Latin American societies. However, similar to the early twentieth century, this renewed partnership has yet to resolve the problems of social and economic justice.

THE CORPORATE STATE ALLIANCE CONTINUES

Having grown briskly in the fifteen years after World War II, U.S. business activity in Latin America skyrocketed during the 1960s. Total U.S. investment in the region shot from $8.3 billion in 1960 to $14.7 billion in 1970.[2] Half of that increase resulted from the continued explosive growth in manufacturing, as U.S. corporations in the automotive, and pharmaceutical industries continued their rapid expansion and were joined by the aggressive growth of other consumer goods industries such as food processing.

Several factors influenced the rapid expansion of American business in the 1960s. U.S. corporations continued to benefit from local protectionist policies once they invested in the region. The rapid urbanization of Latin America served to create a growing market for consumer goods ranging from automobiles to soft drinks. U.S. multinationals also expanded operations in the region in response to intensifying competition from Japanese and European corporations as multinationals increasingly turned to direct investment as a means of entering and competing in global markets. American business also benefited substantially from expanded U.S. government programs to promote foreign investment.

During the 1950s Washington began offering investment guarantees for developing countries including those of Latin America. Under this program corporations could purchase U.S. government policies to insure their foreign investments against such risks as revolution and expropriation. Besides programs to protect overseas investments the government also instituted policies to promote foreign investment. In 1957 Congress approved P.L. 480, which governed the overseas sale of surplus agricultural products. Under that program, part of the foreign currency proceeds from the sales could be lent to U.S. corporations investing in developing countries. The P.L. 480 program came under the control of the Agency for International Development (AID) when it was created in 1961. AID added to P.L. 480 by making dollar loans to U.S. citizens making overseas investments.[3] The government also had other more indirect means of assisting U.S. business in the region.

The 1960s marked the high-water mark of government aid to Latin America. President John F. Kennedy's Alliance for Progress funneled grants and loans into Latin America in return for economic and social reforms in the region. Most of the aid flowing into Latin America came not as grants from U.S. agencies like AID, but as loans from multilateral organizations such as the World Bank, the International Monetary Fund, and the recently created Inter American Development Bank. Although these institutions operated under multilateral designations, they functioned under direct American influence, complimenting U.S. government aid and loan policies. Government and multilateral agency lending accounted for sixty percent of Latin America's public foreign debt during the 1960s.[4] That assistance came with more conditions than simply requirements for repayment.

A 1963 presidential commission on foreign aid concluded that "we cannot insist upon the establishment of our own economic system" in developing countries, but the commissioners went on to state, "We believe the U.S. should not aid a foreign government in projects establishing government-owned industrial and commercial enterprises which compete with existing private endeavors." Making specific reference to the Western Hemisphere, the report's authors recommended that, "Latin America must be encouraged to see its essential choice between totalitarian, inefficient, state-controlled economies and society on the one hand and an economically and politically freer system on the other...."[5] Simply put U.S. foreign aid had the specific purposes of opposing socialism and encouraging capitalism and U.S. business interests. Government programs designed to promote and safeguard American investments received direct assistance and guidance from U.S. foundations and business groups.

Beginning in the 1960s, major U.S. foundations, particularly the Ford Foundation, made a concerted effort to influence the development of university education in Latin America. As a result, much of the training in economics received by the technocratic elite has reflected a developmental orthodoxy propounded by U.S. social scientists. Those development strategies emphasize the importance of private enterprise and particularly foreign investment in the development process. Many members of the elite were educated at U.S. universities, thereby further reinforcing that same thought process.[6] American business leaders, meanwhile, took direct actions to influence U.S. government policy.

During the 1960s, David Rockefeller, brother of Nelson and president of the Chase Manhattan Bank, served as the president of the Business Group on Latin America. He eventually expanded that organization into the Council for the Americas representing 200 corporations accounting for 80 percent of U.S. investment in Latin America. In 1965 President Lyndon Johnson appointed him to the new General Advisory Council on Foreign Assistance Programs where Rockefeller worked to shape foreign aid projects to make Latin America even more attractive to U.S. businesses.[7] His brother would play an evermore public role in shaping U.S. policy in this period.

In 1969, a decade after the Cuban Revolution, and just months before the socialist Salvador Allende was elected president of Chile, Nelson Rockefeller undertook a fact-finding mission to Latin America at the request of President Richard Nixon. As he toured Latin America, Rockefeller became the target of intense popular animosity toward the United States. At virtually every stop in his grand tour, Washington's preeminent Latin American expert encountered ugly demonstrations denouncing his presence and U.S. policy. But Rockefeller remained undeterred by the latest Latin American backlash toward increased U.S. corporate penetration. In the aftermath of his rude reception, Rockefeller prepared the *Report on the Americas*. In that document, Rockefeller honed in on what he saw as the central economic problem in Latin America:

> Private investment, particularly foreign investment, is regarded with suspicion in many quarters. A great many and probably a majority of the citizens of the hemisphere nations regard United States private investment as a form of exploitation or economic colonialism. There is a widespread, mistaken view that such investment takes more out of the area than it contributes to it. Fear of domination by United States companies is expressed frequently.

> The central problem is the failure of governments throughout the hemisphere to recognize fully the importance of private investment. Thus realistic steps have not been taken to encourage private investment, to create a framework within which it can operate and which assures that it will serve the best interests of the entire community.[8]

Rockefeller argued for a new economic strategy of hemispheric integration. That strategy would require the U.S. to reduce its protectionist barriers as well as its health, environmental, and wage standards to permit imports by U.S. corporations which had migrated to Latin America to take advantage of its low wages. Rockefeller had long promoted such a policy but as enunciated near the end of his career in the *Report on the Americas,* his arguments had a prophetic quality.[9] Within two decades they would constitute the central strategy of the United States as it signed the North American Free Trade Agreement (NAFTA) with Mexico and Canada, and sought to incorporate other Latin American nations into a hemispheric free trade zone.

The inducements of foreign aid and the influence of U.S. foundations and prominent individuals like Nelson Rockefeller did not always prove successful in convincing Latin American governments to promote and protect American business. Indeed the Kennedy administration had created the Alliance for Progress as a response to total expropriation of U.S. companies by the Cuban government. In response to challenges like those from Fidel Castro, the government would turn to more aggressive measures, such as imposing trade embargoes, financial blockades, and calling on the covert operatives of the Central Intelligence Agency to alter threatening political trends or even oust unwanted regimes.

In the four decades after the Cuban Revolution, the government, foundations, and business groups all played important roles in influencing the course U.S. corporations followed in Latin America. But American companies did not enjoy uniform success in their activities in the region. Manufacturing corporations surged ahead in their commitments to Latin America. International competition, the low cost of Latin America's skilled labor, a growing regional market for consumer durables, and more lenient treatment by local governments gave the impetus to this rush by U.S. multinationals into the manufacturing sector. U.S. banks which had largely abandoned the area after the massive loan defaults of the Great Depression, would return with a vengeance in the 1970s. Meanwhile, some of the traditional U.S. corporate leaders such as mining and petroleum companies found themselves the targets of nationalization in the 1960s and 1970s. For utility companies the era marked the demise of most of their operations in the region.

CORPORATE EXPANSION

Manufacturing, already the most dynamic segment of U.S. investment in the post-war years, continued to surge forward in the 1960s. During that decade U.S. manufacturing investment tripled to over $4.5 billion, representing nearly a third of all U.S. corporate capital in Latin America. U.S. business grew prodigiously in a variety of undertakings including automobiles, pharmaceuticals, electrical equipment, and food processing.[10] The surge in manufacturing investment made significant regional adjustments in the pattern of U.S. investments. With so many of these enterprises aimed directly or indirectly at the consumer market, these companies sought out those countries, specifically Mexico, Brazil, and Argentina with the largest potential number of consumers. The auto industry generated the most public attention, bringing to Latin America's urban streets and rural roads the single most striking symbol of U.S. corporate culture.

America's big three automakers, General Motors, Ford, and Chrysler had responded with great reluctance to state efforts to create domestically based automobile industries in Brazil, Argentina, and Mexico. They had initially restricted their efforts to the manufacture of trucks with their steadier market demand and less risky investments. But by the mid-1960s, the companies committed themselves to full-scale development of passenger cars. The U.S. automakers had responded in part to changing global realities in their industry. In the United States, the great post-war demand spike for cars had faded by the end of the 1950s, giving way to a far more competitive market for replacement vehicles. That market became all the more challenging with growing imports from such emerging automotive giants as Volkswagen and later Toyota. Indeed, global competition among enormous companies had become the order of the day, and Volkswagen had already taken the lead in the largest potential market in Latin America–Brazil. Hesitancy among the big three gave way to a competitive rush into the region—most notably into their nearest neighbor, Mexico.[11]

In 1962, the Mexican government issued a decree limiting the number of auto manufacturers to seven and requiring that sixty percent of the value of the cars be manufactured in Mexico. The decree in effect carved the domestic market up between the large U.S. and German manufacturers. The U.S. automakers responded quickly with Ford building two new factories in Mexico City, and GM and Chrysler each adding a new factory in the industrial town of Toluca.[12]

Meanwhile, in Brazil, adverse economic conditions led to a similar process of concentration as both Chrysler and Ford bought out foreign and domestically controlled auto manufacturers. By the late 1970s multinational corporations controlled between 85 and 95 percent of auto manufacturing in Brazil, Argentina, and Mexico, with most of the industry in each country dominated by three or four of these firms. U.S. car companies did not enjoy the total dominance U.S. mining companies once held in Latin America because they faced stiff competition from European and Japanese automakers. Nevertheless, in 1973 as Latin American auto production surged past 1.5 million units, the big three accounted for better than 40 percent of that output. In turn, their activities had dramatic impacts upon Latin American societies.

By the early 1970s the multinational auto manufacturers had created a new industrial labor force with more than 180,000 Latin Americans working in their plants. Furthermore, the industry had profound effects on Latin American societies. Cognizant of the need to promote replacement purchases by linking status to specific car models and frequent, albeit minimal, changes in those models, automakers gave an important new impetus to consumer advertising in Latin America with campaigns that stressed as never before the idea that social status and a sense of self-worth were inextricably linked with a specific material possession. The success of those campaigns helped shift infrastructure investment by national governments from public transportation to private vehicles. The success of the multinationals also generated new concerns over the role of foreign corporations in national life, as fledgling domestic manufacturers collapsed or became part of joint ventures with the multinationals.[13] Domination of the local market and the impact of consumerist values also marked the success of the U.S. food and beverage industries.[14]

In Latin America no single brand name has been more widely advertised or more closely associated with American capitalism than Coca-Cola. Even before the First World War, Americans in places like Havana, Cuba, and Panama City, Panama were enjoying the taste of Coke. Unfortunately for the company, these expatriates were about the only market for its product south of the Rio Grande. In Latin America, the only establishments where the name Coca-Cola appeared on the menu were military canteens, and hotels and restaurants catering to Americans. Not until company president Robert Woodruff set up a Foreign Sales Department in the mid-1920s did Coca-Cola make a serious effort to market the beverage overseas. Under this new impetus the company opened bottling plants in Guatemala and Honduras in 1926, and added new franchises in Mexico and Colombia the following year. The company succeeded in cutting shipping costs by reducing the amount of water in coke syrup supplied to its overseas plants. But the Coca-Cola Corporation's foreign marketing efforts remained relatively unsophisticated, and it often selected inexperienced individuals as its franchisees. As a result, most of its recently created operations in Mexico and Colombia had already shut down by the time of the Great Depression. But the story of the U.S. marketing giant proved very different on the eve of World War II.

Having learned lessons from its past failures, Coca Cola now took a very different approach to marketing in Latin America. Mexico, a familiar and nearby market for U.S. business, found itself the target of an intense Coke marketing campaign as giant Coca-Cola "bottles" danced in the bull-fighting rings of Mexico City, and Coke signs sprouted throughout the country's rural villages. By the early 1970s the company controlled 42 percent of a soft drink market where sales had reached 12 billion bottles annually. In Brazil, even the ardent nationalist Getúlio Vargas proved anxious to attract the U.S. beverage company, providing special tax breaks and other legal concessions.

As in the Caribbean decades earlier, Coke followed the flag into Brazil in 1942. Sales began soon after U.S. military bases were set up in 1941 to protect the Southern Hemisphere from the possibility of a Nazi invasion. But this time the beverage giant would not rely on the thin market of GIs and expatriates. Coca Cola encountered a serious challenge in the Brazilian market from a locally produced soft drink, guaraná, made from the seeds of the guaraná tree. However, the Company enjoyed a cost advantage because, unlike guaraná, it did not require pasteurization. Furthermore, the Company launched a highly successful campaign to create local franchisees for the product. The Company carefully selected prominent local citizens for its franchisees, thereby ensuring a reliable base of entrepreneurs and minimizing Coke's image as a foreign corporation. Local bottlers received not just syrup from the Company, but a total package including advertising, promotions, and technical assistance. In turn, bottlers encouraged or pressured retailers to sell only Coke and other products produced by the Company.[15]

By 1952 the Pepsi-Cola company had joined Coke in competing for the Brazilian market. Within two decades, the two U.S. soft drink corporations had captured 40 percent of the Brazilian market. Their success derived in part from the package of services and support they offered local bottlers. In addition, like the auto companies they relied heavily on advertising to expand their market share. As in the United States, part of the success of these ad campaigns came from associating soft drinks with youth, beauty, athletics, and more generally "the good life." The long-established U.S. advertising practice of associating the purchase of a material good with human happiness worked effectively for the U.S. beverage companies in Latin America. But at times they also tailored that marketing to local needs and values. In Brazil, the Pepsi Generation became the Pepsi Revolution because the company's advertising agent recognized that young Brazilians lacked effective means for social protest. Under the slogan, the Pepsi Revolution, they could express generational resentment by abandoning the "old" beverage of Coca-Cola for the "new" soft drink Pepsi. Young Brazilians could now express social protest through product consumption.

Much like the expansion of U.S. automakers, the success of beverage companies raised troubling new questions about the impact of American business in Latin America. Beyond the fact that their success meant the decline of the domestically owned soft drink industry, their activities also raised concerns about public health and cultural values. In terms of health, corporate success in selling their product at every economic and social level meant that millions of impoverished Latin Americans would be spending precious wages on beverages which had little or no nutritional value. Equally troubling was the idea of expressing social protest through consumption in societies with deepseated social injustices and where protest already faced substantial obstacles. Yet the success of U.S. marketing could not be denied; indeed it proved as effective at selling computers as it did at selling soft drinks.[16]

The success of U.S. manufacturers in fields ranging from auto manufacturing to food processing derived from several factors including American technological superiority, as well as responses to global competition. The specific successes of U.S. automotive and beverage corporations in creating consumer demand for their product owed much to the growth of television in Latin America.

By 1968 the number of television sets in Latin America was approaching 10 million. The growth in the number of sets and indeed the entire industry was heavily influenced by U.S. broadcasters. As two Latin Americans explained in a report to the United Nations:

> Throughout the continent the television stations are directly or indirectly dependent upon the major United States networks-and the greater the need for the latest technical equipment and trained technicians, the closer those links are.
>
> In Latin America the United States has a monopoly of the supply of the new technology, the basic film material, the technical experts and, of course, the large-scale capital needed to increase the size of the local investment.[17]

Although this statement exaggerated the degree of U.S. control, it was true that American broadcasters held substantial interests in Latin American television stations. For example, by 1968 ABC held interests in television stations in sixteen Latin American countries with a total audience of

20 million households. ABC's rivals NBC and CBS held much smaller stakes in Latin American networks. However, at this time U.S. influence was most pronounced in the programming area where 80 percent of all Latin American television programs were produced in the United States.

Just as in the United States, television proved an enormously influential medium for conveying ideas and values through the powerful visual images of its programs and advertisements. But in Latin America, those powerful images were being generated by an external culture promoting its own social ideals. The values of that society include consumerism and the underlying assumption that the acquisition of material goods provides the surest path to human happiness.[18] The enormous power and influence of the images created by U.S. corporations once again raised concerns about the reshaping of Latin American culture in the image of American society. Yet not all forms of U.S. corporate activity enjoyed the same success as American manufacturing and communication multinationals. Increasingly, Latin Americans viewed minerals, petroleum, and utilities as part of their national resources, and therefore as parts of their economy which should be under strict national regulation or even national ownership.

CORPORATE VETERANS UNDER SIEGE

For U.S. utilities, primarily G.E. and ITT, the early sixties marked the end of their presence as major corporate players in Latin America. Bowing to the pressures of higher taxation, foreign exchange controls, and tightly controlled rates for electricity, G.E.'s subsidiary, the American and Foreign Power Company (AFP), sold off its holdings to the governments of Argentina, Brazil, Chile, Colombia, and Mexico between 1958 and 1965. ITT followed a similar course of action, divesting itself of the telephone systems it owned in Latin America and turned to other lines of business such as the Sheraton hotel chain.[19] In two other traditional areas of strength, mining and petroleum, U.S. companies proved far less dynamic than they had been in earlier decades.

Mining and petroleum had served as the mainstays of U.S. business activity during the first half of the twentieth century as first the agricultural sector and then banking and utilities faltered. The activity of U.S. enterprises in both these extractive industries continued to grow in the 1960s, but not nearly at the spectacular levels of earlier decades. A variety of factors contributed to this slowdown. In petroleum, for example, the development of vast new oil fields in the Middle East attracted most of the attention of the oil giants, and weakening world prices for petroleum gave little incentive to expand exploration or production in Latin America. As seen in the case of Kennecott and Anaconda in Chile, mining companies were diversifying into manufacturing in the United States and developing minerals in other regions of the world such as Africa. The fear of increased intervention in their affairs by Latin American governments also inhibited investments by mining and petroleum companies.

Extractive industries had become the favorite targets of Latin American nationalists for several reasons. First, they often represented the single largest source of export earnings in individual countries, such as Venezuela and Chile. Second, most Latin Americans came to view foreign control of such valuable natural resources as a serious affront to national sovereignty. And finally, these enterprises tied up their capital in mines or wells which could not be transferred out of the country, making them particularly vulnerable. As the experience of the U.S. copper companies in Chile would clearly illustrate, even attempts to accommodate the nationalist impulse could not guarantee the security of these investments.

The CIA's covert aid to Eduardo Frei in his 1964 race against Salvador Allende for the Chilean presidency was in response to Frei's image as a political moderate. Frei's election brought to power the Christian Democratic Party whose members had developed a reputation as pragmatic politicians. But they too were sensitive to the nationalist impulses within their own society. Soon after his election, President Frei announced his intention to Chileanize the copper industry with the government acquiring part ownership of the U.S. companies which dominated Chile's copper mines. Far more surprising was Kennecott's proposal to sell 51 percent of its local subsidiary to the Chilean government, and launch a development program to increase the output from its El Teniente mine by more than 50 percent.

Kennecott's seemingly magnanimous gesture grew directly out of practical business considerations and the unfavorable light in which the company was viewed in Chile. Since the completion of the El Teniente facilities in the mid-1920s, Kennecott had done little to enhance the production capacity of its enormous mine. As a result, by the mid-1950s the company found it increasingly difficult to maintain existing output levels. Any decline in production would raise Kennecott's tax burden under Chile's Nuevo Trato. But, exploratory activities begun in 1959 indicated that the mineral deposit of El Teniente was in fact much larger than previously estimated. Renovating and expanding its facilities to maintain output and exploit the newly discovered deposits would require the company to make a massive investment in an environment of mounting hostility toward the company.

By the early 1960s, even Chile's most conservative political elements found that there was political capital to be made from denouncing the American copper companies. Kennecott's proposal for Chileanization provided a highly sophisticated response to these problems.

Kennecott made its offer of a 51 percent equity position to the Chilean government in order to shield the company from nationalist criticism and calls for outright expropriation. First, the company would finance $110 million of its $257 million expansion program with a loan secured from the Exim Bank, as well as receiving a guarantee by the Chilean government. An additional $80 million would derive from the government's payment for its 51 percent of the company—a payment the company would then loan back to itself. Kennecott then insured that loan through the AID guarantee program. Finally, the Chilean government would provide another $30 million to help finance the expansion project.[20]

In sum, Kennecott would dramatically increase the total value of its Chilean operations without risking its own money, while at the same time placing the Chilean government on a collision course with the U.S. government should it choose to expropriate Kennecott's interests in El Teniente. As Kennecott's executive vice president for Chilean operations explained, "The aim of these arrangements is to insure that nobody expropriates Kennecott without upsetting relations to customers, creditors and governments on three continents."[21]

Kennecott's principal rival Anaconda proved far less accommodating and creative in its dealings with the Chilean government, conceding only a minority share in a small mine. And even though the Kennecott expansion program and skyrocketing copper prices boosted both output and government copper revenues, the Kennecott program failed to quiet the calls to nationalize the industry. In some ways, Chileanization encouraged advocates of nationalization by demonstrating the capacity of Chileans to manage the industry. The program's success prompted the suggestion that if 51 percent control was good, 100 percent would be even better. By 1969, the copper companies' position in Chile was if anything more perilous than when Frei came to office. Meanwhile, the Cerro de Pasco Corporation had reached an equally critical point in its long relationship with its Peruvian hosts.

Rising metals prices provided record profits for the Cerro de Pasco Corporation in the 1960s, but like Kennecott and Anaconda in the 1950s, the company devoted most of these profits to investments outside the borders of its primary host country. After World War II, Cerro de Pasco began developing mining operations in such countries as Chile, Mexico, Spain, Canada, and Australia. The company also moved into a variety of new areas in the United States including metal refining and manufacturing, oil, aluminum, and cement. By 1965, the Cerro de Pasco Corporation, once focused exclusively on Peru, had devoted 35 percent of its total investments to the United States. At the same time, the company made minimal commitments of capital to its existing Peruvian facilities. It was in those facilities that trouble was brewing for Peru's mining giant.

During the 1960s, Cerro de Pasco's workers took an evermore militant and radical approach to the company. The workers' intensified militancy developed despite the accomodationist policies of APRA and the Communist Party which had alternated in representing the miners before the government and the company. A new generation of young, skilled workers pressed demands that went beyond wages and hours. Union members began to discuss the possible nationalization of the company, and to pledge their support for local peasants who were challenging the company's control of large tracts of grazing land. This more radical and militant stance contributed to the outbreak of 44 strikes between 1961 and 1973—three times as many strikes as the company had experienced in the previous sixty years. During a strike in 1962 workers seized the company town of Oroya, burning company buildings and prompting massive repression by the military. Despite the use of force to suppress strikes and purge the union leadership, the mine workers succeeded in creating an increasingly independent labor movement and placed nationalization of Cerro de Pasco at the top of its agenda.[22] Meanwhile, Peru's American-owned petroleum company was faring little better in its relations with the Peruvian people.

Standard Oil's IPC subsidiary faced its most difficult years during the 1960s. Initially, the election of Fernando Belaunde Terry in 1963 suggested that a solution might be found to the controversy over control of IPC's La Brea and Parinas oil fields. Belaunde Terry, known to be a pragmatic professional much like Eduardo Frei, launched negotiations with the company seeking to resolve the question of control of the fields and IPC's future in the country. But the early hopes of a resolution soon proved illusory as negotiations repeatedly broke down. By 1967 a growing array of political groups had called for the nationalization of IPC. Meanwhile, Belaunde's political position had deteriorated along with the national economy.

IPC also found itself in a weakened state, result of falling output in the La Brea and Parinas fields. Furthermore, it faced serious competition in the production area from the U.S. owned Belco Corporation, and from government and private interests in the area of refining. Its effective monopoly, which had long allowed it to defy Peruvian claims, disintegrated.

Under intense political pressure and facing a badly weakened IPC, Belaunde Terry issued a legal decree in July 1967 which set the stage for the eventual seizure of the company's properties. Nor was IPC's parent firm faring much better in Venezuela.[23]

Market conditions for Venezuelan oil soured in the 1960s. Global oil prices weakened and improved technology placed increasing amounts of Middle Eastern crude on the world market. These developments did not have the same impact on U.S. oil companies and the Venezuelan government. Standard Oil and other companies had effectively ceased making new investments in their Venezuelan properties. In the face of lower prices, they could produce more oil from facilities whose real value was declining. But the government's taxes depended on crude oil prices. Falling oil prices had a serious negative impact on state revenues. During the 1960s, the oil companies fiercely resisted efforts to raise tax rates and government initiatives to put oil field concessions and domestic marketing of oil under the control of a newly created state oil company.

By the end of the decade, however, the increasing successes of the Organization of Petroleum Exporting Countries (OPEC) placed the world's oil producing countries in the strongest position they had ever enjoyed. U.S. oil executives would have done well to take heed of the central role that Venezuela played in the creation of OPEC. Having failed to reach an accommodation with the government in the 1960s when conditions favored the petroleum companies, the oil corporations would find themselves without allies in Venezuela in the 1970s as the power pendulum swung in favor of the government.[24] By then, U.S. investments in Venezuela's Caribbean neighbor, Cuba, had been swept away in a revolutionary upheaval.

Fulgencio Batista's ouster of President Grau San Martín in 1934 had brought Cuba's revolutionary movement to an end, cemented Batista's relations with the United States, and guaranteed him a central place in Cuban politics for the next quarter century. Batista's power rested on his ability to protect U.S. corporations and suppress the revolutionaries' demands for worker control, while at the same time providing at least some material benefits for unionized workers. That compromise guaranteed Batista's influence prior to the end of World War II, even though he would officially serve only one term as president (1940–1944). When Batista returned to power in 1952 by means of a military coup, his seizure of power was met with almost a sense of relief by a populace weary of corrupt and ineffective administrations. But even Batista proved incapable of solving the fundamental social and economic problems that were the legacy of the aborted 1933 revolution.

On the surface, Cuba gave every appearance of a Latin American success story. The island nation ranked second in terms of per capita income among Latin American countries.[25] Its large middle class sported many of the most obvious symbols of modern consumer society. But the apparent national prosperity served as little more than a thin veneer covering the decrepit structure of the national economy. The middle class enjoyed incomes considerably above those of their counterparts in the region, but Havana was also one of the most expensive cities in the world. The middle class faced a cost of living more in line with that in the United States than that of other Latin American countries. Meanwhile, the rural population enjoyed none of the amenities of urban life, living in abject poverty. Sixty percent of the working class suffered from periodic unemployment or underemployment, and the national per capita income in 1958 only slightly exceeded the 1947 figure.[26] Many of Cuba's economic problems stemmed from the nation's continued dependence on a single export crop. In turn, severe inefficiencies weighed down the sugar industry.

Batista's historic compromise had fostered the creation of a union movement promoting the narrow economic interests of its own members through political influence. Union leaders proved highly successful in limiting mechanization and protecting jobs in the short term, but their success also restricted improvements in productivity. As a 1950 study of the Cuban economy noted, "there is much resistance to technical improvements; union pressure often forces employers to retain unnecessary workers; and poor morale affects production by lowering the zeal of both workers and managers." A banker lamented that, "Labor problems are the biggest obstacle to foreign investment in Cuba. It's not so much the wage demands as this *inamovilidad*—job tenure. This blocking of dismissals has interfered so seriously with free management that confidence has been shaken badly."[27] Furthermore, Batista's historic compromise had left Cuba completely open to American imports, frustrating any serious attempt to build an industrial base. These conditions created the underlying causes for the mounting economic and social crisis of the 1950s. That crisis burst to the surface in the rebellion led by the young lawyer Fidel Castro.

Soon after Castro came to power in January 1959, his government sought to implement the revolutionary agenda of 1933 that had called for a more equitable social and economic order on the island. The revolutionary government would redistribute land, reduce utility rates, freeze consumer prices, launch a massive literacy campaign, and ultimately provide free, universal health care. While assisting the poor, the regime's policies had a devastating impact on U.S. businesses.

In May 1959, Castro instituted an agrarian reform law limiting agricultural estates to a maximum of 3,333 acres. The government expropriated all land in excess of that limit, providing compensation in the form of twenty-year bonds.[28] Although not specifically aimed at U.S. properties, the powerful presence of American citizens in the rural economy was certain to be affected. U.S. sugar companies and ranching concerns would lose millions of acres. The renowned King family of Texas lost ninety percent of its ranching property on the island. Over the next two years all American-owned businesses would face expropriation.

The American and Foreign Power Company (AFP), the G.E. subsidiary, which had survived the seizure of its plants by its own workers in 1933, became an early target of the revolutionary government. In the decade prior to the revolution, AFP had more than doubled its generating capacity on the island and had reduced rates to the average residential customer by more than 25 percent. But the company had never escaped its image as a friend of dictators and a foreign monopoly that overcharged Cubans. In August 1959 the Cuban Council of Ministers ordered a reduction in electricity rates. The company estimated the reduction would lower its revenues by more than 20 percent. As a result of the rate adjustment and the unwillingness of the government to allow dollar remittances to the United States, AFP found itself unable to pay the interest on the $8 million in loans it owed to U.S. banks. In some sense, it came as a relief when the government expropriated the company in August 1960. However, the bonds offered in exchange for the company were tied to sales of Cuban sugar in the United States, but the U.S. government had already taken steps to cut off Cuban sugar imports.[29]

In fact, by the time of the AFP expropriation, Cuba and the United States had become engaged in an economic war. Earlier in the year Cuba had signed a trade agreement with the Soviet Union and received a Soviet commitment of economic aid. As a part of that program, the Soviets sold crude oil to Cuba at below world market prices. In June, when Standard, Texaco, and Shell refused to refine the petroleum, the Cuban government seized their refineries. Castro followed up with a wave of expropriations that engulfed not only AFP, but ITT, U.S. sugar mills, banks, hotels, insurance companies, and chemical companies. By December 1960, more than $1 billion in U.S. corporate investments, investments which had dominated the Cuban economy for half a century, had been nationalized. In retaliation the United States imposed a trade embargo on the island. Less than four months later, a CIA-led invasion by 1,200 Cuban exiles quickly collapsed on the shores of the Bay of Pigs.[30]

The U.S. trade embargo, now in its fourth decade, and the CIA-backed invasion offer evidence of the shock inflicted on the United States by the total expropriation of American companies in what corporate leaders had counted as one of their safest havens in Latin America. Over the next decade the attacks on U.S. corporate interests would spread far beyond the shores of Cuba to much of the rest of the region.

In 1968, Peruvian president Fernando Belaunde Terry made a last-ditch effort to reach an agreement with IPC. The tentative agreement, however, only infuriated the Peruvian public because of the concessions made to the company. The agreement proved to be the final straw for an increasingly impatient military which ousted Belaunde Terry.

In the year following its seizure of power, the military regime expropriated the entire $190 million in IPC assets. As two Peruvian intellectuals explained it, the expropriation of the oil companies' operations at La Brea y Parinas and Talara was an act of national liberation from U.S. corporate domination, especially that of the Rockefellers:

> The taking of Talara means not only a symbolic act of national affirmation, but the disappearance of one of the most important corporations in the country, International Petroleum Company, which with its affiliates controlled 80% of the production of oil, almost all of the import of hydrocarbon products and the largest advertising agency (McCann Erickson), without taking into consideration the fact that the Rockefeller family, owners of this corporation, in addition ... controlled a substantial part of the fish meal production (PURINA), a local bank (the Continental Bank), and through IBEC, a large proportion of the supermarkets, chicken production, a system of urban development projects, and so forth. The expropriation of Talara did not destroy an empire, but divested it of one of its main power centers.[31]

Despite threats of economic retaliation from the U.S. government, the Peruvian generals proceeded with a program of drastic economic changes. They nationalized the nine largest sugar estates in the country, including the two owned by W.R. Grace and Company. The government also took over all phone companies, including the ITT subsidiary. Many of these actions and indeed the government itself proved to be less radical than they first appeared.

Ironically, the military had become heir and implementor of the nationalist populist agenda of its archenemy, APRA. Many military officers emerged from the middle class and had been influenced by intellectuals who had become disenchanted with APRA's increasingly conservative drift. But the military's vision of the new Peru was not particularly radical. The military envisioned a top-down solution to Peru's internal social and economic tensions. Workers and capitalists would be reconciled in cooperative ventures in which workers held shares, and worker and peasant organizations would come under the control of a national, state-controlled umbrella organization. As for the nationalizations, both Grace and ITT received compensation with ITT's settlement tied to the company's agreement to invest in large hotels in Peru through its Sheraton subsidiary. Despite the nationalizations, the military had no desire to drive foreign capital out of Peru. In fact, it was making a strenuous effort to attract additional investment in the mining industry.

From the time of its seizure of power, the new Peruvian regime attempted to persuade the consortium of foreign mining companies known as the Southern Peru Copper Corporation (SPCC) to launch its planned investment of $355 million in the massive Cuajone mining project. But those efforts enjoyed only limited success, until the regime settled problems with one of SPCC's principal partners, the Cerro de Pasco Corporation. Despite its swift nationalization of IPC, the Peruvian government showed little inclination to seize the assets of the largest and most influential U.S. company in the country. However, Peruvian mine workers had a very different perspective on Cerro de Pasco's future.[32]

After 1965, the nationalization of the U.S. mining company became a key element in the agenda of the increasingly restless and independent mine workers of the central Andes. Workers showed a growing propensity to strike and to reject the mediation role of APRA and the Communist Party. The miners not only struck for higher wages and better hours, they demanded the nationalization of the Cerro de Pasco Corporation as part of a larger anti-imperialist and anti-capitalist agenda. That program eventually brought the labor movement into direct conflict with the military government.

Between 1970 and 1973 the mine workers launched dozens of strikes at Cerro de Pasco's various mining camps. In 1970 the government sent troops in to arrest the strike leaders on charges of subversion. Then in 1973 the military moved in once again to repress another strike wave. Despite government interventions, the Cerro de Pasco Corporation reported $20 million in lost sales between 1970 and 1971 due to strike activity. Furthermore, the miners made clear that their labor actions had larger goals than better wages and hours. In 1970, the Cerro de Pasco unions analyzed the situation in the following way:

The proletariat of mine workers has always been the motor of developments. These developments, however, have always led to a further extension of the privileges and the enrichment of foreign monopolies and their local representatives. The exploited proletariat of mine workers has fully carried the burdens of a social system in which the exploitation of man by man predominates. The great sums of national and international capital were gathered at the cost of the misery, exploitation and repression of hundreds of thousands of workers.... In this situation the mine workers have the grave duty to debate and analyze in order to develop a strategy that will guarantee a successful treatment of both the concrete class demands and those social, economic and political problems that will eventually lead to the abolition of the capitalist chains. Man's exploitation of man, the basic source of our misery and suppression, must disappear so that a new society may grow in which labor shall be the basis of human existence and shall constitute human dignity....[33]

By December of 1971, Cerro de Pasco offered to sell its operations to the government, but those negotiations dragged on and finally collapsed in September 1973. With the government now denouncing the corporation as an imperialist, antisocial enterprise, the regime ordered the nationalization of Cerro de Pasco on January 1, 1974. Yet consistent with its conservative approach, within three months the government had authorized payments of $150 million to nationalized U.S. corporations including $67 million to the mining company.[34]

The military government of Peru proved in the end that its vision of Peru's future included a substantial role for U.S. corporations. Many other nationalizations in the region such as the nationalization of the oil industry in Venezuela followed a similar line. Latin American governments took control of large-scale U.S. enterprises, particularly in the natural resource sector, which had long been symbols of foreign domination. Yet these actions often did not represent an outright rejection of U.S. corporate investment. These nationalizations usually offered substantial compensation and frequently the regimes provided incentives for investments in other parts of the national economy. Nevertheless, the expropriations had disrupted many U.S. enterprises, and in the midst of these events, another Latin American country had taken a course at least as radical as the one pursued by Cuba since 1959.

Salvador Allende's election as president of Chile in 1970 led to his confrontations with major U.S. corporations like ITT. In March 1972, the Chilean president clearly articulated the perspective that underlay the agenda of his Popular Unity government:

From the economic point of view our country, like so many others in this and other continents, was a dependent one; its basic resources were controlled by foreign capital. . . . Some progress was made, but it was based on techniques brought from abroad and often irrationally applied in the local situation.

Economic dependence essentially affected basic resources like nitrate and copper. . . .

The case of nitrates was dramatic . . . but the case of copper was even more dramatic and instructive. Chile is estimated to have the largest copper reserves in the world. The open pit mine—*Chuquicamata*—is the largest copper mine in the world. Our technicians and economists have estimated that forty years ago foreign capitalists invested $30 million in Chile. Since then they have withdrawn from the country the not exactly insignificant sum of $4,500 million. It should be remembered that copper produces about 70 percent of our foreign exchange and finances a significant part of the fiscal budget. In addition, for more than half a century, Chile itself was allowed no information about levels of production, or the markets, or the price of copper.

For these reasons the Popular Unity Government decided to put an end to this economic dependence, and to retrieve the country's basic resources from the control of foreign capitalists.[35]

In July 1971, the Chilean congress had approved Allende's proposal to nationalize the country's mineral wealth. Although Anaconda and Kennecott claimed a valuation of more than $600 million for their properties, the government deducted from that figure more than $700 million, claiming the companies had earned that amount in excess profits over the years. Other takeovers proved less contentious because the government provided compensation.[36]

The Allende administration spent $70 million dollars acquiring part or all of the interests of Bank of America, First National City Bank, Ralston Purina, RCA, Bethlehem Steel, General Motors, and the Anglo Lautaro Nitrate Company.[37] The nitrate enterprise constituted the remnants of the once great Guggenheim nitrate undertaking which had become the focus of Chilean nationalist ire in the early 1930s. Given public exposure of ITT's efforts to prevent Allende's election, the company faced the prospect of a level of compensation far below its estimated worth. But as noted earlier, that threat never materialized because of the CIA-assisted military coup in which Allende and his Popular Unity government perished.

Clearly U.S. responses to threats to its business interests in Latin America varied widely. While nationalizations in countries like Peru and Venezuela might bring diplomatic protests and at least the threat of economic sanctions, expropriations in Cuba and Chile prompted concerted efforts to oust both governments. The more extreme measures in the latter cases could be attributed to the fact that both Cuba and Chile had launched campaigns which promised not only an end to existing large-scale U.S. investments, but also the transformation of the nations into socialist societies offering minimal opportunities for the future penetration and expansion of U.S. business interests. Such threats of radical change had prompted intervention from both the United States and subversion by domestic interests.

MILITARISTS AND MULTINATIONALS

Although Cuba and then Chile pursued revolutionary change, the military in Brazil, Argentina, and eventually Chile adopted a radically different course of action. During the 1960s and 1970s the armed forces in these and other Latin American countries seized power and imposed long-term military rule. Facing mounting unrest prompted by stagnant economies, rising inflation, and the persistence of social and economic inequalities, the armed forces intervened to crush social and political protests while pursuing economic policies which envisioned a large, albeit regulated, role for multinational corporations. The Brazilian military provided the model for these regimes and their policies.

Brazil, like most Latin American countries, experienced mounting popular protests in the early 1960s. Those protests focused on the failure of both nationalist populist initiatives and more orthodox strategies to achieve development and social justice. Inflation, industrial stagnation, and growing disparities between rich and poor prompted mounting unrest. Under the presidency of João Goulart (1961–1964), workers broke with the hierarchical structures of the state-regulated union system, launching waves of strikes. At the same time, peasants in Brazil's impoverished northeast organized peasant leagues to press their demands for land. After spending $20 million in an attempt to influence local elections, the CIA gave its blessing to a military coup on April 1, 1964.[38]

The Brazilian armed forces had periodically intervened to stabilize the civilian political system, but this time the generals came to stay. Their motto "Security and Development" was eerily reminiscent of the elite's slogan "Order and Progress." Indeed, the military set out to supress domestic social protest while propelling the economy forward with the assistance of foreign capital. Deviating from the nineteenth-century liberal model, this effort involved a partnership with both foreign and domestic capital as well as the state. That effort also involved draconian social and political measures.

The military regime suppressed existing political parties, abolished half of the peasant leagues, intervened in the rest, dismissed union leaders, and took control of their organizations. Dissidents faced the threat of government sanctioned death squads. Social and political repression helped ensure the success of an economic program which effectively froze workers' wages and dramatically reduced the flow of credit in the national economy. Those measures reined in inflation, kept wages low, and shifted wealth toward the upper strata of income earners. The new policies encouraged both domestic and foreign investment as part of a government strategy of promoting the growth of domestic consumer durable (particularly automobiles) and export manufacturing industries.

The Brazilian government hoped to avoid the revenue loss due to declining exports suffered by previous import substitution experiments. Income redistribution would provide a larger market for consumer durables while currency devaluation, tax credits, and other mechanisms would encourage industrialists to export their products.[39] A combination of foreign and domestic corporations along with state-owned enterprises, such as the national oil company Petrobras (see Chapter Four), would carry out the industrialization program. Under this plan, the economy grew in excess of 10 percent annually between 1968 and 1973, prompting many to describe it as the "Brazilian economic miracle." U.S. corporations played a major role in that process.

Between 1965 and 1972, U.S. companies increased their stake in Brazil from $1.1 billion to more than $2.5 billion. Government policies ensuring cheap labor and docile unions as well as incentives for consumer durables and manufacturing exports encouraged U.S. corporations to invest in new activities or expand existing interests. Policies allowing virtual unrestricted profit repatriation and facilitating the takeover of Brazilian-owned firms also attracted U.S. capital. Under these conditions, large U.S. corporations such as Alcoa, Atlantic Richfield, General Motors, General Electric, and Johnson and Johnson poured new capital into the Brazilian economy. Seventy percent of all U.S. investment targeted the manufacturing sector. Government policies helped U.S. and other foreign corporations capture total control or exercise a more dominant role in such sectors as automotives, pharmaceuticals, electrical equipment, and machinery. Yet Brazil did not simply create an open door policy for U.S. multinationals.[40]

Under their own version of economic nationalism, successive Brazilian military administrations retained a leading position in such areas as petroleum exploration and production and utilities through state-run enterprises, and protected domestic corporate control in sectors such as wood and leather products, printing, and textiles. Yet such limitations on foreign investment proved only minor impediments in the otherwise powerful alliance between U.S. companies, Brazilian corporations, and the state during the 1970s. That success led other large Latin American countries such as Argentina and Mexico to experiment with the Brazilian strategy. Those efforts contributed to a dramatic increase in U.S. corporate investment in Latin America.

U.S. corporations rapidly increased their stake throughout Latin America due to a number of factors. The new strategies pioneered in Brazil meant relief from past controls over profit repatriation and new incentives to invest. A growing gap between wages for skilled labor in the United States and Latin America made it economically feasible for manufacturers to develop plants in the area even when their products would be exported back to the United States. U.S. companies also responded to intensifying competition in the region from European and Japanese multinationals. These conditions spurred an increase in U.S. direct investment from less than $15 billion in 1970 to more than $38 billion in 1981. Nearly half of all that capital poured into Brazil, Mexico, and Argentina, with Brazil and Mexico accounting for more than $15 billion. The rush of U.S. multinationals into Latin America accelerated the sectoral concentration of those investments. Of the $38 billion invested in the region, nearly $16 billion had gone into manufacturing. The other major sectors–finance, petroleum, and banking–lagged well behind, ranging between $4 and $6 billion each.[41] But the new investment boom became the focus of widespread popular protest.

As the General Electric Company continued to expand its manufacturing activities in Brazil to include new, more complex consumer products such as televisions, it also sought to impose strict standards of performance on its workers. As a study of G.E.'s Brazilian operations explained:

> For their part, factory workers and office employees must be willing, and must learn to achieve certain minimum standards of personal integrity, conscientious performance of the work task, regularity of attendance, responsible care of machinery and equipment, positive interest in the enterprise's productive performance and so on.

The report went on to note that,

> Preindustrial societies do not generally attach high value to productive labor per se, to disciplined, interdependent teamwork, to impersonal institutional loyalties, and to regularity of attendance at repetitive routine tasks and their conscious and conscientious performance. The transition to the kind of "puritan ethic" required for a modern industrial system . . . is neither easy nor rapid. . . .[42]

Based on the above perspective U.S. companies attempted to impose such standards of performance by turning to a set of management strategies known as Fordism, after American auto magnate Henry Ford. Fordism consists of a combination of high wages, assembly line production, and scientific management practices. While Ford offered his workers exceptionally high wages to make them more amenable to the monotony of the assembly line, U.S. automakers in Brazil combined high wages and the continuing threat of dismissal to make workers more amenable to time/motion studies and the speeding up of the production process. Under this system, Brazilian autoworkers became acutely conscious of the power of supervisors. As one worker explained: "The regime is very much hard-line at the moment. It's enough for two workers to be caught talking together for both to be warned or even suspended. . . . The foremen forgive nothing." In turn, workers had to accept evermore demanding work conditions. As one explained, "The work we have to do is too much. Each one of us on our own has a lot to do. What was being done by two or three is now being done by one or two."[43]

The intensified attempts by U.S. corporations to control the work place and the enormous cost of Brazil's economic miracle for the majority of its population prompted growing resistance to the military and its "master plan" for Brazilian development. Despite the suppression of the labor movement, autoworkers successfully launched a series of strikes. In March 1978, the Brazilian labor leader, Luis Ignacio da Silva or Lula gave voice to the autoworkers' discontent with both the corporations and their government when he exclaimed, "Talk to the bosses? We've already talked. Talk to the authorities? We've already talked. No one cares about the worker. . . . We've given everything for the good of Brazil. And what do we get in return? Nothing."[44]

Two months later a new wave of unrest erupted among Brazilian industrial workers and in 1979 more than 3 million of them went on strike. By this time, the strikers had become part of a much larger resistance movement that included slum dwellers, peasants, and elements of the middle class. Mounting popular protest eventually forced the military to return Brazil to civilian rule in 1985. Popular protests also swept through Argentina, Chile, and Mexico against regimes following similar strategies of export growth based on large, new infusions of foreign capital, the imposition of Fordism in the industrial work place, and enormous sacrifices by most of the population. After 1982 that unrest received new stimulus when an international financial crisis inflicted new suffering on Latin Americans and nearly toppled the largest financial institutions in the United States.[45]

DEBT CRISIS

Much as the Brazilian military's motto offered an eerie echo from the past, the activities of U.S. banks in the 1970s provided worrisome similarities to the 1920s. By the beginning of the 1970s, a huge stock of capital became available to international banking enterprises due to payments by the United States on its trade and budget deficits and then incremented by payments to oil producers as petroleum prices soared. By 1974 these funds, known generally as eurodollars, had reached the staggering sum of $205 billion.[46] As in the 1920s, U.S. banks had large amounts of capital for which they needed to find profitable investments. And once again, they would solve that problem by making large loans in Latin America.

Institutions such as Citibank, which had watched the value of its Latin American bonds evaporate during the Great Depression, now returned with a vengeance. They found anxious customers among Latin American governments, particularly Brazil, Mexico, and Argentina. Latin American regimes sought billions of dollars in credit to finance their development schemes. That meeting of supply and demand in international financial markets led Latin American countries to expand their combined debt from $35 billion in 1972 to over $350 billion in 1983, with over two-thirds of that amount loaned by commercial banks. The nine largest U.S. banks—including Citibank, Bank of America, Chase Manhattan, and Morgan Guaranty—had loaned a total of $26 billion to Latin America's two largest debtors, Brazil and Mexico. Between 1975 and 1981, Citibank alone increased its loans to Brazil from $2 billion to $5 billion.[47] In brief, a handful of U.S. banks extended huge amounts of credit to a few Latin American countries. In 1982, the day of reckoning arrived.

On August 12, 1982, Secretary of the Treasury Donald Regan was planning to leave Washington D.C. for the weekend when a phone call from

Mexican Finance Minister Jaime Silva Herzog interrupted his preparations. Silva Herzog asked Regan if he remembered a conversation they had more than a year earlier. Regan immediately recalled their discussion. Worried about Mexico's mounting debt, Regan had asked Herzog to give him "some warning" if Mexico ran into serious trouble. Herzog was obviously calling with that warning and a plea for help. Silva Herzog told Regan, "Well, the time is here. I need money." When Regan asked how much, Silva Herzog replied, "About a billion." Regan summarily ordered his Mexican counterpart to be in his office within twelve hours.[48]

If Regan could order the Mexican minister about like an obedient servant, it did not disguise the fact that they had now become desperate partners in a financial crisis with the potential to trigger a global economic collapse. If Mexico failed to make payments on its debt, Brazil, Latin America's largest debtor nation with $90 billion in outstanding foreign loans, would quickly follow. Given the large stake Citibank had in those two nations it could easily go under. Once that happened world-class banks from New York to Tokyo would start falling like a row of dominoes. The worst global financial crisis since the Great Depression had grown out of impersonal economic forces and human decisions during the 1970s.

Battered by budget deficits, rising oil prices, mounting inflation, and slow economic growth, the United States by the end of the 1970s experienced its own severe case of stagflation. The imposition of high interest rates to stem inflation helped trigger a recession in 1981 which soon spread to other developed countries. These conditions contributed to a decline in international prices for primary products and a decline in the volume of international trade. Latin America's debtor nations now faced the worst of all possible worlds. The prices and volume of their principal exports (primary products) reduced their ability to repay foreign loans that carried rising interest rates. The crisis erupted on the international scene when Mexico announced in August 1982 that it was unable to make its scheduled debt payments.

In response to the rapidly spreading crisis, banks made a small number of emergency loans to maintain the viability of their debtors and prevent their own collapse. The banks and Latin American governments followed this up with the debt rescheduling. But the most enduring response came in the form of drastic austerity programs overseen by the International Monetary Fund. Under IMF-approved plans, Latin American governments slashed expenditures, kept wages low, and reduced imports, with the purpose of reducing their credit needs and improving their ability to make debt repayments. These measures inflicted widespread suffering among the region's middle and working classes. Reductions in social spending meant reduced resources for health and education. Real wages fell and income distribution within Latin American societies worsened. The effects of economic deterioration impacted on both the middle and working classes as economic growth and per capita income fell throughout the 1980s in virtually every Latin American country.

Even when the worst of the crisis had passed in September 1989, Citibank president John Reed gave a gloomy assessment of the effects of the debt debacle on American business as follows: "The United States is in some important ways withdrawing from the world, and there is no question that American banks are withdrawing from international banking. . . . This means that American companies around the world aren't going to have American banks and I think that is a potential problem for this country."[49] But Reed was wrong.

THE NEW ORTHODOXY

Despite the severe setbacks from the crisis, U.S. businesses, including U.S. banks, did not retreat. And despite the enormous sacrifices by most Latin Americans to pay crushing debts to U.S. banks, and the very large role of U.S. enterprise in the disaster, a new wave of anti-Americanism did not erupt in Latin America as it had in the 1930s. Instead, Latin American economies opened their doors even wider to U.S. and other multinational corporations.[50] These decisions seem extraordinary, given the failure of the experiments of the 1970s and 1980s which relied heavily on foreign corporations and foreign lending to achieve development. A number of factors help explain the decision to embrace foreign corporations even more tightly.

Part of that decision stemmed from regional and global economic realities. By the early 1980s, Latin American debt to developed countries exceeded $350 billion.[51] In the absence of a world depression, which would weaken the ability of creditor nations to penalize countries defaulting on their debts, Latin American governments would find it necessary to toe the line of the International Monetary Fund. The IMF would insist on domestic austerity and greater openness to the world economy as part of the restructuring and repayment plans for the region's debt. Furthermore, the decline of the Soviet Union, and China's decision to pursue a path of capitalist development, left no alternative models or real international support for options other than capitalism. Within the region, national planners were well aware of the enormous problems that Cuba, Chile, and Nicaragua had encountered in pursuing socialist strategies for development. Yet these decisions did not result simply from duress or a lack of options.

By now the technocratic elites of Latin America were largely convinced of the appropriateness of free market policies. Such views were not entirely surprising given the source of much of their training. Many of the region's leading economists and public policy experts had been trained in the United States or had received their education in local institutions featuring programs sponsored by the Ford and Rockefeller Foundations. As a result they were thoroughly versed in the principles of free market orthodoxy. In the years following the overthrow of Allende, Chilean economists trained by noted neoliberal Milton Friedman at the University of Chicago guided the military regime's economic policies. In Mexico, U.S. trained technocrats rose through the ranks of the ruling Institutional Revolutionary Party (PRI). During the 1980s, two Harvard trained men, Miguel de la Madrid and Carlos Salinas de Gortari, attained the Mexican presidency. Consequently, it is hardly surprising that the new Latin American economic orthodoxy bore similarities not only to nineteenth-century Liberalism but to Nelson Rockefeller's vision for the region laid out in the *Report on the Americas*. But even many leftist critics of U.S. economic domination came to be ardent proponents of the new orthodoxy.

In January 1995, Fernando Henrique Cardoso, one of the foremost proponents of Latin American dependency theory, took office as president of Brazil. In an interview with the editor for the Council of Foreign Relations' journal *Foreign Affairs*, Cardoso indicated just how far he had moved away from dependency theory and its protectionist ideas, and toward policies to integrate his country into the global capitalist economy:

> Brazil is a global trader, and it is important for us to keep this profile . . . We see integration schemes as playing an important role in expanding world trade flows even further. . . . In the emerging global economy, we are not . . . in opposition to eventual integration into a hemispheric trade association.[52]

Much like the nineteenth-century development strategy of Mexico's Porfirio Díaz, the new economic policies focused on export promotion and the opening of national economies to foreign investment. With Chile leading the way, Latin American governments reduced import tariffs and quotas, and cut export duties. They also liberalized regulations imposed on foreign corporations and offered debt equity swaps allowing owners of the national debt to swap it for domestic capital investments on highly favorable terms. This strategy also included the privatization of public enterprises. Between 1990 and 1993 alone, foreigners invested more than $4.7 billion in public corporations including petroleum, petrochemicals, telecommunications, electricity, and railroads which had been privatized by the Argentinian government.[53] Throughout Latin America many of the state enterprises created since the Great Depression to protect the national patrimony in sectors such as raw materials and utilities went on the auction block to both domestic and foreign investors. This new era of liberalization led to yet another surge of U.S. corporate activity in the rapidly growing manufacturing sectors, and into areas such as petroleum and mining where U.S. corporations had long been unwelcome. Although the state continues to play a far larger role in the economy and the regulation of foreign corporations than might ever have been imagined one hundred years ago, the new era of internationalization nevertheless bears a striking, even unsettling, resemblance to the liberalism of the last century.

The initial success of neoliberalism in Latin America is undeniable. During the 1990s inflation in the region dropped from 200 percent annually to under 20 percent. Exports have grown by six percent a year compared to less than 2 percent in the mid-1980s. The North American Free Trade Agreement (NAFTA) between Mexico, the United States, and Canada may become the basis of the regional free trade zone envisioned by Nelson Rockefeller. And the enthusiasm of Latin American elites for this process equals that of U.S. leaders. As the Peronist governor of the Argentinian province of Jujuy noted in 1998, "Look, it's simple; there is an Americanization of the world. We cannot go in the opposite direction. At last we are going to make America here."[54]

But these achievements have not translated into a better life for most Latin Americans. Unemployment rates have risen during the decade, real wages have fallen, and income distribution has worsened. As a result, in the 1990s thirty-five percent of the region's people remained trapped in abject poverty—just as they were a decade ago. With their economies growing at rates of 3 or 4 percent annually, Latin American nations are not generating the kind of growth that will lift the majority of their populations out of abject or less life-threatening poverty. Meanwhile, years of hyperinflation, bankruptcies, and the slashing of government social spending have devastated the middle class. As the century closes, Zapatista guerrillas roam the mountains of Chiapas, Mexico, tens of thousands of Brazilian peasants do battle with landowners and the government, middle class Mexicans and Argentinians are rebelling against civilian regimes which have overseen their economic decline, and labor protests have become a way of life in most major Latin American countries.

Protesters from small businesspeople to workers and peasants have made a direct connection between their woes and the increased penetration of their economies by U.S. business. After watching a new Wal-Mart rise on the site of a bankrupt Buenos Aires textile plant, Luis Osvaldo Pazzotta, whose own carpentry business had recently failed, observed ruefully, "This is the new world, and I have no place in it."[55] Gilmar Mauro, a leader of landless peasants in Brazil, conceded that Washington's neoliberal policies had come to dominate the world but he argued that globalization would leave Brazil, "marginal and subjugated."[56] Argentine labor leader Carlos Santillan put the case even more emphatically arguing that, "[President Carlos] Menem thinks that by putting our country at the service of the International Monetary Fund, he brought us into the first world. But workers have lost in a few years rights they fought for over a century. We're a colony here. All that is missing is to have [U.S. President Bill] Clinton come here and plant the American flag."[57]

The dissent and unrest of the late twentieth century is hardly the equal of the turmoil of the early 1930s, but these events are occurring within economies supposedly enjoying a new era of recovery and growth. When the inevitable cyclical downturn comes, the risks of widespread upheaval will rise sharply, and so will the risks to U.S. enterprise.

In the last four decades of the twentieth century, American corporations have weathered an array of attacks from leftist and nationalist regimes from Castro and Allende to the Peruvian military. Not only have they survived such assaults, they have grown and prospered under the economic strategies adopted in the 1970s and the internationalization policies of more recent years. As a result, they have taken a leading position in some of the region's most dynamic manufacturing industries such as automobiles and electrical machinery, while finding renewed opportunities in some of their traditional areas of investment such as natural resources and utilities. Those new investments have been accompanied by intensified efforts to transform the work place. In addition, U.S. corporations, with the support of local governments and the International Monetary Fund, have attempted to broaden the base of consumer societies through increased marketing of products ranging from soft drinks to computers, and continue restructuring of local economies to reallocate additional income to the middle and upper classes.

As the U.S. experience in the Brazilian and Mexican auto industries indicated, U.S. corporations no longer enjoy the totally dominant position they held prior to the end of World War II. They now face constant and vigorous competition from European and Japanese corporations. Yet U.S.

multinationals remain in the eyes of most Latin Americans the epitome of all that is bad and good in foreign corporations. Nelson Rockefeller's vision of internationalizing Latin American economies is fast becoming a reality. In this new environment, U.S. corporations will not enjoy the dominant position Rockefeller might have imagined. But U.S. corporations as the architects of this new order will be held accountable if it fails to produce long-term development for Latin America.

SUMMARY

In the last four decades of the twentieth century, Latin Americans and U.S. businesses seemed to relive all of the extremes that had marked their relationship in the previous one hundred years. The era began with the rise of Fidel Castro and Salvador Allende, who sought to achieve many of the unfulfilled goals of earlier populist movements. Their socialist governments carried out widespread nationalizations of U.S. corporations and engaged in dramatic efforts to achieve domestic social and economic justice. Even more conservative governments such as that of the Peruvian generals felt compelled to pursue some of the same initiatives. Then in the midst of this widespread assault on U.S. corporate interests, a reaction set in which placed the military in power in many Latin American countries. The military regimes and other conservative administrations pursued export-led development models that created a welcoming, albeit regulated, environment for U.S. companies. The ensuing era of dizzying economic expansion ended, much like the frenzied growth of the 1920s, in financial catastrophe with Latin American countries staggering under enormous foreign debt and U.S. banks teetering on the brink of collapse. But instead of a return to populist nationalist policies, the closing decade of the century has been marked by the triumph of neoliberal regimes that have privatized and internationalized their economies much like their liberal predecessors a hundred years ago. As the next millennium approaches, U.S. business is enjoying a new golden age of success in Latin America. Yet the twists and turns of the past four decades are far more than a historical curiosity. These developments have resulted from the mission of transformation launched by U.S. merchants two centuries ago, and Latin American responses to that mission. Over the past four decades, the alliance of American multinationals, private foundations, and the U.S. government has successfully confronted severe challenges to U.S. enterprise. Those challenges have grown out of

Latin American frustration over problems of economic underdevelopment, foreign economic domination, and the attempts of U.S. companies to transform the work habits, and even some of the cultural values of Latin Americans. The success of Americans in overcoming those challenges stems only in part from some of the more drastic actions taken by the U.S. government, such as covert operations and economic sanctions. Far more significant has been the long-term process of transformation. Through concessions to Latin American nationalism such as hiring local managers, development programs promoting private enterprise and foreign investment, the reshaping of the Latin American work place, the promotion of consumerism through the powerful mediums of telecommunications, and the education of managerial and governmental elites, the tripartite U.S. alliance has overcome challenges ranging from revolutionary regimes to the international debt crisis. At the close of the twentieth century, U.S. enterprise appears to have carried out a transformational mission which far exceeds the modest ambitions of nineteenth-century American merchants for political and religious influence. And yet the history of the relationship between Latin Americans and U.S. enterprise also carries with it a cautionary note.

Throughout the past century, U.S. business activity has always prompted complex reactions from Latin Americans. National leaders have frequently welcomed U.S. corporations, and Latin Americans at every level of society have admired, acquired, and imitated numerous elements of U.S. material culture. However, Latin Americans have always been wary of U.S. economic and cultural domination. To the present day, Latin Americans harbor grave reservations about what they view as the free market, materialistic, relentlessly competitive, and individualistic extremism of American society. Should the current era of economic growth come to a sudden and painful end without benefiting most Latin Americans, those concerns may once again be transformed into militant political movements that target Americans and their mission of transformation.

NOTES

CHAPTER ONE

1. John Hart, *Revolutionary Mexico: The Coming and Process of the Mexican Revolution* (Berkeley, 1989), pp. 107–37.

2. Stuart Bruchey, *Enterprise: The Dynamic Economy of a Free People* (Cambridge, 1990), pp. 144–45, and Jacques Barbier and Allan J. Kuethe, eds., *The North American Role in the Spanish Imperial Economy, 1760–1819* (Manchester, 1984).

3. Mira Wilkins, *The Emergence of Multinational Enterprise: American Business Abroad from the Colonial Era to 1914* (Cambridge, 1970), pp. 9–11.

4. William R. Manning, *Diplomatic Correspondence of the United States Concerning the Independence of the Latin American Nations*, 3 vols. (New York, 1925), vol. 2, p. 191. Italics mine.

5. D.C.M. Platt, *Latin America and British Trade, 1806–1914* (London, 1972), pp. 29–30, 259, 275–77.

6. Arnold Bauer, "The Colonial Economy," in Schell Hoberman and Migden Socolow, eds., *The Countryside in Colonial Latin America*, pp. 27–28, 38–39.

7. Steve J. Stern, "The Age of Andean Insurrection, 1742–1782: A Reappraisal," in Stern, ed., *Resistance, Rebellion, and Consciousness*, p. 74.

8. Paul W. Gates, *Landlords and Tenants on the Praire Frontier: Studies in American Land Policy* (Ithaca, 1973).

9. Andreas V. Reichstein, *Rise of the Lone Star: The Making of Texas*, trans. by Jeanne R. Wilson (College Station, Texas, 1989), pp. 68–69, 110–12, 90–91.

10. Reginald Horsman, *Race and Manifest Destiny: The Origins of Racial Anglo-Saxonism* (Cambridge, 1981), pp. 208–13.

11. Fredrick B. Pike, *The United States and Latin America: Myths and Stereotypes of Civilization and Nature* (Austin, 1992), p. 49.

12. Horsman, *Race and Manifest Destiny,* pp. 238–48.

13. Pike, *United States and Latin America,* p. 51. For a brief history of the railroad, see Mira Wilkins, *The Emergence of Multinational Enterprise: American Business Abroad from the Colonial Era to 1914* (Cambridge, 1970), pp. 22–23, 27–28.

14. Mercedes Chen Daley, "The Watermelon Riot: Cultural Encounters in Panama City, April 15, 1856," *Hispanic American Historical Review* 70(February 1990):102. Daley's article contains an excellent analysis of the riot and its causes.

15. William O. Scroggs, *Filibusters and Financiers: The Story of William Walker and His Associates* (New York, 1916), 270–397.

16. Pike, *United States and Latin America,* p. 19.

17. Lowell Gudmundson and Hector Lindo-Fuentes, *Central America, 1821–1871: Liberalism before Liberal Reform* (Tuscaloosa, 1995), pp. 5, 74–76.

18. Nils Jacobsen, *Mirages of Transition: the Peruvian Altiplano, 1780–1930* (Berkeley, 1993), p. 147.

19. Watt Stewart, *Henry Meiggs: Yankee Pizarro* (Durham, 1946).

20. Bruchey, *Enterprise,* pp. 150–51.

21. Paul E. Johnson, *A Shopkeeper's Millennium: Society and Revivals in Rochester, New York, 1815–1837* (New York, 1978), p. 141.

22. John J. Rumbarger, *Profits and Power and Prohibition: Alcohol Reform and the Industrializing of America, 1800–1930* (Albany, 1988), pp. 43–46.

23. Wilkins, *Emergence of Multinational Enterprise,* pp. 38–44, 49–50, 57, and Bruchey, *Enterprise,* pp. 309–10.

24. Charles A. Brand, "The Background of Capitalistic Underdevelopment: Honduras to 1913," Ph.D. diss., University of Pittsburgh, 1972, and Wilkins, *Emergence of Multinational Enterprise,* pp. 12–13.

25. Edwin F. Atkins, *Sixty Years in Cuba* (New York, 1980 [1926]), pp. 95, 109, and Leland H. Jenks, *Our Cuban Colony: A Study in Sugar* (New York, 1928), pp. 34–35.

26. Lawrence A. Clayton, *Grace: W.R. Grace & Co.: The Formative Years, 1850–1930* (Ottawa, Illinois, 1985), pp. 32–81.

27. Ibid., p. 174. Clayton's work contains a thorough treatment of the contract from the company's perspective.

CHAPTER TWO

1. Ralph M. Ingersoll, *In and Under Mexico* (New York, 1924), p. 45.

2. Ibid., pp. 116–17.

3. Ibid., p. 115.

4. Stuart Bruchey, *Enterprise: The Dynamic Economy of a Free People* (Cambridge, 1990), pp. 308–48, and David F. Noble, *America by Design: Science, Technology and the Rise of Capitalism* (New York, 1977).

5. Quoted in William Leach, *Land of Desire: Merchants, Power and the Rise of a New American Culture* (New York, 1993), p. 127.

6. Quoted in Thomas F. O'Brien, *The Revolutionary Mission: American Enterprise in Latin America, 1900–1945* (Cambridge, 1996), p. 28.

7. Burchey, *Enterprise,* p. 382; Victor Bulmer-Thomas, *The Economic History of Latin America since Independence* (Cambridge, 1994),p. 74; Mirta Wilkins, *The Emer-*

gence of Multinational Enterprise: American Business Abroad from the Colonial Era to 1914 (Cambridge, 1970), p. 110; and Wilkins, *The Maturing of Multinational Enterprise: American Business Abroad from 1914 to 1970* (Cambridge, 1974), p. 55.

8. George Philip, *Oil and Politics in Latin America: Nationalist Movements and State Companies* (Cambridge, 1982), pp. 7–8.

9. For a general history of United Fruit in these years, see Charles David Kepner Jr. and Jay Henry Soothill, *The Banana Empire: A Case Study in Economic Imperialism* (New York, 1967[1935]).

10. Wilkins, *Emergence of Multinational Enterprise*, pp. 93–96, and *Maturing of Multinational Enterprise*, pp. 65–68, 131–33.

11. Wilkins, *Maturing of Multinational Enterprise*, pp. 19–23.

12. Frederick B. Pike, *The United States and Latin America: Myths and Stereotypes of Civilization and Nature* (Austin, 1992), p. 168.

13. Ibid., pp. 169–70.

14. John Hart, *Revolutionary Mexico: The Coming and Process of the Mexican Revolution* (Berkeley, 1989), pp. 131–33.

15. Victor Bulmer-Thomas, *The Economic History of Latin America since Independence* (Cambridge, 1994), p. 107.

16. Ibid., p. 104, and Bill Albert, *South America and the World Economy from Independence to 1930* (London, 1983), pp. 29–34.

17. On repressive labor systems, see David J. McCreery, "Debt Servitude in Rural Guatemala," *Hispanic American Historical Review* 63(November 1983):735–59, and Michael Monteón, "The Enganche in the Chilean Nitrate Sector, 1880–1930," *Latin American Perspectives* 6(Summer 1979):66–79.

18. Bulmer-Thomas, *Economic History*, pp. 46–67.

19. Christopher J. Schmitz, *World Non-Ferrous Metal Production and Prices, 1700–1976* (London, 1979), pp. 290–91, and Bill Albert, *South America and the First World War: The Impact of the War on Brazil, Argentina, Peru and Chile* (Cambridge, 1988), p. 11.

20. As quoted in O'Brien, *Revolutionary Mission*, p. 109.

21. As quoted in ibid., p. 41.

22. As quoted in ibid., p. 64.

23. On the history of the fruit companies, see Charles David Kepner Jr., *Social Aspects of the Banana Industry* (New York, 1936); Kepner and Soothill, *The Banana Empire;* and Thomas L. Karnes, *Tropical Enterprise: The Standard Fruit and Steamship Company in Latin America* (Baton Rouge, 1978).

24. Robert Read, "The Growth and Structure of Multinationals in the Banana Export Trade," in Casson, ed., *The Growth of International Business* (London, 1983), pp. 180–213.

25. O'Brien, *Revolutionary Mission*, pp. 186–87, 253–56.

26. Issac F. Marcosson, *Anaconda* (New York, 1957), pp. 33–35, 94–95.

27. Jonathan C. Brown, *Oil and Revolution in Mexico* (Berkeley, 1993), pp. 25–29.

28. Ibid., 13–165.

29. Rosemary Thorp and Geoffrey Bertram, *Peru 1890–1977: Growth and Policy in an Open Economy* (London, 1978), pp. 100–105.

30. Philip, *Oil and Politics*, pp. 13–27.

31. Quoted in ibid., p. 24.

32. Ibid., p. 22.

33. Quoted in Louis A. Pérez Jr., *Cuba: Between Reform and Revolution* (New York, 1988), p. 180.

34. O'Brien, *Revolutionary Mission*, pp. 213–16.

35. Alfonso Bauer Paíz, *Como opera el capital yanqui en Centroamerica: el caso de Guatemala* (México, 1956), pp. 60–79.

36. Robert Sobel, *I.T.T.: The Management of Opportunity* (New York, 1982), pp. 15–67, and Emily S. Rosenberg, *Spreading the American Dream: American Economic and Cultural Expansion, 1890–1945* (New York, 1982), pp. 89–91.

37. Barbara Stallings, *Banker to the Third World: U.S. Portfolio Investments in Latin America, 1900–1986* (Berkeley, 1987), pp. 150–64, 244–46.

38. Hart, *Revolutionary Mexico*, pp. 142–43, and O'Brien, *Revolutionary Mission*, pp. 115, 121, 177, 228.

39. Aviva Chomsky, *West Indian Workers and the United Fruit Company in Costa Rica, 1870–1940* (Baton Rouge, 1996), pp. 46–47, 73–75, and O'Brien, *Revolutionary Mission*, pp. 83, 91.

40. *Commerical Relations of the United States with Foreign Countries during the Year 1903*, U.S. House of Representatives Document #722, 58th Congress, second session, vol. II (Washington, D.C., 1904), p. 178.

41. Charles Morrow Wilson, *Empire in Green and Gold: The Story of the American Banana Trade* (Westport, Connecticut, 1968), pp. 124–25.

42. Carleton Beals, *Banana Gold* (Philadelphia, 1932), p. 145.

43. Quoted in O'Brien, *Revolutionary Mission*, pp. 179–80.

44. For working conditions in the fruteras, see Chomsky, *West Indian Workers*. On Cerro de Pasco, see Adrian DeWind Jr., "Peasants Become Miners: The Evolution of Industrial Mining Systems in Peru," Ph.D. diss., Columbia University, 1977, and Florencia Mallon, *The Defense of Community in Peru's Central Highlands: Peasant Struggle and Capitalist Transition, 1860–1940* (Princeton, 1983). On the Guggenheims, see O'Brien, *Revolutionary Mission*, chapter 7.

45. Peter F. Klarén, *Modernization, Dislocation, and Aprismo: Origins of the Peruvian Aprista Party, 1870–1932* (Austin, 1973), pp. 90–91.

46. Quoted in Chomsky, *West Indian Workers*, pp. 94–95.

47. O'Brien, *Revolutionary Mission*, pp. 177–79, 235, 258–59.

48. Chomsky, *West Indian Workers*, pp. 96–102.

49. Quoted in Gerard Colby with Charlotte Dennett, *Thy Will Be Done–The Conquest of the Amazon: Nelson Rockefeller and Evangelism in the Age of Oil* (New York, 1995), p. 34.

50. George W. Anderson to Victor Cutter, Boston, September 7, 1922, United Fruit Company/orig, General Records of the Department of State, Record Group 59, United States National Archives, Washington, D.C.

51. Pike, *United States and Latin America*, pp. 171–220; Philippe I. Bourgois, *Ethnicity at Work: Divided Labor on a Central American Banana Plantation* (Baltimore, 1989), and O'Brien, *Revolutionary Mission*, pp. 143, 280–81.

CHAPTER THREE

1. Edwin P. Hoyt, Jr., *The Guggenheims and the American Dream* (New York, 1967), p. 261.

2. Eric Hobsbawm, *The Age of Extremes: A History of the World, 1914–1991* (New York, 1994), pp. 89–93.

3. Quoted in Thomas F. O'Brien, *The Revolutionary Mission: American Enterprise in Latin America, 1900–1945* (Cambridge, 1996), p. 117.

4. Memorandum by H.F. Matthews, Division of Latin American Affairs, September 23, 1930, Electric Bond and Share, General Records of the Department of State, Record Group 59, United States National Archive (hereinafter cited as USNA).

5. John Hart, *Revolutionary Mexico: The Coming and Process of the Mexican Revolution* (Berkeley, 1989), pp. 96–97.

6. O'Brien, *Revolutionary Mission*, p. 251.

7. Charles Berquist, *Labor in Latin America: Comparative Essays on Chile, Argentina, Venezuela, and Colombia* (Stanford, 1986), pp. 117–30.

8. Carleton Beals, *Banana Gold* (Philadelphia, 1932), pp. 145–46.

9. Paul J. Dosal, *Doing Business with the Dictators: A Political History of United Fruit in Guatemala, 1899–1944* (Wilmington, 1993), chapter 7, and documents contained in 814, 5045/4–9, reel 20, microfilm–655, Record Group 59, USNA.

10. Quoted in O'Brien, *Revolutionary Mission*, p. 97.

11. O'Brien, *Revolutionary Mission*, pp. 94–98.

12. Roberto Branly, *Minaz–608: coloquios en el despegue* (Havana, 1973), pp. 57–58.

13. Mirta Rosell, ed., *Luchas Obreras Contra Machado: Recopilación e Introducción de Mirta Rosell* (Havana, 1973), p. 62.

14. O'Brien, *Revolutionary Mission*, pp. 213–19.

15. Ibid., p. 265n.

16. Quoted in ibid., p. 274.

17. Ibid., pp. 271–72.

18. Hobsbawm, *Age of Extremes*, pp. 91, 98–99, and J. Fred Rippy, *Globe and Hemisphere: Latin America in the Post-war Foreign Relations of the United States* (Westport, Connecticut, 1972), chapter 3.

19. Hobsbawm, *Age of Extremes*, pp. 88–97.

20. Victor Bulmer-Thomas, *The Economic History of Latin America since Independence* (Cambridge, 1994), pp. 194–201.

21. Gabriel Palma, "From an Export-led to an Import-substituting Economy: Chile 1914–39," in Rosemary Thorp, ed., *Latin America in the 1930s* (New York, 1984), pp. 65–66.

22. Bulmer-Thomas, *Economic History*, pp. 194–209.

23. Henry Leslie Robinson, "American and Foreign Power Company in Latin America: A Case Study," Ph.D. diss., Stanford University, 1967, pp. 35–39, and Schedule 108, Box 0320999, *American and Foreign Power Company Incorporated Annual Report*, 1931, p. 3, in Electric Bond and Share Company Archive, Boise Cascade Corporation, Boise, Idaho.

24. Quoted in O'Brien, *Revolutionary Mission*, p. 127.

25. Ibid., p. 151.

26. Sergio Ramírez, ed., *Sandino: The Testimony of a Nicaraguan Patriot*, trans. by Robert Edgar Conrad (Princeton, 1990), pp. 179, 239, 309.

27. Thomas Ferguson, "From Normalcy to New Deal: Industrial Structure, Party Competition, and American Public Policy in the Great Depression," *International Organization* 38(Winter 1984):41–94.

28. The first Export Import Bank was created by the Roosevelt administration for the specific purpose of financing trade with the Soviet Union.

CHAPTER FOUR

1. Gerard Colby with Charlotte Dennett, *Thy Will Be Done–The Conquest of the Amazon: Nelson Rockefeller and Evangelism in the Age of Oil* (New York, 1995), pp. 81–82, 107–19, 212–13.

2. Emily S. Rosenberg, *Spreading the American Dream: American Economic and Cultural Expansion, 1890–1945* (New York, 1982), pp. 183–84.

3. Rosenberg, *Spreading the American Dream*, pp. 206–08, 222–23.

4. Ibid., p. 195.

5. Mark Russell, "Legitimizing Industrial Capitalism: Philanthropy and Individual Differences," in Robert F. Arnove, ed., *Philanthropy and Cultural Imperialism* (Boston, 1980), p. 88.

6. Quoted in Edward H. Berman, *The Influence of the Carnegie, Ford, and Rockefeller Foundations on American Foreign Policy: The Ideology of Philanthropy* (Albany, 1983), p. 47.

7. Ibid., pp. 54–55.

8. Ibid., pp. 15–17.

9. Rosenberg, *Spreading the American Dream*, pp. 223–24.

10. See Table 3, Introduction.

11. J. Fred Rippy, *Globe and Hemisphere: Latin America in the Post-war Foreign Relations of the United States* (Westport, Connecticut, 1972), pp. 62–89.

12. James D. Cockcroft, *Neighbors in Turmoil: Latin America* (New York, 1989), p. 505.

13. Victor Bulmer-Thomas, *The Economic History of Latin America since Independence* (Cambridge, 1994), pp. 234–35, 276.

14. George M. Ingram, *Expropriation of U.S. Property in South America: Nationalization of Oil and Copper Companies in Peru, Bolivia, and Chile* (New York, 1974), pp. 29–43, and George Philip, *Oil and Politics in Latin America: Nationalist Movements and State Companies* (Cambridge, 1982), pp. 62–64.

15. Mira Wilkins, *The Maturing of Multinational Enterpise: American Business Abroad from 1914 to 1970* (Cambridge, 1974), pp. 361–62.

16. Philip, *Oil and Politics in Latin America*, pp. 10–100.

17. George Philip, *Oil and Politics in Latin America: Nationalist Movements and State Companies* (Cambridge, 1982), pp. 43–67.

18. Charles Berquist, *Labor in Latin America: Comparative Essays on Chile, Argentine, Venezuela, and Colombia* (Stanford, 1986), p. 248.

19. Quoted in ibid., p. 234.

20. Ibid., pp. 214–68.

21. Ingram, *Expropriation of U.S. Property in South America*, pp. 38–44.

22. *Engineering and Mining Journal* 159(December 1958):106.

23. *Engineering and Mining Journal* 162(April 1960):91.

24. Quoted in Dirk Kruijt and Menno Vellinga, *Labor Relations and Multinational Corporations: The Cerro de Pasco Corporation in Peru (1902–1974)* (Assen, The Netherlands, 1979), p. 182.

25. Elizabeth Dore, *The Peruvian Mining Industry: Growth, Stagnation and Crisis* (Boulder, Colorado, 1988), pp. 123–55, and Kruijt and Vellinga, *Labor Relations and Multinational Corporations*.

26. Thomas Klubock, "Exporting the Welfare State: U.S. Capital, Labor Relations, and Gender Ideologies in Chile's El Teniente Mining Enclave," paper presented at Re-

thinking the Post-Colonial Encounter Conference, Yale University, New Haven, Connecticut, October 18–21, 1995. The name Eduardo Pérez is a pseudonym used by the author to protect his source. See also Robert J. Alexander, *Labor Relations in Argentina, Brazil, and Chile* (New York, 1962), p. 335.

27. Isaac F. Marcosson, *Anaconda* (New York, 1957), pp. 208–09.

28. Theodore H. Moran, *Multinational Corporations and the Politics of Dependence: Copper in Chile* (Princeton, 1974), pp. 37–118, and Manuel Berrera, "Desarrollo económico y sindicalismo en Chile, 1938–1970," *Revista Mexicana de Sociología* 42(July–September 1980):1269–96.

29. Theodore Geiger (with the assistance of Liesel Goode), *The General Electric Company in Brazil* (New York, 1961).

30. As quoted in James Schwoch, *The American Radio Industry and its Latin American Activities, 1900–1939* (Chicago, 1990), p. 146. See also Schwoch, pp. 142–43, and Christopher Sterling, *History of Broadcasting: Radio to Television* (New York, 1971).

31. Fernando Henrique Cardoso and Enzo Faletto, *Dependency and Development in Latin America,* trans. by Marjory Mattingly Urquidi (Berkeley, 1979), pp. 160–61.

32. Rhys Jenkins, *Transnational Corporations and Industrial Transformation in Latin America* (London and New York, 1984), pp. 5–82; Jenkins, *Transnational Corporations and the Latin American Automobile Industry* (Pittsburgh, 1987), pp. 17–23; Helen Shapiro, *Engines of Growth: The State and Transnational Auto Companies in Brazil* (New York, 1994), pp. 2–3; Peter Evans, *Dependent Development: The Alliance of Multinational, State, and Local Capital in Brazil* (Princeton, 1979), pp. 75–125; and Mira Wilkins, *The Maturing of Multinational Enterpise: American Business Abroad from 1914 to 1970* (Cambridge, 1974), pp. 311–13.

33. *American and Foreign Power Company Annual Reports, 1938–1943,* Electric Bond and Share Company Archive, Boise Cascade Corporation, Boise, Idaho (hereinafter cited as EBASCO); Wilkins, *Maturing of Multinational Enterprise,* pp. 302–04; and Robert Sobel, *ITT: The Management of Opportunity* (New York, 1982), pp. 67–119.

34. Quoted in Robert MacCameron, *Bananas, Labor, and Politics in Honduras: 1954–1963* (Syracuse, 1983), p. 36.

35. Quoted in ibid., p. 74.

36. Ibid., passim.

37. John Miceli to D'Antoni, n.p., 8/20/45, Folder #17, Papers of the Standard Fruit and Steamship Company, Howard-Tilton Memorial Library, Tulane University, New Orleans, Louisiana.

38. American and Foreign Power Financial Reports 6/30/53 and 6/30/54, Box 0152370, EBASCO.

39. Ibid.

40. Piero Gleijeses, *Shattered Hope: The Guatemalan Revolution and the United States, 1944–1954* (Princeton, 1991), passim.

CHAPTER FIVE

1. Quotes from Robert J. Schoenberg, *Geneen* (New York, 1985), pp. 287–88.

2. See Table 3, Introduction.

3. Mira Wilkins, *The Maturing of Multinational Enterprise: American Business Abroad from the Colonial Era to 1914* (Cambridge, 1974), pp. 330–32.

4. Victor Bulmer-Thomas, *The Economic History of Latin America since Independence* (Cambridge, 1994), p. 359.

5. Quoted in Edward H. Berman, *The Influence of the Carnegie, Ford and Rockefeller Foundations on American Foreign Policy: The Ideology of Philanthropy* (Albany, 1983), pp. 54–55.

6. Ibid., pp. 79–80, 122–23, 169–73.

7. Gerard Colby with Charlotte Dennett, *Thy Will Be Done–The Conquest of the Amazon: Nelson Rockefeller and Evangelism in the Age of Oil* (New York, 1995), pp. 474–75.

8. Nelson Rockefeller, *The Rockefeller Report on the Americas* (Chicago, 1969), p. 89.

9. Colby and Dennet, *Thy Will Be Done*, pp. 666–68.

10. Mira Wilkins, *The Maturing of Multinational Enterprise: American Business Abroad from 1914 to 1970* (Cambridge, 1974), p. 330.

11. Rhys Jenkins, *Transnational Corporations and the Latin American Automobile Industry* (Pittsburgh, 1987), pp. 21–32.

12. Ian Roxborough, *Unions and Politics in Mexico: The Case of the Automobile Industry* (London, 1984), pp. 43–44.

13. On the auto industry, see Jenkins, *Transnational Corporations*, and *Dependent Industrialization in Latin America: The Automotive Industry in Argentina, Chile and Mexico* (New York, 1977).

14. Jenkins, *Transnational Corporations*, chapter 4.

15. Frederick Allen, *Secret Formula: How Brilliant Marketing and Relentless Salesmanship Made Coca-Cola the Best Known Product in the World* (New York: 1994), pp. 170–73.

16. Ibid., pp. 170–73, and Robert J. Ledogar, *Hungry for Profits: U.S. Food and Drug Multinationals in Latin America* (New York, 1975), chapter 8.

17. Alan Wells, *Picture Tube Imperialism? The Impact of U.S. Television on Latin America* (Maryknoll, New York, 1972), p. 120.

18. Ibid., passim.

19. Wilkins, *Maturing of Multinational Enterprise*, pp. 361–62.

20. Theodore H. Moran, *Multinational Corporations and the Politics of Dependence: Copper in Chile* (Princeton, 1974), pp. 129–47.

21. Quoted in ibid., p. 136.

22. Dirk Kruijt and Menno Vellinga, *Labor Relations and Multinational Corporations: The Cerro de Pasco Corporation in Peru (1902–1974)* (Assen, The Netherlands, 1979), pp. 49–53, 114–17, 198.

23. George M. Ingram, *Expropriation of U.S. Property in South America: Nationalization of Oil and Copper Companies in Peru, Bolivia, and Chile* (New York, 1974), pp. 44–54.

24. George Philip, *Oil and Politics in Latin America: Nationalist Movements and State Companies* (Cambridge, 1982), pp. 294–304.

25. Louis A. Pérez Jr., *Cuba: Between Reform and Revolution* (New York, 1988), pp. 296–97.

26. Ibid., p. 297.

27. International Bank for Reconstruction and Development, *Report on Cuba* (Baltimore, 1951), pp. 357, 368.

28. Pérez, *Cuba*, pp. 320–22.

29. American and Foreign Power Financial Reports, 1959, 1960 and Annual Report, 1960, Box 0152370, Electric Bond and Share Company Archive, Boise Cascade Corporation, Boise, Idaho.

30. Ibid., and Pérez Jr., *Cuba*, pp. 295–305, 320–27.

31. Quoted in Ingram, *Expropriation of U.S. Property in South America*, pp. 89–90.

32. Ibid., pp. 72–73, 82.

33. Quoted in Kruijt and Vellinga, *Labor Relations and Mulinational Corporations*, p. 124.

34. Ibid., pp. 116–33, and Ingram, *Expropriation of U.S. Property in South America*, pp. 64–95.

35. Quoted in J. Ann Zammit, ed., *The Chilean Road to Socialism: Proceedings of an ODEPLAN-IDS Round Table, March 1972* (Austin, 1973), pp. 20–21.

36. Ingram, *Expropriation of U.S. Property*, pp. 269–90.

37. Ibid., pp. 290–93.

38. James D. Cockcroft, *Neighbors in Turmoil: Latin America* (New York, 1989), pp. 553–55.

39. Peter B. Evans, *Dependent Development: The Alliance of Multinational, State and Local Capital in Brazil* (Princeton, 1979), pp. 93–100.

40. Bulmer-Thomas, *Economic History*, p. 361.

41. Ramesh F. Ramsaran, *U.S. Investments in Latin America and the Caribbean: Trends and Issues* (New York, 1985), pp. 75–89.

42. Theodore Geiger with Liesel Goode, *The General Electric Company in Brazil* (New York, 1961), p. 81.

43. Quoted in John Humphrey, *Capitalist Control and Workers' Struggle in the Brazilian Auto Industry* (Princeton, 1982), pp. 102–03.

44. Quoted in ibid., p. 159.

45. Bulmer-Thomas, *The Economic History of Latin America*, pp. 323–34; Evans, *Dependent Development*, chapters 3, 4, and 5; and Cockcroft, *Neighbors in Turmoil*, pp. 552–68.

46. Pedro-Pablo Kuczynski, *Latin American Debt* (Baltimore, 1988), p. 36.

47. Ibid., p. 109.

48. Quoted in Phillip L. Zweig, *Wriston: Walter Wriston, Citibank, and the Rise and Fall of American Financial Supremacy* (New York, 1995), pp. 756–57.

49. Quoted in ibid., p. 864.

50. Bulmer-Thomas, *Economic History of Latin America*, pp. 366–94, and Kuczynski, *Latin American Debt*, pp. 107–44.

51. Kuczynski, *Latin American Debt*, p. 10.

52. Quoted in James F. Hoge Jr., "Fulfilling Brazil's Promise: A Conversation with President Cardoso," *Foreign Affairs* 74(July/August, 1995):66–67.

53. Daniel Chudnovsky, Andrés López and Fernando Porta, "New Foreign Direct Investment in Argentina: Privatization, the Domestic Market, and Regional Integration," pp. 57–58, in Manuel Agosin, ed., *Foreign Direct Investment in Latin America* (Washington, D.C., 1995).

54. "A Region at Risk: Argentine Economy Reborn But Still Ailing," *New York Times*, February 6, 1998, p. A7.

55. Ibid.

56. "A Region at Risk: Brazil Pays to Shield Currency and the Poor See the True Cost," *New York Times*, February 5, 1998, p. A10.

57. "A Region at Risk: Argentine Economy . . .," p. A7.

BIBLIOGRAPHY

Agosin, Manuel, ed. *Foreign Direct Investment in Latin America.* Washington, D.C.: Inter-American Development Bank and Johns Hopkins University Press, 1995.

Albert, Bill. *South America and the First World War: The Impact of the War on Brazil, Argentina, Peru and Chile.* Cambridge: Cambridge University Press, 1988.

———. *South America and the World Economy from Independence to 1930.* London: Macmillan Press, 1983.

Alexander, Robert J. *Labor Relations in Argentina, Brazil, and Chile.* New York: McGraw Hill, 1962.

Allen, Frederick. *Secret Formula: How Brilliant Marketing and Relentless Salesmanship Made Coca-Cola the Best Known Product in the World.* New York: Harper Collins, 1994.

American and Foreign Power Company. *American and Foreign Power Company Incorporated Annual Reports,* 1931, 1938–1943. Electric Bond and Share Company Archive, Boise Cascade Corporation, Boise, Idaho.

———. American and Foreign Power Financial Reports, 6/30/53, 6/30/54, 1959, 1960. Electric Bond and Share Company Archive, Boise Cascade Corporation, Boise, Idaho.

Anderson, George W. to Victor Cutter, Boston, September 7, 1922, United Fruit Company/orig. General Records of the Department of State, Record Group 59, United States National Archives, Washington, D.C.

Arnove, Robert F., ed. *Philanthropy and Cultural Imperialism: The Foundations at Home and Abroad.* Boston: G.K. Hall, 1980.

Atkins, Edwin F. *Sixty Years in Cuba.* 1926. Reprint, New York: Arno Press, 1980.

Barbier, Jacques and Allan J. Kuethe, eds. *The North American Role in the Spanish Imperial Economy, 1760–1819.* Manchester: Manchester University Press, 1984.

Bauer, Arnold. "The Colonial Economy." In Louisa Schell Hoberman and Susan Migden Socolow, eds., *The Countryside in Colonial Latin America,* pp. 19–48. Albuquerque: The University of New Mexico Press, 1996.

Bauer Paíz, Alfonso. *Como opera el capital yanqui en Centroamerica: el caso de Guatemala*. México: Editorial Ibero-Mexicana, 1956.

Beals, Carleton. *Banana Gold*. Philadelphia: J.B. Lippincottt Company, 1932.

Berquist, Charles. *Labor in Latin America: Comparative Essays on Chile, Argentina, Venezuela, and Colombia*. Stanford: Stanford University Press, 1986.

Berman, Edward H. *The Influence of the Carnegie, Ford, and Rockefeller Foundations on American Foreign Policy: The Ideology of Philanthropy*. Albany: State University of New York Press, 1983.

Berrera, Manuel. "Desarrollo económico y sindicalismo en Chile, 1938–1970." *Revista Mexicana de Sociología* 42(July-September 1980):1269–1296.

Bourgois, Philippe I. *Ethnicity at Work: Divided Labor on a Central American Banana Plantation*. Baltimore: Johns Hopkins University, 1989.

Brand, Charles A. "The Background of Capitalistic Underdevelopment: Honduras to 1913." Ph.D. diss., University of Pittsburgh, 1972.

Branly, Roberto. *Minaz–608: coloquios en el despegue*. Havana: Girón, 1973.

Brown, Jonathan C. *Oil and Revolution in Mexico*. Berkeley: University of California Press, 1993.

Bruchey, Stuart. *Enterprise: The Dynamic Economy of a Free People*. Cambridge: Harvard University Press, 1990.

Bulmer-Thomas, Victor. *The Economic History of Latin America since Independence*. Cambridge: Cambridge University Press, 1994.

Cardoso, Fernando Henrique and Enzo Faletto. *Dependency and Development in Latin America*. Trans. by Marjory Mattingly Urquidi. Berkeley: University of California Press, 1979.

Casson, Mark, ed. *The Growth of International Business*. London: Allen and Unwin, 1983.

Chen Daley, Mercedes. "The Watermelon Riot: Cultural Encounters in Panama City, April 15, 1856." *Hispanic American Historical Review* 70(1)(1990):85–108.

Chomsky, Aviva. *West Indian Workers and the United Fruit Company in Costa Rica, 1870–1940*. Baton Rouge: Louisiana State University Press, 1996.

Chudnovsky, Daniel, Andrés López and Fernando Porta. "New Foreign Direct Investment in Argentina: Privatization, the Domestic Market, and Regional Integration." In Manuel R. Agosin, ed., *Foreign Direct Investment in Latin America*, pp. 39–104. Washington, D.C.: Inter-American Development Bank and Johns Hopkins University Press, 1995.

Clayton, Lawrence A. *Grace: W.R. Grace & Co., The Formative Years, 1850–1930*. Ottawa, Illinois: Jameson, 1985.

Cockcroft, James D. *Neighbors in Turmoil: Latin America*. New York: Harper & Row, 1989.

Colby, Gerard with Charlotte Dennett. *Thy Will Be Done–The Conquest of the Amazon: Nelson Rockefeller and Evangelism in the Age of Oil*. New York: Harper Collins, 1995.

DeWind Jr., Adrian. "Peasants Become Miners: The Evolution of Industrial Mining Systems in Peru." Ph.D. diss., Columbia University, 1977.

Dore, Elizabeth. *The Peruvian Mining Industry: Growth, Stagnation and Crisis*. Boulder, Colorado: Westview Press, 1988.

Dosal, Paul J. *Doing Business with the Dictators: A Political History of United Fruit in Guatemala, 1899–1944*. Wilmington: Scholarly Resources, 1993.

Engineering and Mining Journal 159(December 1958):109.

Engineering and Mining Journal 162(April 1960):91.

Evans, Peter. *Dependent Development: The Alliance of Multinational, State, and Local Capital in Brazil*. Princeton: Princeton University Press, 1979.

Ferguson, Thomas. "From Normalcy to New Deal: Industrial Structure, Party Competition, and American Public Policy in the Great Depression." *International Organization* 38(1)(1984):41–94.

Gates, Paul W. *Landlords and Tenants on the Prairie Frontier: Studies in American Land Policy*. Ithaca: Cornell University Press, 1973.

Geiger, Theodore with Liesel Goode. *The General Electric Company in Brazil*. New York: National Planning Association, 1961.

Gleijeses, Piero. *Shattered Hope: The Guatemalan Revolution and the United States, 1944–1954*. Princeton: Princeton University Press, 1991.

Gudmundson, Lowell and Hector Lindo-Fuentes. *Central America, 1821–1871: Liberalism before Liberal Reform*. Tuscaloosa: University of Alabama Press, 1995.

Hart, John. *Revolutionary Mexico: The Coming and Process of the Mexican Revolution*. Berkeley: University of California Press, 1989.

Hobsbawm, Eric. *The Age of Extremes: A History of the World, 1914–1991*. New York: Pantheon Books, 1994.

Hoge Jr., James F. "Fulfilling Brazil's Promise: A Conversation with President Cardoso." *Foreign Affairs* 74(July/August 1995):62–75.

Horsman, Reginald. *Race and Manifest Destiny: The Origins of Racial Anglo-Saxonism*. Cambridge: Harvard University Press, 1981.

Hoyt, Edwin P., Jr. *The Guggenheims and the American Dream*. New York: Funk and Wagnalls, 1967.

Humphrey, John. *Capitalist Control and Workers' Struggle in the Brazilian Auto Industry*. Princeton: Princeton University Press, 1982.

Ingersoll, Ralph M. *In and Under Mexico*. New York: Century, 1924.

Ingram, George M. *Expropriation of U.S. Property in South America: Nationalization of Oil and Copper Companies in Peru, Bolivia, and Chile*. New York: Praeger Publishers, 1974.

International Bank for Reconstruction and Development. *Report on Cuba*. Baltimore: Johns Hopkins Press, 1951.

Jacobsen, Nils. *Mirages of Transition: the Peruvian Altiplano, 1780–1930*. Berkeley: University of California Press, 1993.

Jenkins, Rhys. *Dependent Industrialization in Latin America: The Automotive Industry in Argentina, Chile and Mexico*. New York: Praeger Publishers, 1977.

———. *Transnational Corporations and Industrial Transformation in Latin America*. London: MacMillan and New York: St. Martin's Press, 1984.

———. *Transnational Corporations and the Latin American Automobile Industry*. Pittsburgh: University of Pittsburgh Press, 1987.

Jenks, Leland H. *Our Cuban Colony: A Study in Sugar*. New York: Vanguard Press, 1928.

Johnson, Paul E. *A Shopkeeper's Millennium: Society and Revivals in Rochester, New York, 1815–1837*. New York: Hill and Wang, 1978.

Karnes, Thomas L. *Tropical Enterprise: The Standard Fruit and Steamship Company in Latin America*. Baton Rouge: Louisiana State University Press, 1978.

Kepner Jr., Charles David and Jay Henry Soothill. *The Banana Empire: A Case Study in Economic Imperialism*. 1935. Reprint, New York: Russell and Russell, 1967.

Kepner Jr., Charles David. *Social Aspects of the Banana Industry*. New York: Columbia University Press, 1936.

Klarén, Peter F. *Modernization, Dislocation, and Aprismo: Origins of the Peruvian Aprista Party, 1870–1932*. Austin: University of Texas Press, 1973.

Klubock, Thomas. "Exporting the Welfare State: U.S. Capital, Labor Relations, and Gender Ideologies in Chile's El Teniente Mining Enclave." Paper presented at Rethinking the Post-Colonial Encounter Conference, Yale University, New Haven, Connecticut, October 18–21, 1995.

Kruijt, Dirk and Menno Vellinga. *Labor Relations and Multinational Corporations: The Cerro de Pasco Corporation in Peru (1902–1974)*. Assen, The Netherlands: Van Gorcum & Co., 1979.

Kuczynski, Pedro-Pablo. *Latin American Debt*. Baltimore: Johns Hopkins University Press, 1988.

Leach, William. *Land of Desire: Merchants, Power and the Rise of a New American Culture*. New York: Pantheon, 1993.

Ledogar, Robert J. *Hungry for Profits: U.S. Food and Drug Multinationals in Latin America*. New York: IDOC/North America Inc., 1975.

MacCameron, Robert. *Bananas, Labor, and Politics in Honduras: 1954–1963*. Syracuse: Syracuse University, Maxwell School of Citizenship and Public Affairs, 1983.

Mallon, Florencia. *The Defense of Community in Peru's Central Highlands: Peasant Struggle and Capitalist Transition, 1860–1940*. Princeton: Princeton University Press, 1983.

Manning, William R. *Diplomatic Correspondence of the United States Concerning the Independence of the Latin American Nations*, 3 vols. New York: Carnegie Endowment for International Peace, 1925.

Marcosson, Isaac F. *Anaconda*. New York: Dodd, Mead, 1957.

Matthews, H.F. Memorandum. Division of Latin American Affairs, September 23, 1930. Electric Bond and Share/1, Record Group 59, United States National Archive.

McCreery, David J. "Debt Servitude in Rural Guatemala." *Hispanic American Historical Review* 63 (November 1983):735–59.

Miceli, John to D'Antoni, n.p., 8/20/45. Folder #17. Papers of the Standard Fruit and Steamship Company, Howard-Tilton Memorial Library, Tulane University, New Orleans, Louisiana.

Monteón, Michael. "The Enganche in the Chilean Nitrate Sector, 1880–1930." *Latin American Perspectives* 6 (Summer 1979):66–79.

Moran, Theodore H. *Multinational Corporations and the Politics of Dependence: Copper in Chile*. Princeton: Princeton University Press, 1974.

New York Times, "A Region at Risk: Argentine Economy Reborn But Still Ailing," February 6, 1998, p. A7.

New York Times, "A Region at Risk: Brazil Pays to Shield Currency and the Poor See the True Cost," February 5, 1998, p. A10.

O'Brien, Thomas F. *The Revolutionary Mission: American Enterprise in Latin America, 1900–1945*. Cambridge: Cambridge University Press, 1996.

Palma, Gabriel. "From an Export-led to an Import-substituting Economy: Chile, 1914–39." In Rosemary Thorp, ed., *Latin America in the 1930s: The Role of the Periphery in World Crisis*, pp. 50–80. New York: St. Martin's Press, 1984.

Pérez Jr., Louis A. *Cuba: Between Reform and Revolution*. New York: Oxford University Press, 1988.

Philip, George. *Oil and Politics in Latin America: Nationalist Movements and State Companies*. Cambridge: Cambridge University Press, 1982.

Pike, Fredrick B. *The United States and Latin America: Myths and Stereotypes of Civilization and Nature*. Austin: University of Texas Press, 1992.

Platt, D.C.M. *Latin America and British Trade, 1806–1914*. London: Adam and Charles Black, 1972.

Ramírez, Sergio, ed. *Sandino: The Testimony of a Nicaraguan Patriot*. Trans. by Robert Edgar Conrad. Princeton: Princeton University Press, 1990.

Ramsaran, Ramesh F. *U.S. Investments in Latin America and the Caribbean: Trends and Issues*. New York: St. Martin's Press, 1985.

Read, Robert. "The Growth and Structure of Multinationals in the Banana Export Trade." In Mark Casson, ed., *The Growth of International Business*, pp. 180–213. London: Allen and Unwin, 1983.

Reichstein, Andreas V. *Rise of the Lone Star: The Making of Texas*. Trans. by Jeanne R. Wilson. College Station: Texas A&M University Press, 1989.

Rippy, J. Fred. *Globe and Hemisphere: Latin America's Place in the Postwar Foreign Relations of the United States*. Westport, Connecticut: Greenwood Press, 1972 (1958).

Robinson, Henry Leslie. "American and Foreign Power Company in Latin America: A Case Study." Ph.D. diss., Stanford University, 1967.

Rockefeller, Nelson. *The Rockefeller Report on the Americas*. Chicago: Quadrangle Books, 1969.

Rosell, Mirta, ed. *Luchas Obreras Contra Machado: Recopilación e Introducción de Mirta Rosell*. Havana: Instituto Cubano del Libro, 1973.

Rosenberg, Emily S. *Spreading the American Dream: American Economic and Cultural Expansion, 1890–1945*. New York: Hill and Wang, 1982.

Rumbarger, John J. *Profits and Power and Prohibition: Alcohol Reform and the Industrializing of America, 1800–1930*. Albany: State University of New York Press, 1988.

Russell, Mark. "Legitimizing Industrial Capitalism: Philanthropy and Individual Differences." In Robert F. Arnove, ed., *Philanthropy and Cultural Imperialism: The Foundations at Home and Abroad*, pp. 87–122. Boston: G.K. Hall, 1980.

Schell Hoberman, Louisa and Susan Migden Socolow, eds. *The Countryside in Colonial Latin America*. Albuquerque: University of New Mexico Press, 1996.

Schmitz, Christopher J. *World Non-Ferrous Metal Production and Prices, 1700–1976*. London: Cass, 1979.

Schoenberg, Robert J. *Geneen*. New York: W.W. Norton & Co., 1985.

Schwoch, James. *The American Radio Industry and its Latin American Activities, 1900–1939*. Chicago: University of Illinois Press, 1990.

Scroggs, William O. *Filibusters and Financiers: The Story of William Walker and His Associates*. New York: MacMillan, 1916.

Shapiro, Helen. *Engines of Growth: The State and Transnational Auto Companies in Brazil*. New York: Cambridge University Press, 1994.

Sobel, Robert. *ITT: The Management of Opportunity*. New York: New York Times Books, 1982.

Stallings, Barbara. *Banker to the Third World: U.S. Portfolio Investments in Latin America, 1900–1986*. Berkeley: University of California Press, 1987.

Sterling, Christopher. *History of Broadcasting: Radio to Television*. Reprint ed. New York: Arno Press, 1971.

Stern, Steve J. "The Age of Andean Insurrection, 1742–1782: A Reappraisal." In Steve J. Stern, ed., *Resistance, Rebellion, and Consciousness in the Andean Peasant World, 18th to 20th Centuries*, pp. 33–93. Madison: University of Wisconsin Press, 1987.

————, ed. *Resistance, Rebellion, and Consciousness in the Andean Peasant World, 18th to 20th Centuries.* Madison: University of Wisconsin Press, 1987.

Stewart, Watt. *Henry Meiggs: Yankee Pizarro.* Durham: Duke University Press, 1946.

Thorp, Rosemary, ed. *Latin America in the 1930s: The Role of the Periphery in World Crisis.* New York: St. Martin's Press, 1984.

Thorp, Rosemary and Geoffrey Bertram. *Peru, 1890–1977: Growth and Policy in an Open Economy.* London: Macmillan, 1978.

U.S. Bureau of the Census. *Statistical Abstract of the United States: 1992,* 112th ed. Washington, D.C.: Government Printing Office, 1996.

U.S. Bureau of the Census. *Statistical Abstract of the United States: 1986,* 106th ed. Washington, D.C.: Government Printing Office, 1985.

U.S. Department of Commerce, Bureau of the Census. *The Statistical History of the United States: Colonial Times to 1957.* Stamford, Connecticut: Fairfield Publishers, 1965.

U.S. House of Representatives. *Commercial Relations of the United States with Foreign Countries during the Year 1903.* House of Representatives Document #722, 58th Congress, second session, vol. II. Washington, D.C.: Government Printing Office, 1904.

Wells, Alan. *Picture Tube Imperialism? The Impact of U.S. Television on Latin America.* Maryknoll, New York: Orbis Books, 1972.

Wilkie, James, ed. *Statistical Abstract of Latin America,* Vol. II. Los Angeles: University of California, 1995.

Wilkins, Mira. *The Emergence of Multinational Enterprise: American Business Abroad from the Colonial Era to 1914.* Cambridge: Harvard University Press, 1970.

————. *The Maturing of Multinational Enterprise: American Business Abroad from 1914 to 1970.* Cambridge: Harvard University Press, 1974.

Wilson, Charles Morrow. *Empire in Green and Gold: The Story of the American Banana Trade.* 1947. Reprint, Westport, Connecticut: Greenwood Press, 1968.

Zammit, J. Ann, ed. *The Chilean Road to Socialism: Proceedings of an ODEPLAN-IDS Round Table, March 1972.* Austin: University of Texas Press, 1973.

Zweig, Phillip L. *Wriston: Walter Wriston, Citibank, and the Rise and Fall of American Financial Supremacy.* New York: Crown Publishers Inc., 1995.

GLOSSARY

Anarchosyndicalism   A social and political ideology which calls for the end of central governments and their replacement by small, worker controlled communities in order to end social and economic inequalities.

Capital goods   Machinery and tools used in the production of other goods.

Colonos   Small farmers who own or rent land on which they produce tropical agricultural products for large corporations such as the U.S. banana and sugar companies in Central America and Cuba.

Company scrip   Paper money or coins issued by corporations as payment to their workers. Such money is exchangeable for goods only at company owned or designated stores.

Corporate welfare   Policies instituted by companies early in the twentieth century which were designed to produce a less militant, more productive labor force by offering workers education, health services, insurance, and so forth.

Debt peonage   A system for securing labor by making credit advances to peasants who must then provide their labor to the creditor to pay off the debt.

Dependency theory   A theory developed in Latin America during the 1950s and 1960s which argued that underdevelopment in Third World regions such as Latin America resulted from the domination of their economies by the United States and European powers.

Direct investment   A type of foreign investment which gives the investing company influence in or control over the operations of the enterprise in which it has invested.

Dollar diplomacy   A U.S. government policy pursued during the early part of the twentieth century which attempted to control the activities of Caribbean and Central American governments by establishing American control over respective financial systems.

Encomienda A grant allowing a Spaniard to make use of the labor of a specific group of indigenous people. Such grants were made during the colonial era by the Spanish Crown.

Estancia A large commercial cattle or sheep ranch in Latin America.

Exchange controls Government rules designed to prevent or limit the rule of market forces in the exchange of the national currency for foreign currencies.

Expatriate A term which commonly refers to someone voluntarily living outside their own country for an extended period of time in order to pursue business or other professional interests.

Expropriation The seizure of domestic or foreign enterprises or other property (with or without compensation) by a national government.

Featherbedding The policy of hiring more workers than necessary for a job in order to ensure employment to as many people as possible.

Fordism A system of labor control developed by Henry Ford which combined time-motion studies and other scientific management practices with assembly line production, and the payment of high hourly wages to ensure the retention of workers.

Foreign exchange reserves Funds in the form of gold or foreign currencies usually held by governments or financial institutions.

Frutera A large fruit (especially banana) company.

Good Neighbor Policy The policy instituted by Franklin Roosevelt which sought better relations with Latin American countries by foregoing U.S. military intervention and seeking partnerships which would promote Latin American economic growth.

Guano Deposits of bird droppings on islands off the coast of Peru used as an agricultural fertilizer during the nineteenth century.

Hacendados The owners of large agricultural estates or haciendas in Latin America.

Hacienda A large agricultural estate in Latin America.

Hispanization The adoption of Spanish or Latin American values, beliefs, or language.

Infrastructure investment Investments in public works projects such as roads, bridges, dams, and the like designed to promote economic development.

Labor repressive systems Methods of labor control which use mechanisms other than or in addition to wages to attract and manage labor. Such methods involve some degree of coercion and include systems such as the *mita* and debt peonage.

Material culture The manufactured portions of a culture such as consumer products and services.

Mestizos People whose parentage includes Spaniards and Amerindians.

Mita A labor draft used by the Incas. The Spaniards adopted this system to provide labor for public works and mines.

Money economy An economy in which goods or services are bought and sold with currency or credit rather than being exchanged through a barter system.

Multinational A corporation which invests and carries out other business activities in a number of different countries.

Mulattos   People whose parentage includes Africans and Caucasians.

Nationalization   The process by which a national government takes control (with or without compensation) of a foreign enterprise operating within its borders.

Neoliberalism   A set of economic policies promoted during the latter decades of the twentieth century stressing the importance of the free market, and therefore the need to reduce the role of government in the economy by cutting state spending and regulation as well as privatizing public corporations.

Piece work system   A labor system in which workers are paid by the amount of product they produce rather than by the number of hours worked.

Populism   Multiclass political movements calling for the reduction or elimination of social and economic injustices and usually led by a charismatic figure.

Privatization   The sale of government owned companies or other state properties to private domestic or foreign interests.

Profit repatriation   The remittance of profits back to the parent company by overseas subsidiaries.

Protectionism   A type of economic policy such as high import duties or taxes designed to defend and promote domestic industrial development.

Rationalized systems   Systems of production which employ the most efficient combination and utilization of technology and labor.

Real wages   Money wages which have been statistically adjusted for inflation to determine whether buying power has changed over time.

Scientific management   A system of labor control based on scientific methods such as time-motion studies. Such a system is designed to secure the maximum output from workers.

Second Industrial Revolution   The wave of industrialization which began in the United States in the late nineteenth century involving the development of science based industries such as the electrical industry, and the increased application of machinery to the production process.

Socialism   A social and political philosophy which proposes a more equitable distribution of wealth to be achieved through government welfare and tax policies as well as greater worker control over economic activities.

Social darwinism   A sociopolitical theory based on the notion that societies advance through a process of struggle in which the strong come to dominate the weak.

Social engineering   Attempts to create scientifically based social policies which are designed to make a society more productive and tranquil.

Stagflation   Economic condition under which high inflation is combined with slow or negligible economic growth.

Time payment systems   A series of payments made by a consumer to purchase a product. The system allows the consumer to purchase a good with a small initial outlay but total cost exceeds the original price of the product.

Trade embargo   A government policy prohibiting trade with another nation or nations.

INDEX